QUANTITATIVE TECHNIQUES AND METHODS

QUANTITATIVE TECHNIQUES AND METHODS

Shashi Kumar

genNEXT Publication

Quantitative Technique and Methods

ISBN: 978-93-80222-25-7

Published in 2010 in India by
Gennext Publication
23 Main Ansari Road, Darya Ganj,
New Delhi-110002
E-Mail:GenNextpublication@hotmail.com
Phone: 23282060

Printed at: Chawla Offset Printers, Delhi

Contents

Preface

Quantitative Techniques and Methods pertain to the methods essential for managers. It includes Analysis, Data presentation, variables, distribution and simulation. This volume presents complete treatment of the subject with numerous examples. It emphasizes on day to day examples and clearly enlightens all topics. This textbook presents practical simple tools and concepts of Quantitative Techniques and Methods for students as well as managers practicing in business environment. It presents the essentials in a lucid style. This volume exclusively incorporates this discipline to other managerial functions.

Detailed chapters are included on topics such as Linear Models, with Curves, Quantitative Analysis, Pictorial Presentation of Data, Summarizing of Data, Relationships between Two Variables, Money Variables, Time Series Data, Probability, Probability Distributions and Simulation and Sampling Methods.

This volume is a concise introduction to Organizational Behaviour. It is developed specifically for courses and business students. It focuses on the core topics of the organizational behaviour and illustrates to show its application in practice. It is written for students in undergraduate and postgraduate degree programmes. It has been developed to cover extensively various aspects of the field of organizational behaviour. The language is highly lucid so that it becomes interesting and comprehensive.

This book describes the approaches to organizational behaviour, structure and design, theories, motivation, leadership theories, personality, learning, perception, stress, power and authority, organizational development and conflicts & negotiations. It's a text book that is well thought-out, easy to read and a great reference book for anything to do with organizational behaviour.

This volume is an essential addition to any student and business manager library; especially anyone needed to make important, informed decisions in the presence of scarce resources. A valuable source of knowledge for all students, teachers, consultants and lay person who are interested in gaining knowledge of Quantitative Techniques and Methods.

The well-written materials ensure that students are able to understand all topics clearly. Author is confident that this book will be a handy tool for the students learning Quantitative Techniques and Methods. Sincere feedback, suggestions and comments are always welcome.

1

Introduction

Beginning a new programme of study is always a great challenge. To help ease you into the study of quantitative methods this book begins with an outline of the importance of numbers in business life. If you are studying business or interested in any aspect of business you need to know about quantitative methods. Why? Because business is all about quantities: quantities of goods produced and services provided, quantities of inputs and costs, quantities of revenues and profit, and so on. How many times have you seen a news programme that does not mention numbers? How many times have you read a newspaper in which no numbers are quoted? Numbers are integral to our way of life, our understanding of the world around us. This is especially so of the business world that, now and in the future, we relate to as customers, employees, and suppliers.

QUANTITATIVE METHODS, NUMBERS AND BUSINESS

Consider how numbers played a part in the publisher's decision to produce this book. They were interested in the size of the potential market, which meant looking at the number of students on business courses. They needed to set a price, which led them to consider the prices of rival texts on the one hand and their own production costs on the other. The production costs would depend in turn on the number of pages in the book and the number of copies to be produced.

You may feel rather uncomfortable at the prospect of studying numerical subjects. Perhaps memories of Maths at school have left a legacy that leads you to associate analysing numbers with mental numberness. If this is what happened to you, it is best to try to put it behind you. For one thing the focus you will find here is on applications and interpretation rather than proof and derivation. It may help to bear in mind that employers consistently identify numerical and problem-solving skills as highly desirable qualities in potential employees, so try to think of your quantitative studies as building a valuable career asset. For example, in graduate recruitment literature the Exxon Mobil Corporation state that 'Numerical and analytical skills are essential for all vacancies'.

If you do approach the study of quantitative methods with trepidation you may be tempted to think that this is a subject that really doesn't matter because it is of no use for the businesses. It might be comforting to think that the subject is irrelevant because this would excuse not bothering with it. In fact the subjects that you will meet in this book have in many cases been forged in and grown up with the business world. The origins of many of the techniques described in this book are embedded in the history of business sectors as diverse as brewing and insurance.

This is not an opinion held only by people who teach it; a number of researchers have tried to establish the use that companies make of quantitative methods. Usually these studies are aimed at finding how widespread is the use of a particular type of technique, but occasionally researchers canvass the application of the spectrum of techniques that comprise quantitative methods.

Researchers surveyed US companies that were in the 'Fortune 500'. Fortune is an American business magazine that periodically compiles lists of the most prominent companies in the USA. They sent questionnaires to firms in the manufacturing and service sectors, as well as a random sample of small companies. Respondents were asked about the extent to which they used a variety of quantitative techniques.

Thirteen of these techniques feature in this book. Approximately half or more of the respondents' organizations put the majority of these to moderate, extensive or frequent use. Some were very widely used; in the case of forecasting only 6% of respondents reported little or no use.

Researchers found that in general large companies were more likely to use quantitative methods than small companies. He also found that some techniques were widely used in certain sectors; for example, all respondents from the retailing sector reported that they used stock control methods, whereas all the life insurance companies said they used computer simulation.

One interesting aspect of Researchers' study was the reasons companies gave for not using quantitative techniques. Foremost among these were that managers lacked knowledge of them. In other words, many respondents who reported that particular techniques were not used said that it was because they had no training in them, not that the techniques were considered to be of no value.

The comprehensive nature of the study makes work interesting, but it is now some years old. However, in the years since it was published the quality and availability of computer software that performs quantitative analysis has vastly improved, suggesting that the use to which businesses put quantitative methods has increased rather than decreased.

MATHEMATICAL METHODS

Mathematical methods have long played an important role in management and economics but have become increasingly important in the last few decades. "Business mathematics," such as the computation of compound interest, appeared in ancient Mesopotamia but became prevalent in the mercantile economy of the Renaissance. Mathematics later contributed to the engineering advances that made the Industrial Revolution possible. Mathematics crept into economics during the 18th and 19th centuries and became firmly established in the 20th.

It is only in the last few decades that management per se has received the sort of rigorous study that permits the application of mathematics. In the early part of this century "scientific management," called "Taylorism" after its founder F. Taylor, was fashionable. This movement made some worthwhile contributions, such as time-and-motion studies, but it was coupled with dreadful labour relations practices. The symbol of the movement was the efficiency expert policing the shop floor with stopwatch and clipboard.

After Taylorism waned, interest shifted more to making efficient use of labour and other factors than making employees work harder. Shortly before the Second World War a team of scientists solved the operational problems of coordinating Britain's radar stations and thereby created "operational research," called "operations research" in the U.S. During the war this practice of putting scientists and mathematicians to work on operational problems was surprisingly successful in both the British and American military, partly because members of the professional class who had not previously "dirtied their hands" had their first opportunity to apply their training to operational problems. Their success attracted attention, and operations research spread to industry during the fifties.

After the war, G. Dantzig and others developed linear programming at about the same time that computers became available to solve linear programming models. Linear programming proved a remarkably useful tool for the efficient allocation of resources, and this gave a great boost to operations research. In the early postwar years J. von Neumann and O. Morgenstern invented game theory (closely related to linear programming), and H. W. Kuhn and A. W. Tucker broke ground in nonlinear programming. W. E. Deming and others developed statistical techniques for quality control, and the statistical methods first designed for psychometrics in the early 20th century became the mathematical basis for econometrics. Meanwhile business schools began teaching many of these techniques along with microeconomics and other quantitative fields. As a result of all this, mathematical modelling has played an increasingly important role in management and economics.

In fact one can make a case that overreliance on a mathematical approach has sometimes led to neglect of other approaches. After its first few years, operations research focused almost exclusively on mathematical modelling. The reigning orthodoxy in much of economics is the "neoclassical" paradigm, which is heavily mathematical. There is little communication between people in quantitative fields and those in such "soft" fields as organizational science and general management.

In fact both approaches appear to be in a crisis. Economics and operations research have achieved much, but neither can adequately understand phenomena that involve human beings. The soft sciences take on the difficult, ill-structured, human-oriented problems, but it is unclear even what counts as a satisfactory theory in these areas.

One can hope that this double crisis will lead in the coming years to a "paradigm shift" that will supplant the "hard" and "soft" approaches with an integrated science with the rigor of one and the breadth of the other. There are faint signs of such a shift, but they are not sufficiently crystallized to show up in a business school curriculum.

Despite the limitations of the quantitative methods discussed in this course, in many specific areas they are quite useful. In fact the potential of most mathematical techniques, particularly those of operations research, is only beginning to be realized in practice. Affordable personal computers and user-friendly software are motivating managers to learn about mathematical models and use them. Also the line between managerial and technical staff is blurring, so that managers now run models on their notebook computers that systems analysts once ran on mainframes. This again leads to more widespread use.

APPLICATIONS

The applications of mathematical methods in management and economics today are so manifold that it is difficult to find a single person who is aware of their full scope. The following list can only be incomplete.

• *Economists* use linear and nonlinear programming, the theory of variational inequalities, optimal control theory, dynamic programming, game theory, probability choice models, utility theory, regression and factor analysis and other techniques to study equilibrium, optimal investment, competition, consumer behaviour, and a host of other phenomena.

• People in *operations management* use statistical sampling and estimation theory, linear and integer programming, network programming, dynamic programming and optimal control theory, queuing theory, simulation, artificial intelligence techniques, and combinatorial optimization methods to solve problems in quality control, allocation of resources, logistics, project scheduling, labour and machine scheduling, job shop scheduling and assembly line balancing, and facility layout and location. The introduction of flexible manufacturing systems, robots and other automated devices has posed a whole new array of unsolved mathematical problems.

• People in *finance* use linear, nonlinear and integer programming, optimal control theory and dynamic programming, Markov decision theory, regression and time series to determine optimal resource allocation, multiperiod investments, capital budgeting, and investment and loan portfolio design, and to try to forecast market behaviour.

• People in *marketing* use regression and factor analysis, time series, game theory, Markov decision theory, location theory, mathematical programming, probability choice models and utility theory to study consumer preferences, determine optimal location in product space, allocate advertising resources, design distribution systems, forecast market behaviour, and study competitive strategy.

• People in *information systems* and decision support systems use artificial intelligence techniques, propositional and quantified logic, Bayesian methods, probabilistic logic, data structures and other computer science techniques, mathematical programming, and statistical decision theory to design expert and other knowledge-based systems, develop efficient inference and retrieval methods, and evaluate the economic and organizational effects of information systems.

The peculiar nature of mathematics unfortunately raises two obstacles to learning it. One is that students often believe that mathematics can be learned simply by studying a book. Mathematics is learned by working through problems. A second obstacle is that students often believe that they can learn to work problems by studying a book. A book can get one started, but learning to work problems is like learning to play basketball or play the piano—it requires practice, practice, practice.

KEY ARITHMETICAL PROCEDURES

Certain numerical operations feature in many of the techniques that you will face later on, so this section is designed to help remind you of them and introduce you to some which you may not have met.

ADDITION AND SUBTRACTION

Addition, represented by the plus sign '+', is the process of putting two or more numbers together to make a sum or total. As long as the numbers being added together are positive, i.e. more than zero, the resulting total grows as more numbers are added.

Example 1

A sales manager has to drive to a regional office from the company headquarters. The route involves driving 7 miles to a motorway junction, 15 miles along the motorway, 4 miles along a major road, and finally 3 miles across a city. What is the total length of the journey?

You can get the answer by adding together the distances for the four parts of the journey.

$$\text{Total distance} = 7 + 15 + 4 + 3 = 29 \text{ miles}$$

Although you are probably already familiar with addition, you may not have encountered the symbol called 'sigma', which is used to represent it. Sigma is the letter capital S from the Greek alphabet, written as 'Sð'. It is the letter s because s is the first letter of the word 'sum'. It is a Greek letter because at the time that many quantitative techniques were developed, the 'classical' languages of the ancient world were taught in schools and universities. The Greek language, with its specific alphabet, provided the pioneers of these techniques with a source of distinctive symbols.

Although it may seem that the use of letters and symbols by mathematicians is a conspiracy to intimidate the rest of the world, actually they distil the essence of an operation from what would otherwise be a mass of words. The symbol sigma simply stands for 'the sum of'. It is a form of shorthand that is used for convenience. Similarly letters are often used in numerical subjects to represent quantities, sometimes to abbreviate a procedure involving specific numbers and sometimes to represent a procedure in general. For instance, Sðx means 'the sum of a series of numbers, each of which are represented by the letter x'.

Sometimes it is important to identify precisely which of the set of the numbers are to be added together. To show this, the letter 'i' is used to count the numbers, of times of addition.

$\sum_{i=1}^{3} x_i$ means 'the sum of the first to the third numbers'.

The expression 'i =1' below the sigma tells us to start the addition with the first number and the '3' above the sigma sign tells us to finish the addition with the third.

Example 2

In the situation described in Example 1, we could show that the total distance travelled

(which we could represent by 'D') is the sum of the distance for the four parts of the journey (represented by d_1, d_2 etc.) using the expression:

$$D = \sum_{i=1}^{4} d_i = d_1 + d_2 + d_3 + d_4 = 7 + 15 + 4 + 3 = 29$$

If we want to indicate that all of a set of numbers should be added together and we don't know exactly how many there are, we can use the letter 'n' to represent the last number in the set, so $\sum_{i=1}^{3} x_i$ means 'the sum of the first to the last of the numbers'.

At first these types of symbol may appear strange to you, but it is worth learning to recognize and use them as they can become very useful shorthand forms which will save you space and time in future work.

Subtraction, represented by the minus sign '–', is the process of subtracting or 'taking away' one or more numbers from another. As long as the numbers being subtracted are positive, i.e. more than zero, the result reduces as more numbers are subtracted.

Example 3

An on-line music business has a stock of 49 copies of a CD at the beginning of February. In the first week of the month it received orders for 11 copies, in the second week orders for 6 copies, in the third week orders for 9 copies and in the final week orders for 13 copies. How many copies will be left in stock at the end of the month?

You can get the answer by subtracting the orders from the initial stock:

Stock at the end of the month = 49 – 11 – 6 – 9 – 13 = 10

An alternative approach to this operation is to add the orders first and then subtract the total orders from the initial stock. This would be written as:Stock at the end of the month = 49 – (11 – 6 – 9 – 13) = 49 – 39 = 10

The round brackets dictate that the operations shown within them have to be carried out first. They are used to indicate priority. You may well find addition and subtraction fairly easy, but there are cases where they are not so straightforward; first, when negative numbers are involved, and second when the operation involves numbers measured in awkward units, e.g. minutes and hours. Addition and subtraction may give you some difficulty if negative numbers are involved. If a negative number is added to a total, it reduces the total.

Example 4

A customer purchases four items in a supermarket: a pizza costing Rs. 2.50, milk costing Rs.1.50, and two deodorants costing Rs. 3 each. The deodorants are on a 'two-for-one' special offer. What is the total bill the customer should expect?

Because the Bill adjusts for the special offer after the second deodorant has been scanned, the answer may be written as:

Total bill =Rs. 2.50 +Rs. 1.50 +Rs. 3 +Rs. 3 + (–Rs. 3) = Rs. 7

Here round brackets have been used, both to highlight the fact that there is a negative number in the sequence and to indicate that it must be dealt with first. This means deciding how to tackle the apparently contradictory '+ –' sequence of symbols. In fact the minus sign overrides the plus sign, so adding a negative number is the same as subtracting a number. The arithmetical expression used to find the total amount in Example 4 has exactly the same result as the following expression, which combines addition and subtraction:

Total bill = Rs. 2.50 + Rs. 1.50 + Rs. 3 + Rs. 3 – Rs. 3 = Rs. 7

But what do you do if you have to subtract a negative number? In fact subtracting a negative number produces the same result as adding a positive number.

Example 5

The till operator notices that the deodorants the customer has selected are not those on special offer, the offer applies to a similar product. How will this change the total bill? The special offer reduction of Rs.3 has to be taken from the previous total, so now:

Total bill = Rs.7 – (–Rs. 3) = Rs.10

You get exactly the same result if you simply add the amount concerned, Rs. 3.

You may find it helpful to think of the two minus signs 'cancelling each other out' to leave you with an addition. This is rather like the interpretation of double negatives in the English language where, for instance the sentence 'I won't do it for nothing' means 'I want something'. Alternatively it may help to think that taking away a negative is always positive.

Addition and subtraction involving time is something that many people find difficult because time is measured in hours made up of sixty minutes, and minutes made up of sixty seconds, rather than nice neat numerical parcels of ten. The use of the 24-hour clock on top of all this is simply too much for many people.

Example 6

A parcel delivery driver has to deliver packages to four customers. From the depot it takes 15 minutes to reach the first, a further 40 minutes to reach the second, a further 12 minutes to reach the third, and a further 27 minutes to reach the fourth. It takes 1 hour 10 minutes to reach the depot from the last customer. What is the total driving time?

To get the answer we can express all the times mentioned, including the duration of the last stage, in minutes.

Total journey time = 15 + 40 + 12 + 27 + 70 = 164

It may be more useful to express the answer in hours and minutes. To do this we need to find how many lots of sixty minutes there are in 164 minutes. The answer is two, so the total journey time is two hours (120 of the total number of minutes) and 44 minutes (the number of minutes left over if 120 is subtracted from 164).

Example 7

If the driver in Example 6 starts at 11am, at what time will she arrive back at the depot (assuming the time for delivering packages from the van is negligible), and what time is this on the 24-hour clock?

To get the answer, work in hours first, then convert it into minutes.

$$\text{Arrival time} = 11 + 2 \text{ hours} = 1\text{pm} + 44 \text{ minutes} = 1.44 \text{ pm}$$

To express this using the 24-hour clock, add 12 to the number of hours, because the arrival time is after midday:

$$\text{Arrival time} = 1.44 + 12 = 13.44$$

But if the driver started the route at 11.45am what time would she get back to the depot? This is a little more complicated because the departure time and total journey time are measured in both hours and minutes. To find the answer we can start by adding the hours:

$$11 + 2 = 13$$

Then adding the minutes together:

$$45 + 44 = 89$$

Since this amount of minutes is more than 60, i.e. longer than an hour, we have to express it in hours and minutes, and add the result to the sum of the hours:

$$89 \text{ minutes} = 1 \text{ hour and } 29 \text{ minutes}$$

$$13 + 1 = 14 \text{ hours} + 29 \text{ minutes} = 14.29, \text{ or } 2.29 \text{ pm.}$$

MULTIPLICATION AND DIVISION

Multiplication, or 'times-ing', represented either by the asterisk '*' or the 'times' sign '×', is the process of multiplying two or more numbers together. The result is called the product. If a number is multiplied by another number that is greater than one, the product will be greater than the original number.

Example 8

A domestic heating supplier is replacing gas boilers in a housing complex. A new boiler can supply up to 15 litres of hot water per minute. According to the original specifications an old boiler could supply up to 14 quarts of hot water per minute. There are 1.137 litres in a quart. Will a new boiler supply hot water at a greater rate than an old one? We need to convert the quarts given for an old boiler into litres by multiplying the number of quarts by the conversion rate:

$$\text{Litres per minute} = 14 * 1.137 = 15.918$$

We may conclude that a new boiler will not supply hot water at a greater rate than that of the old one.

In this case the number of litres is greater than the number of quarts, the product represents a numerical increase. But if you multiply a number by another number that is less than one, you will get a product that is lower than your first number.

Example 9

An exporter needs to send a package weighing 20 lb. abroad. The airfreight company they use require the weight to be given in kilograms. If one pound is 0.4536 kilograms, what is the weight of the package in kilograms?

Find the answer by multiplying the number of pounds by the conversion rate:

$$\text{Weight in kilograms} = 20 * 0.4536 = 9.072$$

But what if the multiplication involves negative numbers? If you have to multiply a positive number by a negative number, the product will be negative. However if you multiply two negative numbers together, the product will be positive:

$$4 * (-2) = -8 \text{ but } (-4) * (-2) = 8$$

The two negatives 'cancel each other out' when they are multiplied together. If more than two negative figures are multiplied together, whenever the number of figures is odd the result will be negative, whereas when the number of figures is even the result will be positive:

$$(-3) * (-2) * (-2) = -12 \text{ but } (-3) * (-2) * (-2) * (-2) = 24$$

Division, or finding how many times one amount 'goes into' another, is the process of dividing one number by another. It is represented either by the forward slash '/' or the sign '÷'.

If you divide a number by another number that is greater than one, the result will be smaller than the original number.

Example 10

A small design partnership makes a profit of Rs.94,200. If the profit is shared equally between the six partners in the business, how much should each partner receive?

Find the answer by dividing the profit by the number of partners.

Profit share = Rs.94,200/6 = Rs.15,700

If you divide a number by another number that is less than one, the result will be larger than the original number.

Example 11

A businessman from abroad travels 341 miles in the UK. On his return he must enter the number of kilometres he has travelled on his expense claim.

A kilometre is 0.62 of a mile (to 2 decimal places), so how many kilometres should he record?

To get this you have to divide 341 by 0.62:

Kilometres travelled = 341/0.62 = 550

SQUARES, POWERS AND ROOTS

Taking the square of a number is the process of multiplying a number by itself. The process is represented by the number with a superscript showing the number two, for example the square of three, or three squared would be written 32, which tells us to multiply three by three. If the number you want to square is more than one, the result will be larger than the number itself, for instance the square of three is nine. However, if the number you want to square is less than one, the result will be smaller than the number itself, for example the square of a half is a quarter.

Example 12

A company changes its logo and must order a new square brass plate measuring 65 cm long by 65 cm wide for the main office. The cost of the plate will be based on the area of the plate. There are two possible suppliers: Boldazbrass, who need the area in square centimetres, and Striking Plates, who need the area in square metres. What figures should be given to the suppliers?

To find an area multiply the length by the width. Here because the plate is square, that is, the length and width are the same, we can simply square 65 to get the figure for the first supplier:

$$\text{Plate area for Boldazbrass} = 65^2 = 4225 \text{ square centimètres}$$

To get a figure in square metres for the second supplier we have to divide 65 by 100 so that the dimensions are expressed in metres before we square them:

$$\text{Plate area for Striking Plates} = 0.65^2 = 0.4225 \text{ square metres}$$

Squaring a positive number will always give you a positive result. But because multiplying one negative number by another always gives you a positive product, squaring a negative number will always give you a positive result as well.

$$\text{So, } 3^2 = 9 \text{ and } (-3)^2 = 9$$

The fact that we always get a positive result when we square a negative number is worth remembering because it plays a vital role in several techniques you will come across.

The number 2 in 3^2 is known as the power to which 3 is raised, which means the number of threes that have to be multiplied together. Three to the power three indicates that three should be cubed, that is three threes should be multiplied together:

$$3^3 = 3 * 3 * 3 = 27$$

Multiplying with numbers expressed in powers involves adding the powers, so:

$$3^2 * 3^3 = 35$$

Three to the power five (3 * 3 * 3 * 3 * 3) is 243 so this is simply another way of saying nine times twenty-seven. At first sight it might seem odd to be adding something when the sign '*' says multiply but in adding the powers (two plus two to give four) we are simply counting the number of threes that would have to be multiplied together to get the answer.

Before electronic calculators became widely available powers were used to carry out multiplication because adding powers was easier. This is what logarithms were about; converting numbers into the powers of ten meant that any multiplication, no matter how complex, could be undertaken using only addition.

While our access to calculators today means that we have no such need for logarithms for arithmetical convenience, you will probably find powers of ten used when very large numbers are shown in calculator displays and computer software.

Example 13

An economist wants to find out how much it would cost to give every resident of the India half a million Rupees, assuming the India's population is 56 million.

If you multiply fifty-six million by half a million on your calculator (56,000,000 * 500,000) it will probably show something like:

$$2.8^{13} \text{ or } 2.8*^{10}\ 13 \text{ or } 2.8E + 13$$

The calculator produces the answer 28000000000000 but has insufficient space to fit in all the zeroes, so it uses powers of ten to represent them and expresses the answer as 2.8 times ten to the power thirteen. The power, thirteen, is the number of times you would have to multiply 2.8 by ten to get 28,000,000,000,000. The letter E in the third version of the expression stands for exponent, another word for power.

You will also come across negative powers or exponents in calculator and computer work. To understand negative powers it helps if you are aware that dividing with numbers involving powers means subtracting the powers, for instance:

$$3^3 \div 3^2 = 3^1$$

This is another way of saying three cubed (27) divided by three squared (9) is three; the result is three to the power one since a number raised to the power one is simply the number itself. If we use the same approach to divide three cubed by three cubed, we get three to the power zero:

$$3^3 \div 3^3 = 3^0$$

The cube of three is twenty-seven, so this is the same as dividing twenty-seven by twenty-seven, which gives us one. So three to the power zero is one; in fact any number to the power zero is one.

If we divide three squared by three cubed we get a negative power:

$$32 \div 33 = 3^{-1}$$

Here we are dividing nine by twenty-seven, which gives us one-third. A number raised to the power minus one is one over that number, which is known as the reciprocal of the number. A number raised to the power minus two is one over the square of the number:

$$3^2 \div 3^4 = 3^{-2}$$

This is the same as saying nine divided by eighty-one is one-ninth, or one over the square of three. In the same way as positive powers of ten are used in calculator displays and computer software to represent very large numbers, negative powers of ten are used to represent very small numbers.

Example 14

Half a kilogram of a hazardous chemical is deposited by accident in a tank holding 800 million litres of water. If the chemical disperses throughout the contents of the tank, how much will there be per litre of water?

If you divide one-half by 800 million on your calculator (0.5 ÷ 800000000) you will probably see:

$$6.25^{-10} \text{ or } 6.25*10 - 10 \text{ or } 6.25E{-}10$$

The answer is 0.000000000625 kilograms per litre but there is not enough room for all the zeroes, so the calculator uses negative powers of ten and the answer is shown as 6.25 divided by ten to the power ten, in other words 6.25 divided by ten ten times. Taking the square root of a number, represented by the radical or 'tick' sign, $\sqrt{\ }$, means finding what has to be squared to produce the number. The square root of nine, shown as $\sqrt{9}$, is three because the number three multiplied by itself gives you nine. You should bear in mind that the result of $\sqrt{9}$ could be – 3, since the square of – 3 is also nine. Having said that, in most business contexts it is the positive root that is of interest.

Example 15

A mobile phone retailer has been sent a pack of merchandising material that has to be assembled in the shop window for the launch of a new 'Square Deal' product. At the heart of the display is a fluorescent mosaic in the shape of a square that must be made up of centimetre square stickers. If the pack contains 234 stickers, what are the maximum dimensions of the mosaic square, assuming that the stickers cannot be cut?

You can determine the answer by taking the square root of 234:

$$\text{Length/width} = \sqrt{234} = 15.297$$

The maximum dimensions would be 15 centimetres long by 15 centimetres wide. Although $\sqrt{234}$ is also –15.297 the concept of negative dimensions makes no sense here. An alternative form of representing the square root of a number is to show the number to the power of a half, so:

$$\sqrt{3} = 3^{1/2}$$

If you square the square root of a number you get the number itself, so:

$$\sqrt{3} * \sqrt{3} = 3$$

We get the same result o n adding powers:

$$3^{1/2} * 3^{1/2} = 3^{1} = 3$$

FRACTIONS, PROPORTIONS AND PERCENTAGES

Fractions, proportions and percentages sound different, but they are only different ways of doing the same thing: expressing a part of something in relation to its whole. If, for example, a company employs 100 people of whom 25 are women, this could be expressed as:

women make up one-quarter of the labour force

or women make up 0.25 of the labour force

or women make up 25% of the labour force.

One-quarter is a fraction, 0.25 is a proportion and 25% is a percentage. There are different ways of saying the same thing because there are four quarters in one, four lots of 0.25 in one and four lots of 25% in 100%. You should bear in mind that each of them is a number less than one, including the percentage, which doesn't look as if it is less than one.

It is easier to use percentages if you understand that the literal meaning of 'percent' is per hundred. (Centum meant one hundred in Latin, cent is French for a hundred, cento is Italian for a hundred, and a century is a hundred years.) This can help especially when you have to perform arithmetical operations using percentages.

Example 16

A bookshop gets Rs.20 for every copy of a particular book sold, 70% of which is paid to the publisher. The publisher pays 10% of the 70% they get to the writer of the book. If the bookshop sells 270 copies, how much will the writer get?

The bookshop gets 270 * Rs. 20 = Rs. 5400

To work out how much of this the publisher will get you may be tempted to multiply Rs. 5400 by 70 and get Rs. 378,000. Although the publisher would be delighted by your result it far exceeds the amount the bookshop received for the books! The result is distorted because we have multiplied by 70 not 70%.

To do it properly we need to multiply by 0.7, the proportion form of 70%, or by 70/100, the fraction form of 70%.

5400 * 0.7 = Rs. 3780 = 5400 * 70/100

To find the amount the writer will get we need to take 10% or one-tenth of this, Rs. 378. We could represent the whole procedure as:

270 * 20 * 0.7 * 0.1 = Rs. 378

Proportions are the easiest form of numbers less than one to deal with because they are 'calculator friendly', but you may occasionally come across arithmetical operations involving fractions.

Addition and subtraction with fractions is straightforward if the figures below the line, the denominators, are the same:

$$\frac{1}{5}+\frac{2}{5}=\frac{3}{5}$$

But if the denominators are different we need to make them compatible. The easiest way of doing this is to multiply them together to find a compatible or common denominator, a unit that can be used for both numbers.

Example 17

A third of visitors to an Internet site use the Alpha service provider and a quarter use Omega. What fraction of visitors uses Alpha or Omega?

To find this we need to add a quarter to a third,

$$\frac{1}{3}+\frac{1}{4}$$

But these are incompatible; thirds are not the same as quarters. If we multiply three by four we get twelve. Since both a third and a quarter can be expressed in twelfths (4/12 and 3/12 respectively), we can conduct the addition using twelfths as follows:

$$\frac{4}{12}+\frac{3}{12}=\frac{7}{12}$$

Subtracting fractions also involves identifying a common denominator, so:

$$\frac{1}{3}-\frac{1}{4}=\frac{4}{12}-\frac{3}{12}=\frac{1}{12}$$

To multiply two fractions, multiply the figures above the line, the numerators, and divide the result by the product you get from multiplying the denominators together, so:

$$\frac{2}{5}*\frac{3}{4}=\frac{2*3}{5*4}=\frac{6}{20}$$

It is better to express fractions in the smallest denominator possible. Here we could divide both the numerator and denominator by two (doing the same thing with the top and bottom does not alter the value of the expression), and giving the answer as 3/10.

Dividing is the reverse of multiplying. If you multiply a number by two then divide the result by two you get the number you started with. Bear this in mind when you divide fractions, as it involves 'reversing' or inverting the second fraction and then multiplying:

$$\frac{1}{4}\div\frac{2}{5}=\frac{1}{4}*\frac{5}{2}=\frac{1*5}{4*2}=\frac{5}{8}$$

APPROXIMATION AND ROUNDING

You may find it easy to work out numbers in your head, or you may find such a skill incomprehensible and envy those who have it. The truth is that anyone can learn how to carry out mental arithmetic, the tricks are to round the numbers first so they are easier to deal with, and then use them to get a rough figure that can be refined with a little more work.

People who find it easy to work out numerical problems in their head often use rounding and approximation intuitively, that is without thinking about it. In fact you probably round certain numbers automatically. If someone asked your age, you would say '18' or '24' as appropriate, you would not say '18 years, 3 months and 22 days' or '24.12 years'. You round down to the nearest completed year of your age. In the same way when you check how much money you have you probably look at the notes and large denomination coins in your purse or wallet and make an estimate. Only when you are particularly concerned about how much you have, or you have time to spare would you count every coin.

You must be familier with approximation and rounding. If you get used to applying them in your numerical work you will gain a better 'feel' for numbers, become better able to spot mistakes and think numerically 'on your feet'.

Example 18

You enter a burger bar where a member of staff asks for your order. You know what you want to order but you don't know how much it will cost. As you give your order you look at the prices of the things you want: one burger Rs.2.59, another burger Rs.1.99, a portion of fries Rs.0.89, a cold drink Rs.0.99, a hot drink Rs.0.79. You want some idea of the total cost so you know whether to count up your change or get out a note.

To get a quick answer, round up each item to the nearest Rupee:

Rough cost = Rs. 3 + Rs. 2 + Rs. 1 + Rs. 1 + Rs. 1 = Rs. 8

Every figure has been rounded up so this is an over-estimate. We know that the total cost will be no more than this, but it is a rather rough approximation. You could get a more accurate idea if you rounded each figure to the nearest ten pence:

Approximate total cost = Rs. 2.60 + Rs. 2.00 + Rs. 0.90 + Rs. 1.00 + Rs. 0.80 = Rs. 7.30

Each of the figures here is rounded up by one penny, so you can get the precise total by taking five pence away from Rs.7.30, which gives you Rs. 7.25.

SIGNIFICANT FIGURES AND DECIMAL PLACES

We tend to use rounding to produce informative figures when complete precision is not necessary. You should round down figures under 5 and round up figures of 5 and over. The degree of rounding is expressed as the number of significant figures.

Example 19

A total of 291,538 people visit a trade exhibition. Round this figure so that it is expressed to:

(a) five significant figures

(b) four significant figures

(c) three significant figures

(a) 291,540 round the 8 up, so 38 becomes 40

(b) 291,500 round the 4 down, so 540 becomes 500

(c) 292,000 round the 5 up, so 1500 becomes 2000

If rounding is applied to numbers with figures after the decimal point, the degree of rounding is expressed as the number of decimal places.

Example 20

A bureau de change offers an exchange rate of 3.2856 for one currency against another.

Express this figure to:

(a) three decimal places

(b) two decimal places

(c) one decimal place

(a) 3.286

(b) 3.29

(c) 3.3

Note that in Example 20 zeroes have not been written to the right of the last specific or significant figure, whereas zeroes were included in the answers to Example 19. This is because in Example 19 the zeroes are vital in expressing the size of the numbers.

When you are working with numbers involving decimals you will need to work to a certain number of decimal places, in other words a certain degree of precision, but exactly how many decimal places? To ensure that your work is not too approximate, avoid rounding until you have reached the answer, and express the answer to one more place of decimals than the original figures were in. For example, if the numbers you began with were given to two places of decimals, give your answer to three places of decimals.

PRECEDENCE OF ARITHMETICAL OPERATIONS

Often you will find that the forms of arithmetical operations we have looked at in this chapter are used in combination. An expression may for instance involve addition, multiplication and squaring. If this is the case it is important that you carry out the operations in the right sequence, with some operations preceding others. The order of precedence can be summarized as follows:

- First carry out any operations in brackets.
- Then do any squaring and square rooting.
- Then multiplication and division.
- Finally, addition and subtraction to be done.

The priority given to brackets is particularly important because they can be used to change the sequence of other operations completely, for example:

$$4 + 7 + 2 * 3 = 17 \text{ but } (4 + 7 + 2) * 3 = 39$$

In the first case the multiplication is carried out before the additions. The effect of the brackets is to prioritize the addition over the multiplication. Addition would normally be undertaken after multiplication, but enclosing the additions in brackets makes them 'jump the queue' ahead of the multiplication.

You may find nested brackets used to specify a sequence of operation, for instance:

$$((3 + 2) * 4)^2 = (5 * 4)^2 = 20^2 = 400$$

You need to carry out this sort of sequence by starting inside the innermost brackets and working outwards. Note that without the brackets we would get a completely different answer:

$$3 + 2 * 4^2 = 3 + 2 * 16 = 3 + 32 = 35$$

If you come across an expression involving operations with equal priority, carry them out from left to right, for example:

$$16/2 * 4 = 8 * 4 = 32 \text{ not } 16/2 * 4 = 16/8 = 2$$

If we wanted to specify that the multiplication should be undertaken first, we should use brackets:

$$16/(2 * 4) = 16/8 = 2$$

Example 21

A contractor has to prepare an estimate for resealing the damaged floor of a square swimming pool that has an area measuring 17 metres by 17 metres. The cost of sealing materials is Rs.15 per square metre. He estimates the job will take 3 days. The cost of labour will be Rs. 80 per day and equipment hire will cost Rs. 50 per day. He adds a mark-up of 35% to the total cost to cover overheads and profit. Work out his estimate.

Total cost = 172 * 15 + 3 * 80 + 3 * 50

The mark-up of 35% means that to get the estimate we must take the total cost and increase it by 35%. We can do this by taking 135% of the total cost, in other words multiplying by 135/100 or 1.35. Since we should only do this after the total cost has been worked out, we will use brackets to clarify the sequence:

$$1.35 * (17^2 * 15 + 3 * 80 + 3 * 50)$$

Start inside the brackets, squaring first:

Estimate = 1.35 * (289 * 15 + 3 * 80 + 3 * 50)

Then multiplying:

Estimate = 1.35 * (4335 = 240 + 150)

Then adding:

Estimate = 1.35 * (4725)

Finally the multiplication outside the brackets:

Estimate = Rs.6378.75

The rules about precedence apply where capital sigma (Sð) is used to represent addition. You may find the process of taking a set of numbers and multiplying them in turn by a set of related numbers before adding up the resulting set of products is expressed as:

$$\sum_{i=1}^{n} x_i y_i$$

Here the x values, x_1 to x_n are the numbers in the first set and the y values, y_1 to Y_n are the numbers in the second set. When you see an expression like this remember that the multiplication must be carried out before the addition. You should note that when we use letters to represent numbers as we have done here, the multiplication is implicit or assumed because the y_i is written right after the x_i. This convention avoids the confusion that might arise from using one 'x' to represent a number and another 'x' to represent multiply.

Example 22

A cinema manager checks the revenue, R, from the screening of a film by working out:

$$R=\sum_{i=1}^{3} p_i q_i$$

The p values are the ticket prices; p_1 is the adult price of Rs. 6, p_2 the children's price of Rs.3, p_3 is the concessionary price of Rs. 4 for pensioners. The q values are the quantities of tickets sold; q_1 the number of adult tickets, q_2 the number of children's tickets and q_3 the number of concessionary tickets. What is the revenue from a screening attended by 25 adults, 32 children and 15 pensioners?

$$R=\sum_{i=1}^{3} p_i q_i = p_1 * q_1 + p_2 * q_2 + p_3 * q_3$$

$$= 6 * 25 + 3 * 32 + 4 * 15$$

$$= 150 + 96 + 60 = \text{Rs. } 306$$

2

Basic Linear Algebra

LINEAR EQUATION

The Gauss- Jordan elimination procedure is a systematic method for solving systems of linear equation. It work on one variable at a time, eliminating it in all rows but one, and then moves on to the next variable. We illustrate the procedure on three examples.

Example: (Solving linear equation)

$$x_1 + 2x_2 + x_3 = 4$$
$$2x_1 - x_2 + 3x_3 = 3$$
$$x_1 + x_2 + x_3 = 3$$

In the first step of the procedure, we use the first equation to eliminate x_1 from the other two. Specifically, in order to eliminate x_1 from the second equation, we multiply the first equation by 2 and subtract the result from the second equation. Similarly, to eliminate x_1 from the third equation we subtract the first equation from the third. Such are called elementary row operations. We keep the first equation and the modify second and third equations. The resulting equation are

$$x_1 + 2x_2 + x_3 = 4$$
$$-5x_2 + x_3 = -5$$
$$-x_2 - 2x_3 = -1$$

Note that only one equation was used to eliminate x_1 in all the others. This guarantees that the new system of equations had exactly the same solution(s) as the original one. In the second step of the procedure, we divide the second equation by -5 to make the coefficient of x_2 equal to 1. Then, we use this equation to eliminate x_2. This yields the following new system of equations.

$$x_1 + \frac{7}{5}x_3 = 2$$

$$x_2 - \frac{1}{5}x_3 = 1$$

$$-\frac{11}{5}x_3 = 0$$

Once again, only one equation was used to eliminate x_2 in all the others and that guarantees that the new system has the same solution(s) as the original one.

$$x_1 = 2$$

$$x_2 = 1$$

$$x_3 = 0$$

So, there is a unique solution. Note that, throughout the procedure, we were careful to keep three equation that have the same solution (s) as the original three equations. Why is it useful? Because, linear systems of equation do not always have a unique solution and it is important to identify such situations.

Another example: $x_1 + 2x_2 + x_3 = 4$

$$x_1 + x_2 + 2x_3 = 1$$

$$2x_1 + 3x_2 + 3x_3 = 2$$

First we eliminate x_1 from equation 2 and 3.

$$x_1 + 2x_2 + x_3 = 4$$

$$-x_2 + x_3 = -3$$

$$-x_2 - 2x_3 = -6$$

Then we eliminate x_2 from equation 1 and 3.

$$x_1 + 3x_3 = -2$$
$$x_2 - x_3 = 3$$
$$0 = -3$$

A third example:
$$x_1 + 2x_2 + x_3 = 4$$
$$x_1 + x_2 + 2x_3 = 1$$
$$2x_1 + 3x_2 + 3x_3 = 5$$

Doing the same as above, we end up with

$$x_1 + 3x_3 = -2$$
$$x_2 - x_3 = 3$$
$$0 = 0$$

Now equation 3 is an obvious equaliy. It can be discarded to obtain

$$x_1 = -2 - 3x_3$$
$$x_2 = 3 + x_3.$$

The situation where we can empress some of the variables (here x_1 and x_2) in terms of the remaining variables (here x_3) is important. These variables are said to be basic and nonnbasic respectively. Any choice of the nonbasic variable x_3 yields a solution of the linear system. Therefore the system has infinitely many solutions.

It is generally true that a system of a linear equations in n variables has either :

(a) no solution,

(b) a unique solution,

(c) infinitely many solutions.

The Gauss Jordan elimination procedure solves the system of linear equation using two elementary row operations:

- Modify some equation by multiplying it by a nonzero scalar (a scalar is an actual real number, such as $\frac{1}{2}$ or-2 it cannot be one of the variables in the problem),
- Modify some equation by adding to it a scalar multiple of another

equation.

The resulting system of m linear equations has the same solution (s) as the original system. If an equation 0= 0 is produced, it is discarded and the procedure is continued. If an equation 0= a is produced where a is a nonzero scalar, the procedure is stopped: in this case, the system has no solution. At each step of the Procedure a new variable is made basic: it is coefficient 1 in one of the equation 0 in all the other. The Procedure stop when each equation is a basic variable associated with it. Say p equation remain (remember some of the original equation may have discarded), when n = p the system has a unique solution. When n > p then p variables are basic and the remaining n-p are nonbasic. In this case, the system of infinitely many solution.

Exercise- Solve the following system of linear equation using the Gauss- Jordan elimination procedure and state whether case, (a), (b), and (c) holds.

(1)
$$3x_1 + 4x_3 = 2$$
$$x_1 + x_2 + x_3 = 4$$
$$2x_2 + x_3 = 3$$

(2)
$$2x_1 + 2x_2 - x_3 = 1$$
$$4x_1 + x_3 = 2$$
$$x_1 - x_2 + x_3 = 2$$

(3)
$$x_1 - x_2 + x_3 = 1$$
$$-2x_1 + 2x_2 - 2x_3 = -2$$
$$-x_1 + x_2 - x_3 = -1$$

Exercise- Indicate whether the following linear system if equation has 0, 1 and infinitely many solutions.

$$x_1 + 2x_2 + 4x_3 + x_4 + 3x_5 = 2$$
$$2x_1 + x_2 + x_3 + 3x_4 + x_5 = 1$$
$$3x_2 + 7x_3 - x_4 + 5x_5 = 6$$

VECTORS AND MATRICES

It is useful to formalize the operation of vectors and matrices that form the basis of linear algebra. For our purpose, the most useful definition are the following:

A matrix is a rectangular array the number written in the from

$$A = \begin{pmatrix} a_{11} & a_{12} \, \Lambda \, a_{1n} \\ \mathrm{M} & \mathrm{M} \quad \mathrm{M} \\ a_{m1} & a_{m2} \, \Lambda \, a_{mn} \end{pmatrix}$$

A matrix A has dimensions m x n, if it has m rows and n columns, When n=1, the matrix is called a row vectors, When n=1 the matrix is called the column vector. A vector can be represented either by a row or a column vector.

Equation of two matrices of some dimension:

$$\text{Let } A = \begin{pmatrix} a_{11} & \Lambda & a_{1n} \\ \mathrm{M} & & \mathrm{M} \\ a_{m1} & \Lambda & a_{mn} \end{pmatrix} \text{ and } B = \begin{pmatrix} b_{11} \, \Lambda \, b_{1n} \\ \mathrm{M} \qquad \mathrm{M} \\ b_{m1} \, \Lambda \, b_{mn} \end{pmatrix}$$

Than A=B means that $a_{ij} = b_{ij}$ for all i, j

Multiplication of a matrix A by a scalar k:

$$kA = \begin{pmatrix} ka_{11} & ka_{12} \, \Lambda & ka_{1n} \\ \mathrm{M} & \mathrm{M} & \mathrm{M} \\ ka_{m1} & ka_{m2} \, \Lambda & a_{mn} \end{pmatrix}$$

Addition of two matrices of some dimension

$$\text{Let } A = \begin{pmatrix} a_{11} & \Lambda & a_{1n} \\ \mathrm{M} & & \mathrm{M} \\ a_{m1} & \Lambda & a_{mn} \end{pmatrix} \text{ and } B = \begin{pmatrix} b_{11} \, \Lambda \, b_{1n} \\ \mathrm{M} \qquad \mathrm{M} \\ b_{m1} \, \Lambda \, b_{mn} \end{pmatrix}$$

$$A+B\begin{pmatrix} a_{11}+b_{11}\ \Lambda\ \ a_{1n}+b_{1n} \\ \mathrm{M} \qquad\qquad \mathrm{M} \\ a_{m1}+b_{m1}\ \Lambda\ \ a_{mn}+b_{mn} \end{pmatrix},$$

Then

Not that A+B is not defined when A and B have different dimension.

Exercise: Compute:

$$3\begin{pmatrix} 2\ 3\ 1 \\ 0\ 5\ 4 \end{pmatrix} - 2\begin{pmatrix} 0\ 4\ 1 \\ 1\ 6\ 6 \end{pmatrix}$$

Multiplication of a matrix of dimensions $m\times n$ by a matrix of dimensions $n\times p$:

$$\text{Let } A+B\begin{pmatrix} a_{11}\Lambda\ b_{1n} \\ \mathrm{M} \qquad \mathrm{M} \\ a_{i1}\Lambda\ a_{in} \\ \mathrm{M} \qquad \mathrm{M} \\ a_{m1}\Lambda\ a_{mn} \end{pmatrix} \text{ and } B=\begin{pmatrix} b_{11}\ \Lambda\ b_{1j}\Lambda\ b_{1n} \\ \mathrm{M} \qquad \mathrm{M} \qquad \mathrm{M} \\ b_{m1}\Lambda\ b_{mj}\Lambda\ b_{mn} \end{pmatrix}$$

Then AB is a matrix of dimensions $m\times p$ computed as follows.

$$AB\begin{pmatrix} a_{11}\,b_{11}+\Lambda+a_{1n}\,b_{n1} & \Lambda & a_{11}\,b_{1p}+\Lambda+a_{1n}\,b_{np} \\ \mathrm{M} & a_{i1}\,b_{1j}+\Lambda+a_{in}\,b_{nj} & \mathrm{M} \\ a_{m1}b_{11}+\Lambda+a_{mn}\,b_{n1} & \Lambda & a_{m1}\,b_{ip}+\Lambda+a_{mn}\,b_{np} \end{pmatrix},$$

As an example, let us multiply the matrices

$$A=\begin{pmatrix} 2\ 3\ 4 \\ 5\ 1\ 0 \end{pmatrix} \text{ and } \quad B=\begin{pmatrix} 11\ 12 \\ 14\ 15 \\ 17\ 18 \end{pmatrix}$$

The result is

$$AB = \begin{pmatrix} 2\times11+3\times14+4\times17 & 2\times12+3\times15+4\times18 \\ 5\times11+1\times14+0\times17 & 5\times12+1\times15+0\times18 \end{pmatrix}$$

$$= \begin{pmatrix} 132 & 141 \\ 69 & 75 \end{pmatrix}$$

Note that AB is defined *only* when the number of columns of A equals the number of rows of B. An important remark: even when both AB and BA are defined, the results are usually different. A property of matrix multiplication is the following:

$$(AB)C = A(BC)$$

That is, if you have three matrices A, B, C to multiply and the product is legal (the number of columns of A equals the number of rows of B and the number of columns of B equals the number of rows of C), then you have two possibilities: you can first compute AB and multiply the result by C, or you can first compute BC and multiply A by the result.

Exercise: Consider the following matrices

$$x = \begin{pmatrix} 1 & 1 & 1 \end{pmatrix} \; y = \begin{pmatrix} 3 & 2 & 1 \end{pmatrix} \; z = \begin{pmatrix} 1 \\ 1 \\ 1 \end{pmatrix}$$

When Possible, Compute the following quantities

(a) xz

(b) zx

(c) yzx

(d) xzy

(e) $(x+y)z$

(f) $(xz)+(yz)$

Remark -A system of linear equations can be written conveniently using matrix notation. Namely,

$$a_{11}x_1 + \cdots + a_{1n}x_n = b_1$$

$$\cdots \quad \cdots \quad \cdots$$

$$a_{m1}x_1 + \cdots + a_{mn}x_n = b_m$$

can be written as

$$\begin{pmatrix} a_{11} & \cdots + a_{1n} \\ \vdots & \vdots \\ a_{m1} & \cdots + a_{mn} \end{pmatrix} \begin{pmatrix} x_1 \\ \vdots \\ x_n \end{pmatrix} = \begin{pmatrix} b_1 \\ \vdots \\ b_m \end{pmatrix}$$

or as

$$\begin{pmatrix} a_{11} \\ \vdots \\ a_{m1} \end{pmatrix} x_1 + \cdots + \begin{pmatrix} a_{1n} \\ \vdots \\ a_{mn} \end{pmatrix} x_n = \begin{pmatrix} b_1 \\ \vdots \\ b_m \end{pmatrix}$$

So a matrix equation Ax=B where A is a given m x n matrix, b is a given M- column vectors and x is an unknown n-column vector is a linear system of m equation in n can be written as

Variables Similarly a vector equation $a_1x_1 + \cdots + a_nx_n = b$ where $a_1, \cdots, a_n b$ are given m- column vector and $x_1, \cdots, x_n$ are unknown real number is also a system of m equation in n variables

Exercise-

(a) Show the matrix equation-

$$\begin{pmatrix} 1 & 2 & 1 \\ 2 & -1 & 3 \\ 1 & 1 & -1 \end{pmatrix} \begin{pmatrix} x_1 \\ x_2 \\ x_3 \end{pmatrix} = \begin{pmatrix} 4 \\ 3 \\ 3 \end{pmatrix}$$

(b) Show the vector equation

$$\begin{pmatrix}1\\2\\1\end{pmatrix}x_1+\begin{pmatrix}2\\-1\\1\end{pmatrix}x_2+\begin{pmatrix}1\\3\\-1\end{pmatrix}x_3=\begin{pmatrix}4\\3\\3\end{pmatrix}$$

The following standard definition will be useful:

A square matrix is a matrix with same number of rows as columns.

The identity matrix I is a square matrix with 1's of the main diagonal and 0's else where i.e.

$$I=\begin{pmatrix}1 & 0 & \cdots & 0\\ 0 & 1 & \cdots & 0\\ \cdots & \cdots & \cdots & \cdots\\ 0 & 0 & \cdots & 1\end{pmatrix}$$

The zero matrix contains only 0's. In particular, the zero vector has all components equal to 0. A nonzero vector is one that contains at least one nonzero component.

The transpose of matrices $A=\begin{pmatrix}a_{11} & a_{12} & \cdots & a_{1n}\\ \vdots & \vdots & & \vdots\\ a_{m1} & a_{m2} & \cdots & a_{mn}\end{pmatrix}$ is the matrix

$$A^T=\begin{pmatrix}a_{11} & \cdots & a_{m1}\\ a_{12} & \cdots & a_{m2}\\ \vdots & & \vdots\\ a_{1n} & \cdots & a_{mn}\end{pmatrix}$$

A square matrix A is symmetric it its elements satisfy $a_{ij}=b_{ij}$ for all i and j. So a symmetric matrix satisfies AT= A.

LINEAR COMBINATION

Suppose that the vector (1, 3) represents the content of a "Regular" can of mixed nuts (1lb cashews and 3 1b Peanuts) while (1.1) represents a "Deluxe" Can (1 1b cashews and 1 1b Puanuts) Can you obtain a mixture of 2 1b cashews and 3 Ib peanuts, by combining the two mixtures in appropriate amounts? The answer is to us x_1 cans of regular and x_2 cans Deluxe in order to satisfy the equality

$$x_1\begin{pmatrix}1\\3\end{pmatrix}+x_2\begin{pmatrix}1\\1\end{pmatrix}=\begin{pmatrix}2\\3\end{pmatrix}$$

This is none other than a system of two linear equation

$$x_1 + x_2 = 2$$
$$3x_1 + x_2 = 3$$

The solution of these equation is $x_1 = 1/2, x_2 = 3/2$ So the desired combination is the mix 1/2 can of regular nuts with 3/2 can of the Delux nuts. Thus if some recipe calls for the mixture (2,3), you can subsititute 1/2 can of regular mix and 3/2 can of Delux mix.

Suppose now that you want to obtain 1 lb cashews and no peanuts. This poses the equations,

$$x_1\begin{pmatrix}1\\3\end{pmatrix}+x_2\begin{pmatrix}1\\1\end{pmatrix}=\begin{pmatrix}1\\0\end{pmatrix}$$

The solution is $(x_1, x_2) = (-1/2, 3/2)$.Thus you can obtain a pound of pure cashews by buying 3/2 can of Delux mix and removing enough nuts to from 1/2 can regular mix, which can be sold. In this case it is physically possible to use a negative amount of some ingredient, but in other cases it may be impossible, as when one is mixing paint.

A vector of the form $x_1\begin{pmatrix}1\\3\end{pmatrix}+x_2\begin{pmatrix}1\\1\end{pmatrix}$ is called a linear combination of the vectors $\begin{pmatrix}1\\3\end{pmatrix}$ and $\begin{pmatrix}1\\1\end{pmatrix}$. In particular we just save that the vector $\begin{pmatrix}2\\3\end{pmatrix}$ Is a linear combination of the vectors $\begin{pmatrix}1\\3\end{pmatrix}$ and $\begin{pmatrix}1\\1\end{pmatrix}$ And so it $\begin{pmatrix}1\\0\end{pmatrix}$

The question arises : can one obtain any mixture whatever by taking the appropriate Combination of regular and Deluxe cans? Is any vector $\begin{pmatrix}b_1\\b_2\end{pmatrix}$ a linear combination of $\begin{pmatrix}1\\3\end{pmatrix}$ and $\begin{pmatrix}1\\1\end{pmatrix}$?

To answer the question, solve the equation of general. You want of mixture of b_1 cashews and b_2 peanuts and set.

$$x_1\begin{pmatrix}1\\3\end{pmatrix}+x_2\begin{pmatrix}1\\1\end{pmatrix}=\begin{pmatrix}b_1\\b_2\end{pmatrix},$$

or equivalently,

$$\begin{aligned}x_1+x_2 &= b_1\\ 3x_1+x_2 &= b_2\end{aligned}$$

These equation of a unique solution, no matter what are the values of b_1 and b_2 namely,

$$x_1\frac{b_1-b_2}{2}, x_2\frac{3b_1-b_2}{2}$$

No matter the vector (b_1, b_2)you want, you can get it as a linear combination of (1,3) and (1,1), The vectors (1,3) and (1,1) are said to be linearly independent.

Not all pair of vectors can yield an arbitrary mixture (b_1, b_2). For instance, to linear combination of (1,1) and (2,2) yields (2,3). In other works and equations.

$$x_1\begin{pmatrix}1\\1\end{pmatrix}+x_2\begin{pmatrix}2\\2\end{pmatrix}=\begin{pmatrix}2\\3\end{pmatrix}$$

have no solution of (1, 1) the vectors, (1, 1) and (2, 2) are said to be linearly independent

If (2,2) represents, for instance, a large Deluxe can of nuts and (1,1) a small one, it is clear that you cannot obtain any mixture you want by combining large and small Deluxe The reason is that (2, 2) is already a multiple of (1,1), that is (2, 2) is a linear combination cans. In fact, once you have small cans, the large cans contribute nothing at all to the mixtures you can generate, since you can always substitute two small cans for a large one.

A more interesting example is (1,2,0), (1,0,1) and (2,2,1). The third vector is clearly a linear combination of the other two (it equals their sum). Altogether, these three vectors are said to be linearly dependent. For instance, these three vectors might represent mixture of nuts as follows:

Brand	A	B	C
cashews	1	1	2
peanuts	2	0	2
almonds	0	1	1

Then once you have brands A and B, brand C adds nothing whatever to the variety of mixtures you can concoct. This is because you can already obtain a can of brand C from brands A and B anyway. In other words, if a recipe calls for brand C, you can always substitute a mixture 1 of a can brand A and 1 can brand B.

Suppose you want to obtain the mixture (1,2,1) by combining Brands A, B, and C. The equation are

$$x_1 + x_2 + 2x_3 = 1$$
$$2x_1 + x_3 = 2$$
$$x_2 + x_3 = 1$$

If you try to solve these equation, you will find that there is no solution, So that vector (1,2,1) is not a linear combination of (1 ,2 0,) (1,0 ,1) and (2,2,1).

The concepts of linear combination, linear dependence and linear independence introduced in the above examples can be defined more formally, for any number of *n*-component vectors. This is done as follows:

- A vector B having n component is a linear combination of the k vectors $v_1,........,v_k$ each having n components, if it is possible to find k real numbers $x_1,........,x_k$ satisfying :

$$x_1v_1 + ...x_kv_k, = b \quad (1.1)$$

To find the numbers $x_1,.......,x_k$ view (1.1) as a system linear equations and solve by the Gauss- Jordan Method.

- A set of vectors (All having n components) is linearly dependent if at least vectors linear combination of the others. Otherwise they are linearly independent.
- Given n linearly independent vectors $v_1,..............,v_n$, each having n components, any desired vector b with n component can be obtained as a linear combination of them:

$$x_1v_1,..............,x_nv_n = b \quad (1.2)$$

The desired weights $x_1,..............,x_n$ are computed by solving (1.2) with the Gauss-Jordan method: there is a unique solution whenever the vectors $v_1,..............,v_n$ are linearly independent:

Exercise: A can of Brand A mixed not has 1Ib cashews, 1Ib almonds, 2Ib peanuts. Brand B gad 1Ib cashews and3Ib peanuts. Brand C has 1 Ib almonds and 2 Ib peanuts. Show how much of each brand to by/ sell so as to obtain a mixture containing 5 Ib of each type of nut.

Exercise: Determine whether the vector $\begin{pmatrix} 1 \\ 2 \\ -2 \end{pmatrix}$ is a linear combination of

(*a*) $\begin{pmatrix} 1 \\ 0 \\ 2 \end{pmatrix}, \begin{pmatrix} 2 \\ 0 \\ 1 \end{pmatrix}$

(*b*) $\begin{pmatrix} 2 \\ 1 \\ -1 \end{pmatrix}, \begin{pmatrix} 1 \\ 2 \\ -1 \end{pmatrix}, \begin{pmatrix} -1 \\ 1 \\ -2 \end{pmatrix}$

In linear programming. there are typically many more variables then equation. So, this case warrants looking at another example.

Example: A craft shop makes deluxe and regular belts. Each deluxe belt requires a strip of leather and 2 hours of labour. Each regular belt requires a leather strip and 1 hour of labour. 40 leather strips and 60 hours of labour are available. How many belts of either kind can be made?

This is really a mixing problem. Rather than peanuts and cashews, the mixture will contain leather and labour. The items to be mixed are four activities: manufacturing a deluxe belt manufacturing a regular belt leaving a leftover leather strip in inventory and leaving an hour of labour idle (or for other work). Just as each Regular can of mixed nuts contributes 1 pound of cashews and 3 pounds of peanuts to the mixture, each regular belt will consume 1 leather strip and 2 hours of labour. The aim to combine the four activities in the right proportion so that 40 strips and 60 hours are accounted for :

$$x_1\begin{pmatrix}1\\2\end{pmatrix}+x_2\begin{pmatrix}1\\1\end{pmatrix}+s_1\begin{pmatrix}1\\0\end{pmatrix}+s_2\begin{pmatrix}0\\1\end{pmatrix}=\begin{pmatrix}40\\60\end{pmatrix}$$

So,

x_1 = number of deluxe belts made

x_2 = number of regular belts made

s_1 = number of leather strips left over

s_2 = number of labour hours left over

In tableau from, the equations are:

x_1	x_2	s_1	s_2	*RHS*
1	1	1	0	40
2	1	0	1	60

(1.3)

Since there are only two equations, you can only solve for two variables. Let's solve for x_1 and x_2 using Gauss-Jordan elimination. After the first integration you get,

x_1	x_2	s_1	s_2	RHS	
1	1	1	0	40	(1.4)
0	-1	-2	1	-20	

A second iteration yields the solution,

x_1	x_2	s_1	s_2	RHS	
1	0	-1	1	20	(1.5)
0	1	2	-1	20	

This tableau represents the equations

$$x_1 - s_1 + s_2 = 20$$
$$x_2 + 2s_1 - s_2 = 20$$

or

$$x_1 = 20 + s_1 - s_2$$
$$x_2 = 20 - 2s_1 - s_2$$

You can't say how many deluxe belts x_1 and regular belts x_2 the plants will make until you specify how much leather s_1 and labour s_2 will be left over. But (1.6) is a formula for computing how many belts of either type must be made, for any given s_1 and s_2. So the equation have many solutions (infinitely many)

For example if you want to have nothing left over ($s_1 = s_2 = 0$) you will make 20 of each. If you want to have 5 strips and 5 hours left over, you will make $x_1 = 20$ deluxe and $x_2 = 15$ regular belts.

The variables x_1, x_2 you solved for are called basic variables. The other variables are nonbasic. You have control of the nonbasic. Once you give them values, the value of the basic variables follow. A solution in which you make all the nonbasic variables zero is called a basic solution.

Can you have basic variables other then x_1, x_2? Sure. Any pair of variables can be basic provided the corresponding column sin (1.3) are linearly independent (otherwise, you can't solve for the basic variables).

Equations (1.3), for instance are already solved in (1.3) for basic variables s_1 , s_2 . Here the two basic activities are having leftover leather and having leftover labour. The basic solution is $(s_1, s_2) = (40,60)$. This means that if you decide to produce no belts($x_1 = x_2 = 0$) You must have 40 leftover leather strips and 60 leftover labour hours.

The intermediate step (1.4) solves the equations with basic variables x_1 and x_2. Here the basic solution is unrealizable. If you decide to participate only in the basic activities (making deluxe belts and having leftover labour), you must 40 belts and have -20 leftover hours (i.e., use 20 more than you have), which you can't do within your current resources.

Exercise: Consider the system of equations

x_1	x_2	x_3	x_4	RHS
1	1	2	4	100
3	1	1	2	200

where the first columns on the left represent a regular mixture of nuts a Deluxe mixture a small can of Premium mixture and a large can of Premium.

(a) Solve the system with x_1 and x_2 basic

(b) You want 100 cans of mixed nuts each of which contains 1 Ib cashews and 2 Ib peanuts (i.e-,you want the right -hand side of the above equation)- How can you get them by blending 10 small cans of Premium with proper amounts of the regular and deluxe blends? Hint Set $x_3 = 10$ and $x_4 = 10$ in the expression for the solution values of x_1, x_2 found in (a).

(c) How can you obtain a small can of premium mix by combining (and decombining) the regular and Deluxe blends?

(d) How can you obtain one can of regular mix by combining large and small cans of premium? If you cannot do it, why not? Hint It has to do with linear dependence.

Exercise: A can of paint A has 1 quart red, 1 quart yellow, A can of paint B has 1 quart, 1 quart blue. A can or paint C has 1 quart yellow, 1 quart blue.

(a) How much of each paint must be mixed to obtain a mixture of 1 quart red, 1 quart yellow and 1 quart blue?

(b) How much of each paint must be mixed to obtain one quart of pure red? What do you conclude about the physical feasibility of such a mixture?

Exercise: An electronics plant wants to make stores and CB's. Each Store requires 1 power supply and 3 speakers. Each CB requires 1 power supply and 1 speaker. 100 power supplies and 200 speakers are in stock. How many stores and CB's can it make if it wants to use all the power supplies and all but 10 of the speakers? Hint. Use the following equations.

x_1	x_2	s_1	s_2	RHS
1	1	1	0	100
3	1	0	1	200

Exercise:. A construction foreman needs cement mix containing 8 cubic yards (yd^3) cement, 12 yd^3 sand and 16 yd^3 water. On the site are several mixer trucks containing mix A (1 yd^3 cement, 3 yd^3 sand, 3 yd^3 water) several containing mix B (2 yd^3 cement, 2 yd^3 sand, 3 yd^3 water) and several containing mix C (2 yd^3 cement, 2 yd^3 sand, 3 yd^3 water)

How many truckloads of each mix should the foreman combine to obtain the desired blend?

INVERSE OF A SQUARE MATRIX

If A and B are square matrices such that AB = 1 (the identity matrix), then B is called the inverse of A and is denoted by A^{-1}. A square matrix A has either no inverse or a unique inverse A^{-1}. In the first case, it is said to be singular and in the second case nonsingular. Interestingly, linear independence of vectors plays a role here: a matrix is singular if its columns from a set of lenearly dependent vectors; and it is nonsingular if its columns are linearly independent. Another property is the following: if B is the inverse of A, then A is the inverse of B.

Exercise: (a) Compute the matrix product

$$\begin{pmatrix} 1 & 3 & -2 \\ 0 & -5 & 4 \\ 2 & -3 & 3 \end{pmatrix}\begin{pmatrix} -3 & -3 & 2 \\ 8 & 7 & -4 \\ 10 & 9 & -5 \end{pmatrix},$$

(b) What is the inverse of

$$\begin{pmatrix} -3 & -3 & 2 \\ 8 & 7 & -4 \\ 10 & 9 & -5 \end{pmatrix}?$$

(c) Show that the matrix $A = \begin{pmatrix} 0 & 0 & 0 \\ 0 & 1 & 1 \\ 1 & 0 & 1 \end{pmatrix}$ is singular.

Hints: Assume That the inverse of A *is* $B = \begin{pmatrix} b_{11} & b_{12} & b_{13} \\ b_{21} & b_{22} & b_{23} \\ b_{31} & b_{32} & b_{33} \end{pmatrix}$ and perform the matrix product AB. Than show that no choice can make this product equal to the identity matrix $I = \begin{pmatrix} 1 & 0 & 0 \\ 0 & 1 & 0 \\ 0 & 0 & 1 \end{pmatrix}$

An important property of nonsingular square matrices is the following Consider the system of linear equations-

$$\begin{pmatrix} a_{11} & \Lambda & a_{1n} \\ a_{21} & \Lambda & a_{2n} \\ \text{M} & & \text{M} \\ a_{n1} & \Lambda & a_{nn} \end{pmatrix}\begin{pmatrix} x_1 \\ \text{M} \\ x_n \end{pmatrix} = \begin{pmatrix} b_1 \\ b_2 \\ \text{M} \\ b_n \end{pmatrix},$$ simply written as Ax=b

When A is a square nonsingular matrix this linear system has a unique solution, which can be obtained as obtained as follows. Multiply the matrix equation Ax=b by A^{-1} on the left:

$$A^{-1}Ax = A^{-1}b,$$

This yields $Ix = A^{-1}b$ and so the unique solution to the system of linear equations is

$$x = A^{-1}b.$$

Exercise: Solve the system

$$\begin{aligned} -3x_1 - 3x_2 - 2x_3 &= 1 \\ 8x_1 + 7x_2 - 4x_3 &= -1 \\ 10x_1 + 9x_2 - 5x_3 &= 1 \end{aligned}$$

Finding the Inverse of Square Matrix

Given, $A = \begin{pmatrix} a_{11} & \Lambda & a_{1n} \\ M & & M \\ a_{n1} & \Lambda & a_{nn} \end{pmatrix}$ we must find $B = \begin{pmatrix} b_{11} \Lambda & b_{1n} \\ M & M \\ b_{n1} \Lambda & b_{nn} \end{pmatrix}$ such that AB= 1 (the identity matrix). Therefore, the first column of B must

safisfy $A\begin{pmatrix} b_{11} \\ M \\ b_{n1} \end{pmatrix} = \begin{pmatrix} 1 \\ 0 \\ M \\ 0 \end{pmatrix}$ (this vector is the 1st column of I) Similarly, for the other columns of B, For example, the jth column of B

satisfies $A\begin{pmatrix} b_{ij} \\ M \\ b_{nj} \end{pmatrix} = \begin{pmatrix} 0 \\ M \\ 0 \\ 1 \\ 0 \\ M \\ 0 \end{pmatrix}$ (the jth column of I). So in order to get the inverse of an $n \times n$ matrix, we must solve n linear systems. However, the same steps of the Gauss-Jordan elimination procedure are needed for all of these systems. So we solve them all at once, using the matrix from.

$$A=\begin{pmatrix} 3 & -2 \\ -4 & 3 \end{pmatrix}$$

Example: Find the inverse of

We need to solve the following matrix equation

$$\begin{pmatrix} 3 & -2 \\ -4 & 3 \end{pmatrix} B = \begin{pmatrix} 1 & 0 \\ 0 & 1 \end{pmatrix}$$

We divide the first row by 3 to introduce a 1 in the top left corner

$$\begin{pmatrix} 1 & -\frac{2}{3} \\ -4 & 3 \end{pmatrix} B = \begin{pmatrix} \frac{1}{3} & 0 \\ 0 & 1 \end{pmatrix}$$

Then we add four times the first row to the second row to introduce a 0 in the first column.

$$\begin{pmatrix} 1 & -\frac{2}{3} \\ 0 & \frac{1}{3} \end{pmatrix} B = \begin{pmatrix} \frac{1}{3} & 0 \\ \frac{4}{3} & 1 \end{pmatrix}$$

Multiply the second row by 3.

$$\begin{pmatrix} 1 & -\frac{2}{3} \\ 0 & 1 \end{pmatrix} B = \begin{pmatrix} \frac{1}{3} & 0 \\ 4 & 3 \end{pmatrix}$$

Add $\frac{2}{3}$ the second row to the first. (All this is classical Gauss- Jordan elimination)

$$\begin{pmatrix} 1 & 0 \\ 0 & 1 \end{pmatrix} B = \begin{pmatrix} 3 & 2 \\ 4 & 3 \end{pmatrix}$$

As IB = B, we get

$$B=\begin{pmatrix} 3 & 2 \\ 4 & 3 \end{pmatrix}$$

It is important to note that, in addition to the two elementary row operations introduced earlier in the context of the Gauss-Jordan elimination procedure, a third elementary row operation may sometimes be needed here, namely permuting two rows.

$$A = \begin{pmatrix} 0 & 1 & 0 \\ 2 & 1 & 0 \\ 0 & 0 & 1 \end{pmatrix}$$

Example : Find the inverse of

$$\begin{pmatrix} 0 & 1 & 0 \\ 2 & 1 & 0 \\ 0 & 0 & 1 \end{pmatrix} B = \begin{pmatrix} 1 & 0 & 0 \\ 0 & 1 & 0 \\ 0 & 0 & 1 \end{pmatrix}$$

Because the top left entry of A is 0, we need to permute rows 1 and 2 first.

$$\begin{pmatrix} 2 & 1 & 0 \\ 0 & 1 & 0 \\ 0 & 0 & 1 \end{pmatrix} B = \begin{pmatrix} 0 & 1 & 0 \\ 1 & 0 & 0 \\ 0 & 0 & 1 \end{pmatrix}$$

Now we divide the first row by 2.

$$\begin{pmatrix} 1 & \frac{1}{2} & 0 \\ 0 & 1 & 0 \\ 0 & 0 & 1 \end{pmatrix} B = \begin{pmatrix} 0 & \frac{1}{2} & 0 \\ 1 & 0 & 0 \\ 0 & 0 & 1 \end{pmatrix}$$

Next we add $-\frac{1}{2}$ the second row the first.

$$\begin{pmatrix} 1 & 0 & 0 \\ 0 & 1 & 0 \\ 0 & 0 & 1 \end{pmatrix} B = \begin{pmatrix} -\frac{1}{2} & \frac{1}{2} & 0 \\ 1 & 0 & 0 \\ 0 & 0 & 1 \end{pmatrix}$$

and we are done, since the matrix in front of B is the identity.

Exercise: Find the inverse of the matrix

$$A = \begin{pmatrix} 1 & 4 & 2 \\ 0 & 1 & 0 \\ -1 & -4 & 2 \end{pmatrix}$$

Exercise: Find the inverse of the matrix

$$A = \begin{pmatrix} 0 & 1 & -2 \\ 4 & 0 & 5 \\ 3 & 0 & 4 \end{pmatrix}$$

DETERMINANTS

To each square matrix, we associate a number called its determinant, defined as follows:

if $A = (a_{11})$ then det $(A) = a_{11}$

if $A = \begin{pmatrix} a_{11} & a_{12} \\ a_{21} & a_{22} \end{pmatrix}$ then det $(A) = a_{11}\, a_{22} + a_{12}a_{21}$

For a square A of dimensions $n \times n$, the determinant can be obtained as follows. First define A_{1j} as the matrix of dimensions $(n-1)\times(n-1)$ obtained from a by deleting row 1 and column. j Then.

det $(A) = a_{11}$ det $(A_{11}) - a_{12}$ det $(A_{12}) + a_{13}$ det $(A_{13}) - ...a_{1n}$ det (A_{1n})

Note that, in this formula the single alternate between + and -

For example if $A = \begin{pmatrix} a_{11} & a_{12} & a_{13} \\ a_{21} & a_{22} & a_{23} \\ a_{31} & a_{32} & a_{33} \end{pmatrix}$, then

$$\det(A) = a_{11}(a_{22}\, a_{33} - a_{23}\, a_{32}) - a_{12}(a_{21}a_{33} - a_{23}\, a_{31})$$
$$+ a_{13}(a_{21}a_{32} - a_{22}a_{31}).$$

Determinants have several interesting properties. For example the following statements are equivalent for a square matrix A:

- det(A) = 0
- A has no inverse, i.e. A is singular,
- the columns of A from a set of linearly dependent vectors,
- the rows of A form a set of linearly dependent vectors.

For our purpose, however, determinants will be needed mainly in our discussion of classical optimization, in conjunction with the material from the following section.

Exercise: Compute the determinant of

$$A = \begin{pmatrix} 4 & 2 & 3 \\ 1 & 0 & 1 \\ 0 & 1 & 2 \end{pmatrix}$$

POSITIVE DEFINITE MATRICES

When we study functions of several variables, we will need the following matrix notions.

A square matrix A is positive definite if $x^T Ax > 0$ for all nonzero column vectors x. It is negative define if $x^T Ax < 0$ for all nonzero x. It is positive semidefinite if $x^T Ax \geq 0$ and negative semidefinite if $x^T Ax \leq 0$ for all x. These definitions are hard to check directly and you might as well forget them for all practical purposes.

More useful in practice are the following properties, which hold when the matrix A is symmetric (that will be the case of interest to us), and which are easier to check.

The ith principal minor of A is the matrix A^i formed by the first i rows and columns of A.

So, the first principal minor of A is the matrix $A_1 = (a_{11})$, the second principal minor is the matrix $A_2 = \begin{pmatrix} a_{11} & a_{12} \\ a_{21} & a_{22} \end{pmatrix}$ and so an

- The matrix A is positive definite if all its principal

minors $A_1\ A_2,.......A_n$ have strictly positive determinants.

- If these determinants are nonzero and alternate in signs, starting with det $(A_1)<0$ then the matrix A is negative definite.
- If the determinants are all nonnegative then the matrix is positive semidefinite.
- If the determinants alternate in signs, starting with det$(A_1)\leq 0$ than the matrix is negative semidefinite.

To fix ideas consider a 2×2 symmetric matrix $A=\begin{pmatrix} a_{11} & a_{12} \\ a_{12} & a_{22} \end{pmatrix}$

It is positive definite if:

(i) det $(A_1)=a_{11}>0$

(ii) det $(A_2)=a_{11}a_{22}-a_{12}a_{12}>0$

and negative definite if:

(i) det $(A_1)=a_{11}<0$

(ii) det $(A_2)=a_{11}a_{22}-a_{12}a_{12}>0$

It is positive semidefinite if:

(i) det $(A_1)=a_{11}\geq 0$

(ii) det $(A_2)=a_{11}a_{22}-a_{12}a_{12}\geq 0$

and negative semidefinite if:

(i) det $(A_1)=a_{11}\leq 0$

(ii) det $(A_2)=a_{11}a_{22}-a_{12}a_{12}\geq 0$

Exercise: Check whether the following matrices are positive definite, negative definite positive semidefinite, negative semidefinite or none of the above.

$(a)\, A=\begin{pmatrix} 2 & 1 \\ 1 & 4 \end{pmatrix}$

$$(b)\ A = \begin{pmatrix} -2 & 4 \\ 4 & -8 \end{pmatrix}$$

$$(c)\ A = \begin{pmatrix} -2 & 2 \\ 2 & -4 \end{pmatrix}$$

$$(d)\ A = \begin{pmatrix} 2 & 4 \\ 4 & 3 \end{pmatrix}$$

3

Getting Linear Models Straight

This chapter is intended to introduce you to the use of algebra in solving business problems. For some people the very word algebra conjures up impressions of abstract and impenetrable jumbles of letters and numbers that are the preserve of mathematical boffins. Certainly parts of the subject of algebra are complex, but our concern here is with algebraic techniques that help to represent or model business situations. In doing this we are following in the footsteps of the 'father of algebra', Mohammed ibn-Musa al-Khwarizmi. In the ninth century al-Khwarizmi wrote Al-jabr wa'l-muqabala, which might be translated as 'Calculation Using Balancing and Completion'. The first part of the Arabic title gives us the word algebra. Although al-Khwarizmi was a scholar working at the House of Wisdom in Baghdad, he saw his task in very practical terms, namely to focus on.

In the course of this chapter we will confine our attention to simple algebra and how you can use it to solve certain types of business problem. We will focus on linear equations, which are those that are straight lines when they are plotted graphically. They form the basis of linear models that assist business problem-solving.

LINEAR EQUATIONS

Central to algebra is the use of letters, most frequently x and y, to represent numbers. Doing this allows us to deal systematically with quantities that are unknown yet of importance in an analysis. These unknown quantities are often referred to as variables, literally things that vary over a range of numbers or values. Sometimes the point is to express a quantitative procedure in a succinct way, and the use of letters merely constitutes convenient shorthand.

Example 1

A sales agent is paid a basic wage of Rs. 200 per week plus 10% commission on sales.

The procedure for working out his/her total wage may be written as:

Total wage = 200 + 10% of sales

It is often more useful to abbreviate this by using letters. If y is used to represent the total wage and x to represent sales we can express the procedure as:

$$y = 200 + 0.1x$$

Using this we may find the total wage for a week when sales were Rs.1200:

$$y = 200 + 0.1 * 1200 = 200 + 120 = \text{Rs. } 320$$

These types of expression are called equations because of the equals sign, '=', which symbolizes equality between the quantity to its left and the quantity to its right. An equation is literally a state of equating or being equal.

An equation that involves just two unknown quantities can be drawn as a line or a curve on a graph. Each point along it represents a combination of x and y values that satisfies, or fits the equation.

To plot an equation start by setting out a scale of possible values of one unknown along one axis, or dimension, and a scale of the possible values of the other unknown along the other axis. Ensure the scales cover the range of plausible values, and start them at zero unless interest in the line is limited to part of it well away from zero. Plot the x values along the horizontal axis, known as the x axis, and the y values along the vertical axis, known as the y axis. This conveys that y depends on x.

Once each axis has been prepared, portraying an equation in its graphical form involves finding two points that lay along the line that will represent the equation. This means you have to identify two pairs of x and y values both of must satisfy the equation. The way to do this is to specify an x value and use the equation to work out what value y would have to take in order to satisfy the equation, then repeat the process for another x value. To ensure that your line is accurate it is important to take one x value from the far left hand side of the horizontal axis and the other from the far right hand side.

Example 2

Plot the equation that represents the procedure for working out the weekly wage for the sales agent in Example

The equation is:

$$y = 200 + 0.1x$$

where y represents the wage and x the sales.

To help us design the x axis let us suppose that the maximum sales the agent could achieve in a week is Rs.5000. Using the equation we can use this to find the maximum wage:

$$y = 200 + 0.1(5000) = 700$$

This means the highest value we need to include in the scale on the y axis is Rs.700.

We are now in a position to construct the framework for our graph, which might look like Figure 1.

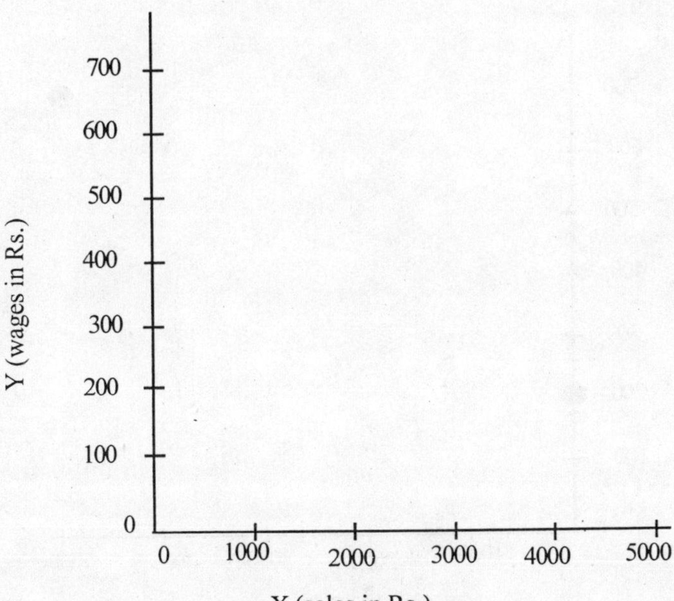

Figure 1: Framework for plotting the equation in Example 1

To plot the line that represents the equation we need to find two points that lie on the line. One of these should be on the left hand side. The lowest number on the left of the horizontal axis is zero, so we could use the equation to work out the wage when sales are zero:

$$y = 200 + 0.1(0) = 200$$

When sales are Rs.0 the wage is Rs. 200, this pair of values gives us the position, or coordinates of one point on the line. The sales value, 0, positions the point along the horizontal axis and the wage value, 200, positions the point along the vertical axis. To get a second set of coordinates we should take a sales figure from the right hand side of the horizontal axis, say the maximum figure of 5000, and work out the wage when sales are Rs.5000, again using the equation:

$$y = 200 + 0.1(5000) = 700$$

When sales are Rs. 5000 the wage is Rs.700. The point we plot to represent this pair of values will be positioned at 5000 along the horizontal axis and at 700 along the vertical axis.

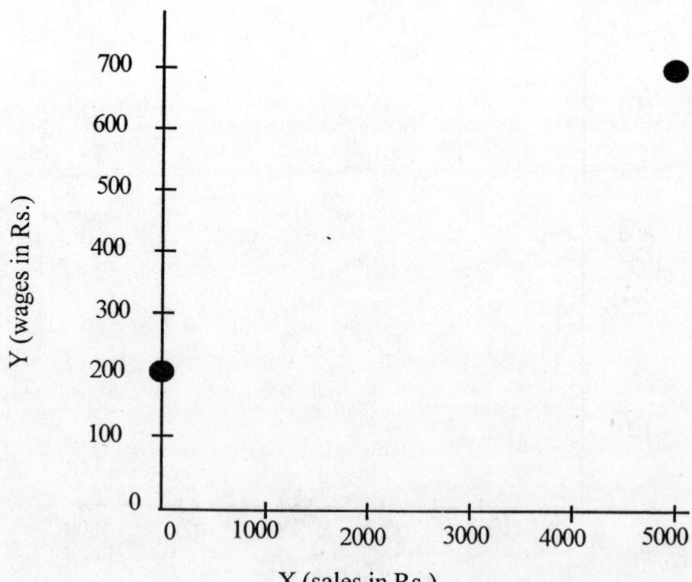

We can now plot both points as in Figure 2:

Figure 2 : Points on the line of the equation in Example 1

If plotting an equation is new to you, or just something you haven't done for a while, it is a good idea to plot a third point between the first two. A third point should lie in line with the first two so it is a good way of checking that you have plotted the other points correctly. A suitable position for our third point in this case might be when sales are Rs.2000 and the wage will be:

$$y = 200 + 0.1(2000) = 400$$

The points that represents these coordinates, sales of Rs. 2000 and a wage of Rs. 400, have been plotted in Figure.

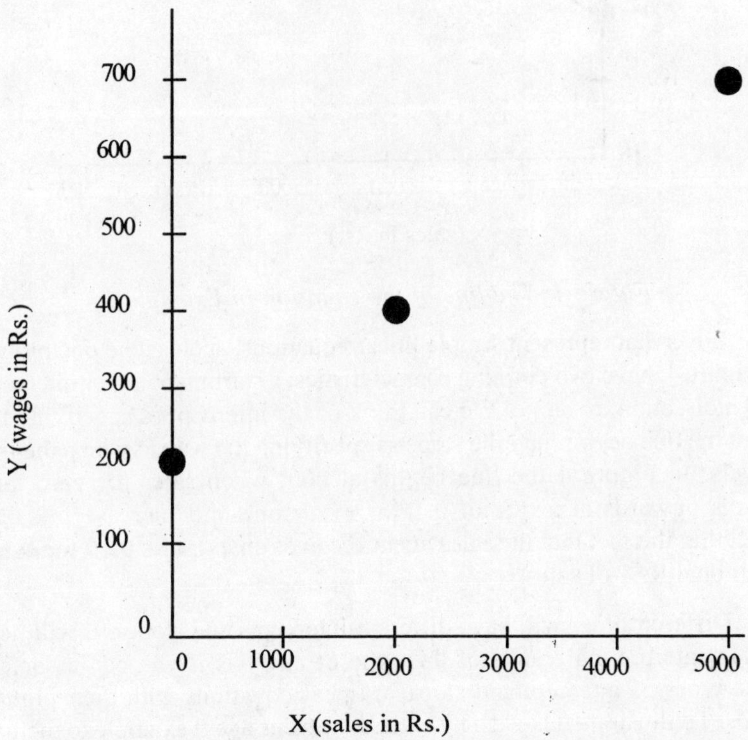

Figure 3: Three points on the line of the equation in Example 1

The final stage in plotting the equation is to draw a straight line linking the plotted points. This is shown in Figure 4 given above.

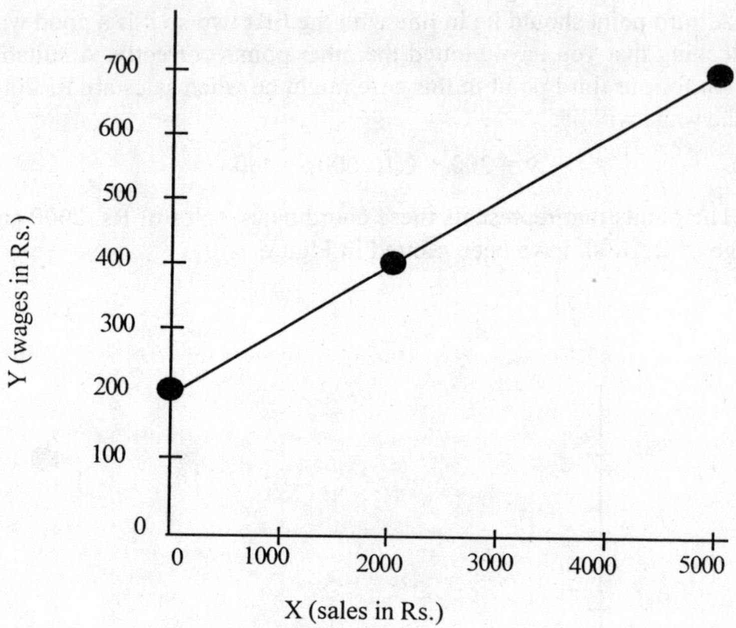

Figure 4: The line of the equation in Example 1

Lines that represent simple linear equations, such as the one plotted in Figure 4, have two defining characteristics: a starting point, or intercept, and a direction, or slope. We can think of the intercept as specifying the point the line begins, and the slope as specifying the way in which the line travels. In Figure 4 the line begins at 200, when sales are zero, and travels upwards at a rate of 0.1 for every one-unit increase in sales, reflecting the fact that the sales agent receives an extra Rs.0.10 for every additional Rs.1 of sales.

Different lines will have different intercepts and slopes. It will help you in interpreting results of this type of analysis if you can associate basic types of intercept and slope in linear equations with their plotted forms. To illustrate this we may extend the sales agent example to include contrasting approaches to wage determination.

Example 3

Suppose the basic wage of the sales agent in Example 1 is increased to Rs.300 and the commission on sales remains 10%. Express the procedure for determining the wage as an equation and plot it.

The total wage (y) in terms of sales (x) is now:

$$y = 300 + 0.1x$$

The line representing this has an intercept of 300 and a slope of 0.1. It is the upper line in Figure

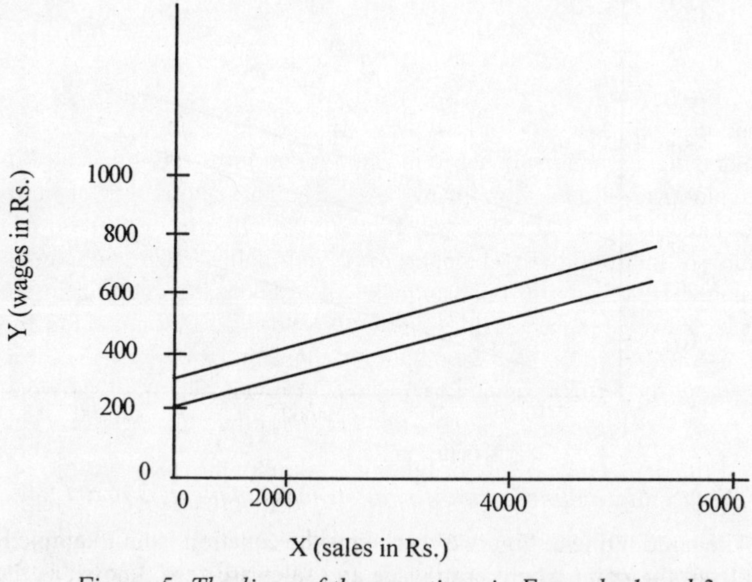

Figure 5: The lines of the equations in Examples1 and 3

You can see two lines plotted in Figure. The lower is the line plotted in Figure 4, the original formulation for finding the wage. The upper represents the equation from Example 3, where the basic wage is increased to Rs. 300. It is higher because the intercept is 300 compared to the 200 in the original equation but note that the two lines are parallel since they have exactly the same slope. Lines that have the same slope will be parallel whatever their intercept.

Example 4

Identify the equation that would express the calculation of the wages of the sales agent in Example 1 if there were no basic wage and the commission rate remained 10%.

The total wage would be:

$$y = 0 + 0.1x$$

This is plotted in Figure 6 given below together with the equations from Examples1 and 3.

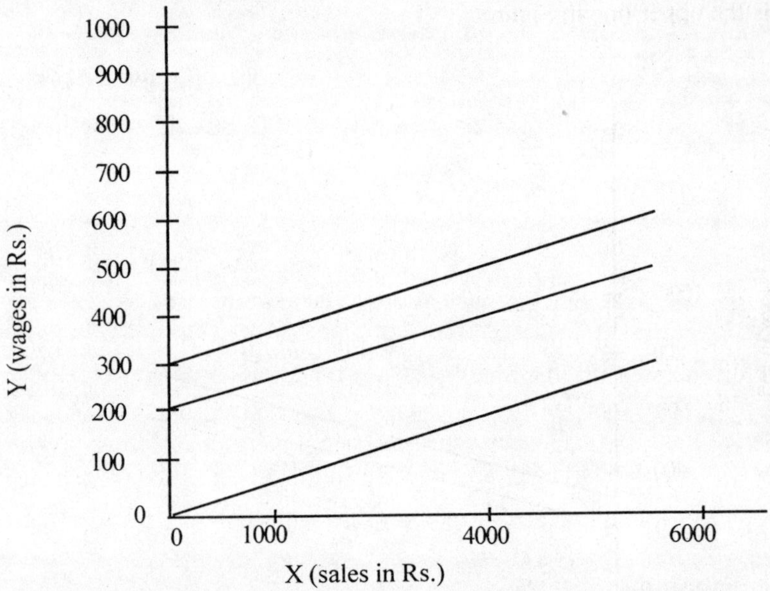

Figure 6: The lines of the equations in Examples1, 3 and 4

The bottom line in Figure 6 represents the equation from Example It starts from the point where both wage and sales are zero, known as the origin, since the intercept of the line is zero. It is parallel to the lines above it because it has the same slope as them.

Example 5

The basic wage of the sales agent in Example 1 is to remain at Rs.200, but the rate of commission increases to 20%. Express the procedure for determining the wage as an equation and plot it.

The total wage (y) in terms of sales (x) is now:

$$y = 200 + 0.2x$$

The line representing this has an intercept of 200 and a slope of 0.2. It is plotted in Figure 7 together with the equation from Example.

The equations plotted in Figure 7 given above have the same

intercept, 200, but different slopes. This means they start at the same point on the left hand side of the graph but their paths diverge. The upper, steeper line represents the equation from Example. It has a slope of 0.2, twice the slope of the line representing the equation in Example 1, 0.1, reflecting the greater rate at which commission is earned, 20% rather than 10%. The slope is twice as steep since the same sales will result in the sales agent earning double the commission.

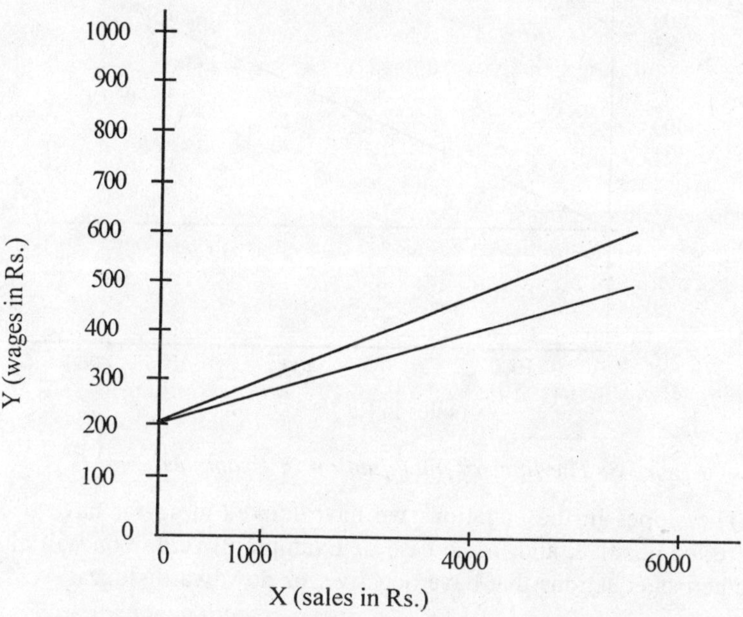

Figure 7: The lines of the equations in Examples1 and 5

Example 6

Identify the equation that would express the calculation of the wages of the sales agent in Example 1 if the basic wage is Rs. 200 and there is no commission.

The total wage would be:

$$y = 200 + 0x$$

This is plotted in Figure 8 together with the equation from Example

The equation in Example 6 is plotted as the bottom, horizontal line in Figure. It has a zero slope; literally it goes neither up nor down. Whatever the level of sales the wage will be unaffected. It may be drawn that the level of sales is not going to affect the wage.

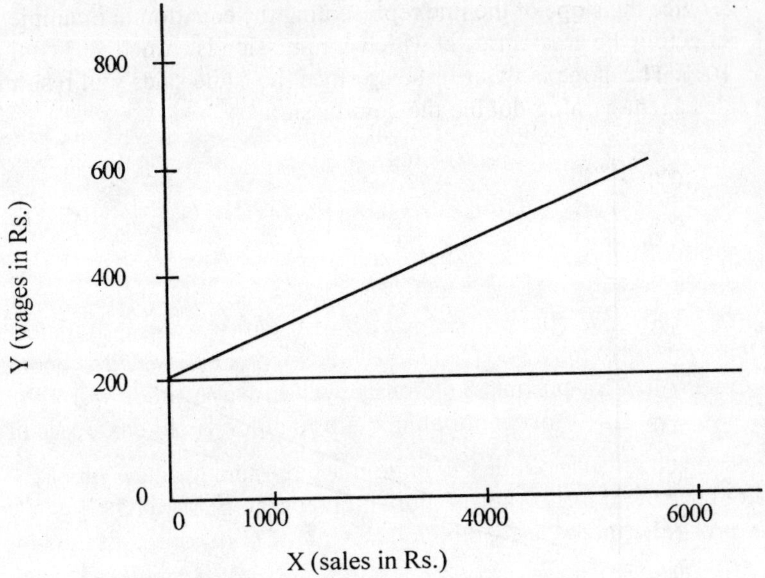

Figure 8: The lines of the equation in Examples1 and 6

The slopes in the equations we have looked at so far have been upward, or positive, and in the case of Example 6, zero. You will also come across equations that have negative, or downward slopes.

Example 7

The company that employs the sales agent in Example 1 believes that its sales vary according to the price charged for its product. They summarize the relationship in the form of the following equation:

$$y = 800 - 10x$$

where y represents the number of units sold and x the price at which they are sold in Rs.

The equation is plotted in Figure

In Figure 9 the line slopes downwards because the slope, – 10, is negative.

It means that for every increase of Rs.1 in the price of the product the number of units sold will decrease by ten.

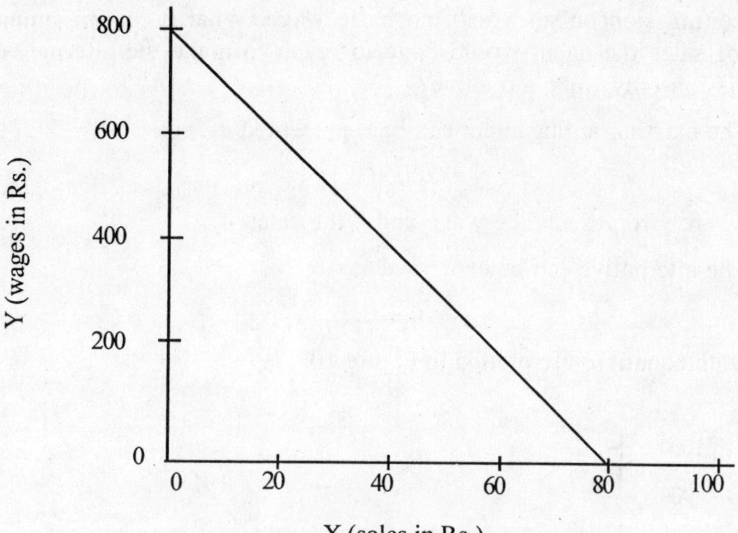

Figure 9: The line of the equation in Example 7

SIMULTANEOUS EQUATIONS

In the previous section we looked at how linear equations can be used to show the connection between two variables. Such equations represent the relationship in general terms; they are in effect recipes or formulae that specify how the value of one quantity can be established with reference to another quantity. This is how a wage that consists of a basic component plus sales commission can be calculated or how a phone bill made up of a fixed charge plus a cost per unit can be worked out. In each case a single linear equation provides a clear numerical definition of the process involved and can be used to work out the appropriate y value for any given x value.

Sometimes it is necessary to consider two linear equations jointly, or simultaneously, hence the fact that such combinations of equations are known as simultaneous equations. Typically the aim is to find a pair of specific values of x and y that satisfy both equations. You can achieve this by plotting both equations on the same pair of axes and identifying the point where the lines cross.

Example 8

The sales agent in Example 1, currently receiving a wage of Rs.200 plus 10% commission on sales, is offered the alternative of receiving

20% commission on sales with no basic wage. What is the minimum level of sales the agent would have to reach to make the alternative commission-only wage attractive?

The existing arrangement can be represented as:

$$y = 200 + 0.1x$$

where y represents the wage and x the sales.

The alternative can be expressed as:

$$y = 0 + 0.2x$$

Both equations are plotted in Figure 10.

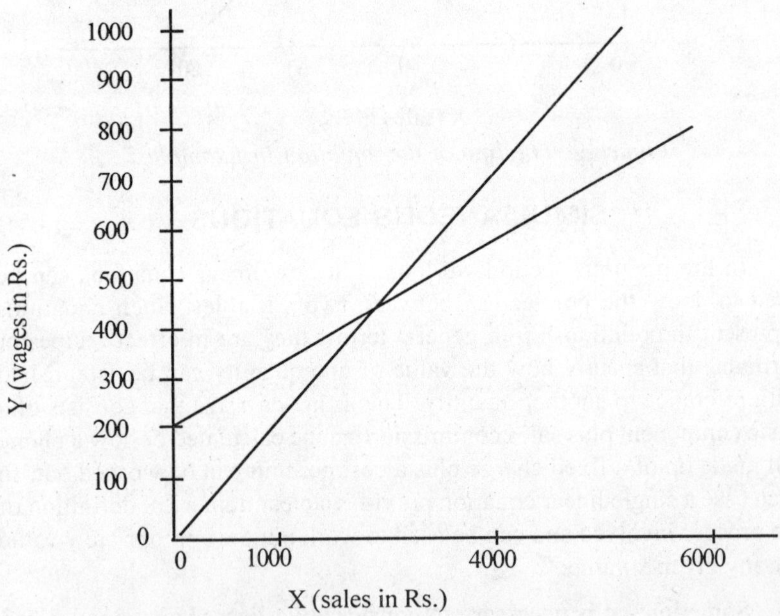

Figure 10: The lines of the equations in Example 8

In Figure 10 the lines cross at the point representing sales of Rs.2000 and a wage of Rs.400. The line representing the current method of determining the wage is the higher line when sales are below Rs.2000, indicating that it would be the better arrangement for the agent when sales are less than Rs.2000. The line representing the alternative arrangement is the higher line when sales are greater than Rs. 2000, indicating that it would be the better arrangement when sales exceed Rs.2000. The minimum level of sales the agent would have to reach to make the alternative commission-only wage attractive is therefore Rs. 2000.

Finding values that fit both of two equations is known as solving simultaneous equations. In Example 8 the point where the lines cross meets the requirements of both equations because it is a point on both lines. The fact that it is the only point where the lines cross tells us that it represents the only combination of wage level and sales that fits both equations.

You can solve simultaneous equations without plotting their lines on a graph using a method known as elimination. As the name implies this involves removing or eliminating one of the unknown quantities with the intention of leaving a numerical value for the other.

In order to end up with a clear result conventionally simultaneous equations are arranged so that the unknown quantities and the factors applied to them, their coefficients, are located on the left hand side of the equals sign and the intercept, or constant appears to its right. This may involve rearranging the equations. In doing this we need to ensure that any manipulation preserves the equality inherent in the equation by balancing every operation performed on one side with the exact same operation on the other side.

Following this we proceed to the removal of one of the unknown quantities, either x or y. This is straightforward if the number of x's or y's in both equations is the same, in which case if you subtract one equation from the other you will be left with an expression which has just one unknown on the left of the equals sign and a number on its right. Using suitable multiplication or division you can then establish the value of this remaining unknown, one of the pair of x and y values that fits both equations.

Having found one of the pair of values mutually compatible with both equations you can substitute it into one of the original equations and find the value of the other unknown that, in combination with the value of the first unknown, satisfies the original equations jointly, or simultaneously.

Example 9

In Example 8 the sales agent is presented with two possible wage arrangements represented as:

$$y = 200 + 0.1x \quad \text{(the original arrangement)}$$

and $y = 0 + 0.2x$ (the commission-only alternative)

where y represents the wage and x the sales.

We will start by rearranging both equations so the components, or terms, involving x and y are on the left of the equals sign and the 'stand-alone' numbers are on the right. In the case of the first equation, representing the original arrangement, this entails moving the 0.1x from the right of the equals sign over to the left. In doing this we have to reverse the sign in front of it, as strictly speaking we are subtracting 0.1x from both sides of the equation, and hence preserving the balance:

$$y = 200 + 0.1x$$

Subtract 0.1x from both sides:

$$y = 0.1x = 200 + 0.1x - 0.1x$$

to get:

$$y = 0.1x = 200$$

For the second equation:

$$y = 0 + 0.2x$$

Subtract 0.2x from both sides:

$$y - 0.2x = 0 + 0.2x - 0.2x$$

to get:

$$y - 0.2x = 0$$

We can now set these rearranged equations alongside each another and subtract one from the other to eliminate y:

$$y = 0.1x = 200$$

$$y = 0.2x = 0$$

$$+ 0.1x = 200$$

We can break this operation down into three parts:

$$y - y = 0y \text{ no } y$$

$$- 0.1x - (-0.2x) = + 0.1s$$

$$200 - 0 = 200$$

giving us:

$$0.1x = 200$$

This tells us that one-tenth of x is 200. If we multiply both sides of this by ten we find that a 'whole' x is worth 2000:

$$0.1x * 10 = 200 * 10 \text{ so } 1x = 2000$$

In other words both wage determination models produce the same wage when sales are Rs. 2000. But what will the wage be? To find out this put the sales figure of 2000 into the equation representing the original arrangement:

$$y = 200 + 0.1 * 2000 = 200 + 200 = 400$$

The original approach to establish the sales agent's wage will produce a wage of Rs. 400 when sales are Rs. 2000. The alternative, commission-only formulation will of course yield the same wage when sales are Rs. 2000:

$$y = 0 + 0.2 * 2000 = 400$$

The values of 2000 and 400 for sales and wages respectively therefore satisfy both wage determination equations simultaneously.

Applying elimination in Example 9 was made easier because in both equations there was only one 'y', that is the coefficient on y in each equation was one. If the coefficients on an unknown are different you have to apply multiplication or division to one or both equations to make the coefficients on the unknown you wish to eliminate equal before you can use subtraction to remove it.

Example 10

Find the level of wages at which the two procedures for determining the sales agent's wage in Example 8 result in the same wage by eliminating x, the level of sales. The equations representing the procedure, as rearranged in Example 9, are:

$$y - 0.1x = 200$$

$$y - 0.2x = 0$$

If we multiply the first equation by two we get:

$$2y - 0.2x = 400$$

Subtracting the second equation from this:

$$2y - 0.2x = 400$$

$$y - 0.2x = 0$$

$$y = 400$$

Again we find that the wage level at which the two wage determination models produce the same result is Rs. 400. If we substitute that value of y into the equation representing the original arrangement we may find the level of sales that will yield a wage of Rs. 400:

$$400 - 0.1x = 200$$

Subtract 400 from both sides of the above equation we get as:

$$400 - 400 - 0.1x = 200 - 400$$

$$-0.1x = -200$$

Multiply both sides by minus one to the above equation:

$$(-1) * (-0.1x) = (-1) * (-200)$$

$$0.1x = 200$$

And multiply both sides by ten to the above equation :

$$x = 2000$$

The level of sales at which both approaches to wage determination will produce a wage of Rs. 400 is therefore Rs. 2000.

Not all pairs of equations can be solved simultaneously. These are either cases where one equation is a multiple of another, such as:

$$3x + 2y = 10 \text{ and } 6x + 4s = 20$$

or cases where one equation is inconsistent with the other, such as:

$$2x + y = 14 \text{ and } 2x + y = 20$$

In the first case the equations are the same; if you try to plot them you will find they produce the same line. In the second case plotting them produces lines that are parallel and therefore do not cross.

BREAK-EVEN ANALYSIS

The type of linear model that we have looked at in the previous section can be used to analyse the relationship between the costs and revenue of a company. The aim in doing this is to identify the point at which the revenue matches the costs, known as the break-even point, the output level at which the company makes neither profit nor loss but breaks even.

In setting up a break-even analysis we need to make several definitions and assumptions. First we assume that there are two types of cost, fixed and variable. Fixed costs, as the name implies, are those costs that are constant whatever the level of production. These might be the costs of setting up the operation such as the purchase of machinery as well as expenses, such as business rates, that do not vary with the level of output. Variable costs on the other hand are costs that change in relation to the amount produced, such as the costs of raw materials and labour.

We can define the total costs (TC) as the sum of the total fixed costs (TFC) and the total variable costs (TVC):

$$TC = TFC + TVC$$

The total variable costs depend on the quantity of output. We will assume that the variable cost of producing an extra unit is the same however many units we produce; in other words, it is linear or varies in a straight line with the amount produced. We can therefore express the total variable cost as the variable cost per unit produced, known as the average variable cost (AVC) multiplied by the quantity produced (Q), so the total cost is:

$$TC = TFC + AVC * Q$$

The total revenue (TR) is the price per unit (P) at which the output is sold multiplied by the quantity of output (Q):

$$TR = P * Q$$

Once we have defined the total cost and total revenue equations we can plot them on a graph and look at exactly how total revenue compares to total cost. This is a key comparison as the total revenue minus the total cost is the amount of profit made:

$$Profit = TR - TC$$

The point at which the lines representing the two equations cross is the point at which total cost is precisely equal to total revenue, the break-even point.

Example 11

The Ackrana Security Company intends to manufacture video security cameras. The costs of acquiring the necessary plant and machinery and meeting other fixed costs are put at Rs. 4.5 million. The average variable cost of producing one of their cameras is estimated to be Rs.60 and the company plans to sell them at Rs. 150 each. How many will they need to produce and sell in order to break even?

Total cost, $TC = 4500000 + 60Q$

Total revenue, $TR = 150Q$

These equations are plotted in Figure 11. Conventionally the money amounts, cost and revenue are plotted on the vertical or y axis and the output is plotted on the horizontal or x axis. This arrangement reflects the assumption that the money amounts depend on the output and makes it easier to interpret the diagram.

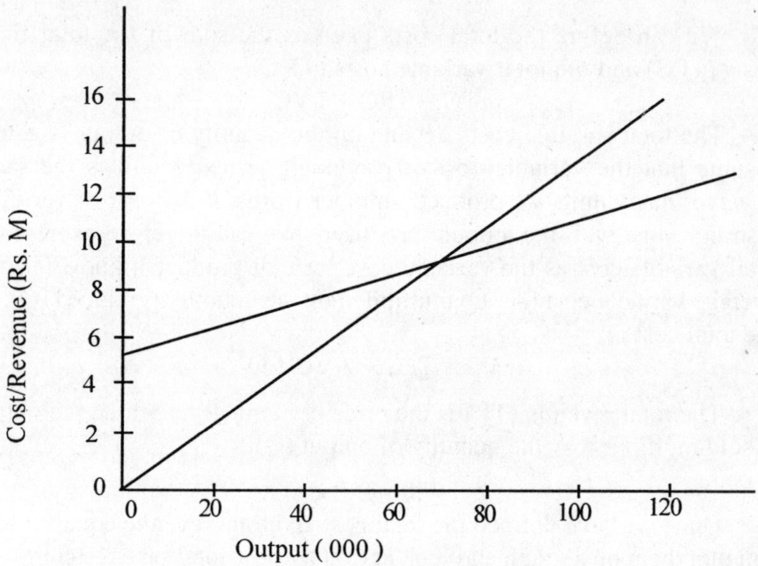

Figure 11: Total cost and total revenue lines in Example 11

In Figure 11 the steeper line that starts from the origin represents the total revenue equation and the other line represents the total cost equation. You can see that the lines cross when output is about 50,000 units. At this level of production both the total cost and total revenue are equal, at about Rs.7.5 million. This is the break-even point, at which costs precisely match revenues.

We can verify the break-even point by solving the total cost and total revenue equations simultaneously:

$$TC = 4500000 + 60Q \text{ so } TC - 60Q = 4500000$$

$$TR = 150Q$$

so $$TR - 150Q = 0$$

When total cost and total revenue are equal, subtracting one from the total revenue will leave us with an expression in which the only unknown is the level of output, Q:

$$TC - 60Q = 4500000$$
$$TR - 150Q = 0$$
$$+ 90Q = 4500000$$

Dividing both sides by 90 means that the level of output at which total cost and total revenue are equal is 50,000:

$$4500000/90 = 50000$$

The total cost and total revenue when 50000 units are produced will be:

$$TC = 4500000 + 60 * 50000 = 4500000 + 3000000 = Rs.7,500,000$$
$$TR = 150 * 50000 = Rs.7,500,000$$

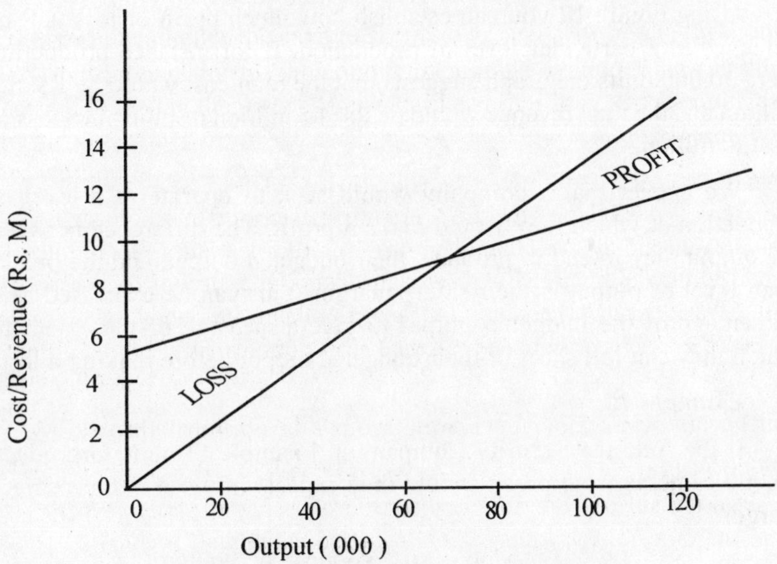

Figure 12: Break-even graph for Example 11 with areas representing profit and loss

Break-even analysis may be extended to illustrate the levels of output that will yield a loss and those that will yield a profit. A level of output less than the break-even level, and hence to the left of the position of the break-even point along the horizontal axis of the graph, will result into a loss. A level of output higher than the break-even level, to the right of the break-even point on the horizontal axis, will yield a profit.

Break-even analysis may be extended to illustrate the levels of output that will yield a loss and those that will yield a profit. A level of output less than the break-even level, and hence to the left of the position of the break-even point along the horizontal axis of the graph, will result into a loss. A level of output higher than the break-even level, to the right of the break-even point on the horizontal axis, will yield a profit.

At any point to the left of the break-even point the total cost line is the higher line indicating that total cost is higher than total revenue; the greater the difference between the two lines, the larger the loss. At any point to the right of the break-even point the total revenue is the higher line, which means that the total revenue is higher than the total cost; the bigger the difference between the two lines, the larger the profit. The areas representing loss and profit are shown in Figure 12.

Using Figure 12 you can establish how much profit or loss will be achieved at a particular level of production. If for instance production were 30,000 units the graph suggests that the total cost would be Rs. 6.3 million and the total revenue would be Rs. 4.5 million resulting in a loss of Rs.1.8 million.

We expect that a company would seek to operate at a level of production at which they would make a profit. The difference between the output they intend to produce, their budgeted output, and the break-even level of output is their safety margin. This can be expressed as a percentage of the budgeted output to give a measure of the extent to which they can fall short of their budgeted output before making a loss.

Example 12

If the Ackrana Security Company in Example 11 aims to produce 80,000 cameras what profit should they expect and what is their safety margin?

$$TR = 4500000 + 60 * 80000 = 9,300,000$$

$$TC = 150 * 80000 = 12,000,000$$

Profit = 12000000 – 9300000 = 2,700,000 that is Rs.2.7 million

In Example 11 we found that their break-even point was 50,000 cameras so their safety margin is:

$$\frac{Budget\ output - Break - even\ output}{Budget\ Output} * 100 = \frac{80000 - 50000}{80000} * 100 = 37.5\%$$

The break-even analysis we have considered is the simplest case, where both costs and revenue are assumed to be linear, that is to form straight lines when plotted graphically. In practice companies might find that with greater levels of production come economies of scale that mean their variable cost per unit is not constant for every unit produced but falls as output increases. Furthermore, they may have to reduce their price if they want to sell more products so that their total revenue would not have a linear relationship to their output level.

Despite these shortcomings the basic model can be a useful guide to the consequences of relatively modest changes in output as well as a framework for considering different levels of initial investment, pricing strategies and alternative sources of raw materials.

INEQUALITIES

So far we have focussed on the use of equations to model business situations. Under some circumstances it is appropriate to use inequalities, also known as inequations, expressions of relationships in which one or more unknowns are not necessarily equal to a specific numerical value.

The basic forms of inequalities are not equal ($\neq$), less than (<), and greater than (>):

$x = 10$ means x must take a value other than 10

$x < 10$ means x must be less than 10

$x > 10$ means x must be greater than 10

It may help you to distinguish between < and > if you think of the sharp end of each symbol as pointing to the lesser quantity, and the open end to the greater. In $x < 10$ the sharp end points the x so it is the smaller quantity and 10 is the larger quantity whereas in $x > 10$ the sharp end points to 10 so that is the smaller quantity and x is the larger.

There are two types of composite inequality that you will meet later in this chapter. These are less than or equal to ($\leq$) and greater than or equal to ($\geq$). In both cases the lines beneath the < and > signs signifies the possibility that the two sides in the relationship are equal is included.

These composite inequalities are useful to represent the ways in which business operations might be limited or constrained by factors such as the amount of raw material or time available for the production of different products or services. In such cases all or some of the limited resource might be used, but it is not possible to use more than the amount on hand. The available quantity of resource is a ceiling or constraint on the business activity. An inequality can be used to represent the relationship between the amounts of the resource required for the products and the quantity in stock so that we can tell which combinations of products or services can be produced with the given materials, in other words what output levels are feasible.

Example 13

The Sirdaria Citrus Company produces juices using exotic fruits including two made from hoormah, 'Anelle' and 'Emir'. Fruit concentrate for these products is imported and the supply is erratic. Sirdaria has 4000 litres of hoormah concentrate in stock. The Anelle brand consists of 8% concentrate. Emir, the luxury product, consists of 10% concentrate.

Represent the fruit concentrate constraint as an inequality. Since we don't know exactly how much of each product can be produced, indeed we want an inequality to identify what the possibilities are, we must start by defining the key variables: the amounts of each product produced. We will use x to represent the amount of Anelle produced and y to represent the amount of Emir produced.

Anelle requires 0.08 litres of concentrate per litre, so if we produce x litres of Anelle we will need 0.08x litres of concentrate. Emir requires 0.1 litres of concentrate per litre so producing y litres of Emir will use up 0.1y litres of concentrate. Whatever the volume of Anelle and Emir produced the amount of concentrate needed will be the amount required for Anelle production added to the amount required for Emir production:

Concentrate required = $0.08x + 0.1y$

The concentrate required must be balanced against the available supply of 4000 litres. To be feasible the output of products must not give rise to a demand for concentrate that exceeds the available supply, in other words the demand must be less than or equal to the available supply:

$$0.08x + 0.1y \leq 4000$$

Inequalities, like equations, represent the connection or relationship between amounts either side of the appropriate sign. Like equations they can also be represented graphically, but whereas the graphical form of an equation is a line the graphical form of an inequality is an area bounded or limited by a line. To portray an inequality graphically you have to start by plotting the line that bounds the area. If the inequality is a composite type the line to plot is the line for the equation that represents the limits of feasibility, output combinations that use up all of the available resource.

LINEAR PROGRAMMING

The inequalities we considered in the previous section are important ways of representing the factors that can constrain or limit business operations, but they only demonstrate the possibilities open to a company. They do not indicate which possible, or feasible arrangement would be best for the company.

To provide guidance on making the best choice between the available alternatives we need to bring the intentions or objectives the company wants to achieve into the analysis. This can be done using a technique called linear programming that is designed to solve problems of constrained optimality, problems in which best, or optimal choice has to be made from the alternatives that the constraints collectively permit, the feasible solutions.

As the name implies, linear programming assumes that the problem to be solved involves linear or straight-line relationships. Constraints in linear programming are portrayed as inequalities in exactly the same way as we used in the examples in the previous section.

The constraints we have considered so far reflect tangible limitations to operations. There are also non-negativity constraints that reflect the logical limitation that the output quantities cannot be negative. They simply state that each variable representing output of a product must be more than or equal to zero, for instance if x represents the quantity of a product made, then $x \geq 0$.

Once the constraints have been plotted and the area representing all the operational possibilities that the constraints collectively allow, the feasible region, has been identified, the company objective can be brought into consideration. To do this we need to specify it in algebraic form, as what is called an objective function. We assume that the company objective might involve maximizing something, like profit or revenue, but it could be to minimize something, such as cost.

If the company whose operations are being modelled want to maximize their profit they will want to select the feasible solution that yields the most profit. To help them find this we need to know the amount of profit generated from units of the different products they can produce with their limited resources. These figures are key components of the objective function.

The objective function is the profit per unit from the first product multiplied by the quantity of that product made, added to the profit per unit of the second product multiplied by the quantity of the second product made. Since we do not know the level of output for each product when we represent or formulate the problem, indeed the point of the analysis is to establish exactly what are the best levels of output, we have to use symbols for the amounts produced. An objective function will look like:

Maximize:

$$ax + by$$

where

a is the profit per unit of the first product

x is the quantity of the first product made

b is the profit per unit of the second product

y is the quantity of the second product made

Whatever the level of output, we may use the objective function to find out the resulting profit.

Formulating the objective function is one thing, but how can we use it to find the best feasible solution, the optimal solution? There are two ways of doing this: either using the objective function to work out the total profit for each feasible solution, or plotting the objective function graphically. We will look at both methods.

The first approach seems as daunting because there are simply so many feasible solutions that working out the total profit for each one would be laborious. In fact the vast majority of feasible solutions can be ruled out because logically they cannot be the optimal solution. These are the feasible solutions that are inside, as against on the edges of, the feasible region. Any solution within the feasible region is surrounded by other feasible solutions, including solutions with higher output levels of one or both products. As long as the products yield a profit, a higher level of output of them will yield a higher profit, so a feasible solution inside the feasible region can always be bettered.

Excluding the solutions inside the feasible region still leaves us with all the solutions along its edges, which still amount to so many that working out the profit for each one of them would be tedious. Fortunately we can ignore the vast majority of these because the optimal solution will be located at one of the corners of the feasible region, except in special circumstances that we will consider later. Because the corners are fundamental to solving the problem they are referred to as basic feasible solutions.

Since one corner will be the optimal solution we need only work out the total profit for the output mixes represented by the corner points. The optimal solution is the one that results in the highest profit.

Instead of working out the total profit for each corner of the feasible region it is possible to identify the optimal solution by plotting the objective function. This approach is more elegant and can be quicker, especially when the feasible region has more corners. But before you can do this you have to assign a value to the objective function.

When an objective function is given a value and plotted the resulting line is called an iso-profit line. The points on such a line all have one thing in common: they represent output combinations that yield exactly the same profit. The prefix iso- means equal so an iso-profit line shows production mixes that give equal profit, in the same way as isobars on weather maps link places with the same level of atmospheric pressure.

By plotting an iso-profit line that runs through the feasible region we can identify those feasible combinations giving that level of profit. You can use such a line to see how far above it you can go without leaving the feasible region; the furthest you can go is the optimal solution.

However, you may find it equate easy to plot a value of the objective function that is above the feasible region and look for the point on the feasible region that is nearest to the plotted iso-profit line. This point is the optimal solution. Once we have identified it we can find the levels of production it represents by reading from the graph or solving simultaneously the equations of the lines that cross at the optimal solution.

Plotting an iso-profit line to identify the optimal solution is particularly useful if the problem is a little more complex.

MINIMIZATION PROBLEMS

The examples in the previous section featured a maximization problem, one in which the company was seeking to maximize its profits. There are also linear programming problems in which the objective is to minimize something, typically total costs.

The approach to solve a minimizing problem is essentially the same as that we use for a maximization problem. We start by formulating the problem, i.e. defining the variables, then setting out the constraints and the objective function. We can then proceed to represent the problem graphically, indicate the feasible region, and use the objective function to find the optimal solution.

Apart from the contrasting form of the objective the main difference between maximization and minimization problems is the type of constraint involved. In maximization problems the constraints are typically 'less than' constraints that impose upper limits on output that generates profit. In minimization problems the constraints are usually 'more than' constraints that impose lower limits on inputs that incur costs.

Example 23

The Jeevan Aid Agency has to evacuate the residents of a volcanic island and their belongings by boat. The island's small harbour can only handle small boats. There are two types of boat the agency can hire locally: the Sea Hawk and the Sea Travel. A Sea Hawk can take 25 passengers and 10 tons of cargo, and costs Rs. 800 per day to charter. A Sea Travel can take 40 passengers and 4 tons of cargo, and costs Rs. 1000 per day to charter. The agency needs capacity for at least 2000 passengers and 440 tons of cargo. How many of each type of boat should be chartered to minimize the agency's costs per day, and what is the minimum daily cost?

If we define x as the number of Sea Hawk they charter and y as the number of Sea Travel they charter then their objective is to minimize:

$$800x + 1000y$$

Subject to the following constraints:

$$25x + 40y \geq 2000 \text{ (passengers)}$$

$$10x + 4y \geq 440 \text{ (cargo)}$$

$$x \geq 0 \text{ and } y \geq 0$$

Figurc 13 shows the constraints and the feasible region. You can see that the feasible region is above the plotted constraints, which is typical for a minimization problem. Note that it has no upper boundary.

The objective is to minimize cost, so a specific value of the objective function line that we plot is called an iso-cost line.

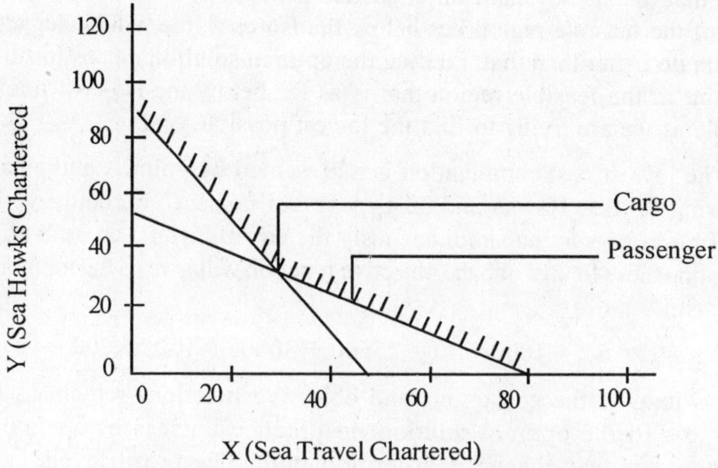

Figure 13 : Sea Hawks Chartered Example 13

The value we choose should be easy to divide by the coefficients in the objective function, in this case 800 and 1000, and should be large enough to position the line near the edges of the feasible region. The iso-cost line for Rs.80,000 will meet both requirements; it is the dotted line in Figure 14.

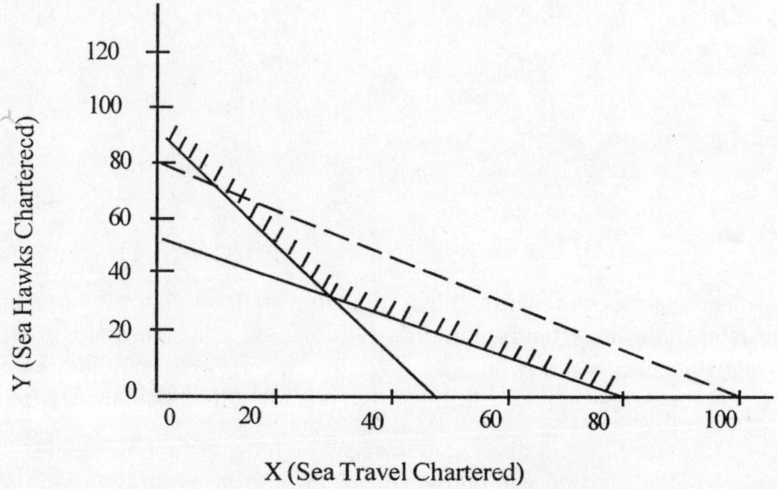

Figure 14 : Sea Hawks Chartered Example 14

Much of the iso-cost line passes through the feasible region, which means that the agency can charter sufficient capacity for Rs.80,000, but much of the feasible region lies below the iso-cost line, which suggests they can do better than that. Finding the optimal solution means locating the point in the feasible region that is as far below the iso-cost line as possible as we are trying to find the lowest possible cost.

The lowest cost combination is represented by point A and entails chartering 32 Sea Hawks and 30 Sea Travel boats. (You could verify these figures by solving simultaneously the equations that cross at point A.) Putting these figures into the objective function will give us the minimum total cost:

$$800 * 32 + 1000 * 30 = 25600 + 30000 = \text{Rs. } 55,600$$

As long as the constraints and objective functions remain as the same so will the optimal solution. In practice businesses operate in environments that change, that are dynamic. The profit levels in an objective function may need to change because new competition is squeezing margins. Constraints may relax if new sources of supply can be located. To cope with such eventualities and answer questions beginning 'what if', we can use sensitivity analysis to explore around the optimal solution of a linear programming problem.

4

Dealing with Curves

In the previous chapters we looked at how linear equations, equations that represent straight lines, can be used to model business situations and solve business problems. Although important, their limitation is that the relationships they are used to model need to be linear for them to be appropriate. There are circumstances when this is not the case, for instance the sort of model economists use to represent the connection between volume of production and cost per unit. In such a model economies of scale mean that the average cost of production per unit gets lower as output increases. The equation representing the situation would be non-linear and we might be interested in analysing it to find the least cost level of output.

In this chapter we will look at the features of basic non-linear equations and use them to analyse business operations. Following this we will consider how to find optimal points in non-linear business models using simple calculus. Later in the chapter you will meet the Economic Order Quantity model, a non-linear business model that organizations can use in determining their best stock ordering policy.

SIMPLE FORMS OF NON-LINEAR EQUATIONS

One thing you might have noticed about the linear equations was the absence of powers. We met terms like 60Q and 0.08x but not $3Q^2$ or 3/x. The presence of powers (or for that matter other non-linear forms like sines and cosines, although we will not be concerned with them here) distinguishes a non-linear equation. In order to appreciate why, consider two possible relationships between x and y:

$$y = x$$

$$y = x^2$$

In the first case we have a linear equation: y will increase at the same pace with x however big x is. If x is 4, y will be 4. If x goes up to 5, so will y.

If x is 10 and goes up to 11, so will y. Even if we had something that looks more elaborate, the effect on y that is caused by a change in x is the same, whether x is small or large.

Example 1

A train operating company sets ticket prices using the equation:

$$y = 0.8 + 0.2x$$

where y is the ticket price in Rs. and x is the number of miles travelled.

To use this equation to work out the cost of a ticket for a 4-mile journey we simply substitute the 4 for x:

$$y = 0.8 + 0.2 * 4 = 0.8 + 0.8 = \text{Rs.}1.60$$

The cost of a 5-mile journey will be:

$$y = 0.8 + 0.2 * 5 = 0.8 + 1.0 = \text{Rs.}1.80$$

The cost of a 10-mile journey will be:

$$y = 0.8 + 0.2 * 10 = 0.8 + 2.0 = \text{Rs.}2.80$$

The cost of an 11-mile journey will be:

$$y = 0.8 + 0.2 * 11 = 0.8 + 2.2 = \text{Rs.}3.00$$

Notice the difference an extra mile makes to the cost, Rs.0.20, is the same whether the difference is between 4 and 5 miles or between 10 and 11 miles. This is because the equation is linear; the slope is constant so the rate at which the value of y changes when x is changed is the same however big or small the value of x. The equation is plotted in Figure 1.

If an equation is not linear the size of the change in y that comes about when x changes does depend upon how big x is.

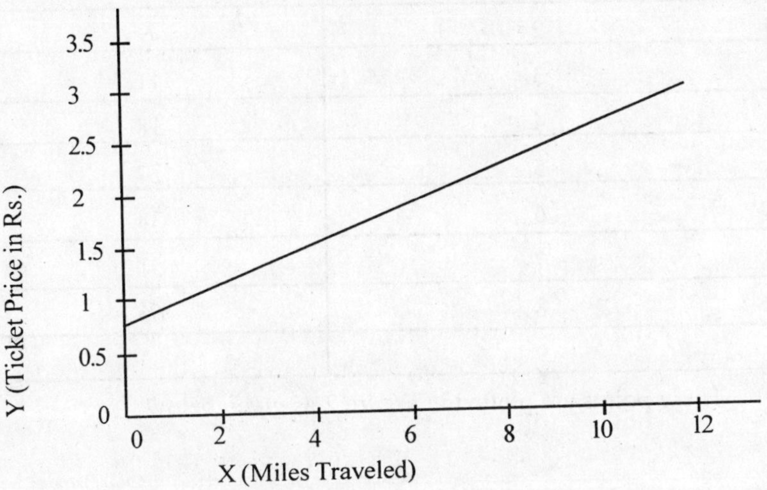

Figure 1: The ticket price equation in Example 1

With a non-linear equation a one-unit increase in x when x is small may result in a modest change in y whereas a one-unit change in x when x is large may cause a much larger change in y.

Example 2

The inventor of the new Slugar household labour-saving gadget prepares a business plan to attract investors for the venture. She anticipates that over time sales of the product will grow according to the equation:

$$y = 2 + x^2$$

where y is the sales in thousands of units and x is the number of years elapsed since the product launch. Show the expected sales growth over 9 years graphically.

To plot a linear equation you only need two points since the line is straight. To plot a non-linear equation we need a series of points that track the path of the curve that represents it. This entails calculating y values using the range of x values in which we are interested, in this case from 0 (product launch) to 9.

x (years since product launch)	y (sales in 000s)
0	2
1	3
2	6
3	11
4	18
5	27
6	38
7	51
8	66
9	83

These points are plotted in Figure 2 as given below:

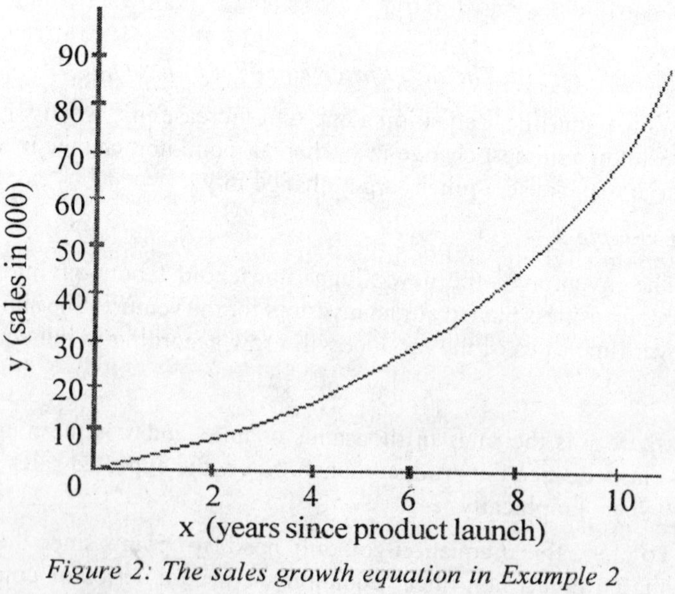

Figure 2: The sales growth equation in Example 2

An equation that includes x to the power two is called a quadratic equation, derived from the Latin word quadrare, which means to square. Similarly an equation that includes x to the power three is known as cubic. You may also meet reciprocal or hyperbolic equations. These include x to a negative power, for instance: $y = x^{-1} = 1/x$.

Example 3 An economist studying the market for a certain type of digital camera concludes that the relationship between demand for the camera and its price can be represented by the equation: $y = 800/x$

where y is the demand in thousands of units and x is the price in Rs. To plot this equation we need a series of points such as the following:

x (price in Rs.)	y (demand in 000s)
100	8.000
200	4.000
300	2.667
400	2.000
500	1.600
600	1.333
700	1.143
800	1.000

The equation is plotted in Figure 3 as given below.

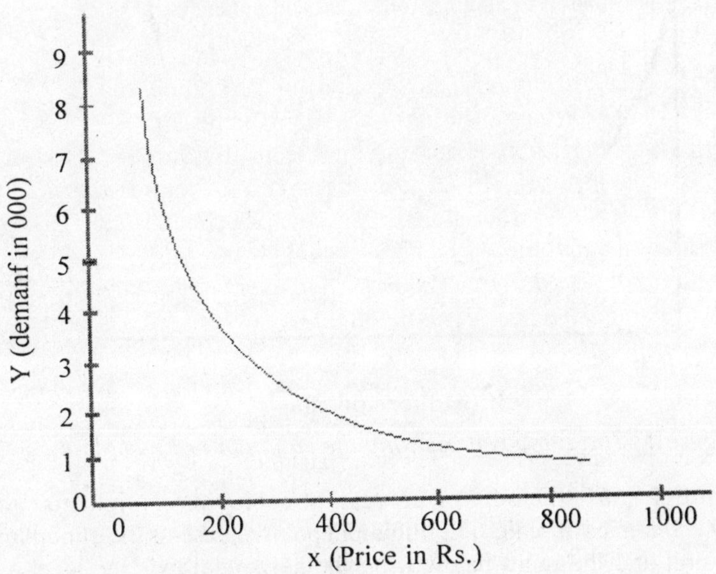

Figure 3: The demand equation in Example 3

Some curves feature peaks and troughs, known as maximum and minimum points respectively. These sorts of points are often of particular interest as they may represent a maximum revenue or a minimum cost, indeed later in the chapter we will be looking at how such points can be identified exactly by the techniques of calculus.

Example 4

The project manager of the new Machine car plant suggests to the board of directors that the production costs per car will depend on the number of cars produced according to the equation:

$$y = x^2 - 6x + 11$$

where y is the cost per car in thousands of pounds and x is the number of cars produced in millions.

The equation is plotted in Figure

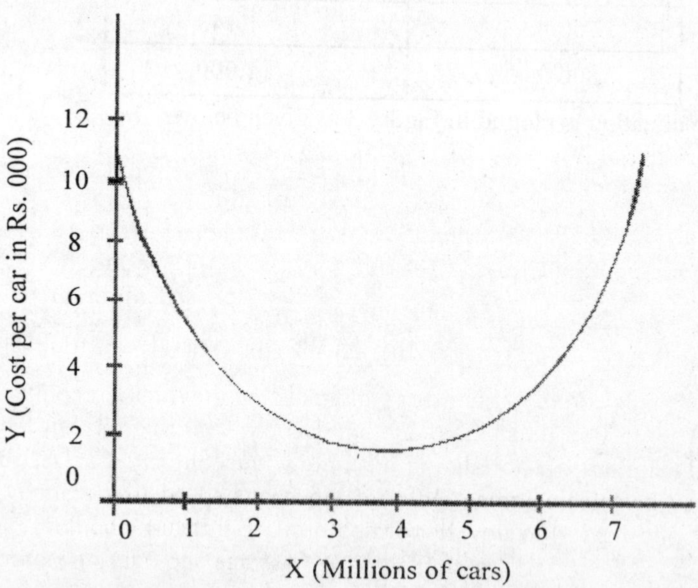

Figure 4: The curve representing the equation in Example 4

Figure 4 show the sort of curve that economists might use to represent economies of scale. The minimum point represents the minimum cost per unit and the point below it on the horizontal axis the level of output that should be produced if the firm wants to produce at that cost. Other models economists use include maximum points.

BASIC DIFFERENTIAL CALCULUS

We can find the approximate location of the maximum and minimum points in Examples above by studying the graphs carefully, marking the maximum or minimum point then identifying the values of x and y at which the point is located using the scales along the axes. At best this would give us an idea of where the point lies in relation to x and y, but it is almost impossible to pinpoint it accurately by inspecting the graph.

To find the precise location of maximum and minimum points we can use techniques from the branch of mathematics known as calculus. The word calculus conveys an impression of mystery to some people. In fact it, like the word calculate, is derived from the Latin word calculare which means to reckon with little stones, a reflection of the method of counting in ancient times. Calculare is related to the Latin word calx which means a stone, the source of the word calcium.

Calculus is composed of the two main components, differential calculus and integral calculus. The former, which involves the process of differentiation, is about finding how curves change, whereas the latter is about finding areas underneath curves. Our concern in this section is with differentiation.

Differentiation is concerned with slopes, and slopes in equations reflect the way that the x variable changes the y variable. In a simple equation such as:

$$y = 5 + 3x$$

the slope, +3, tells us that an increase of one in the value of x will result in the value of y increasing by three. The slope is the rate of change in y that is brought about by a unit change in x. The other number in the equation, 5, is a constant or fixed component; whatever the value of x, the amount added to three lots of x to get y is always 5.

The slopes of more elaborate equations are not so straightforward. So how does differential calculus help us find slopes? It consists of a fairly mechanical procedure that is applied to all the components in an equation that contains x in one form or another; either simply with a coefficient, like 3x, or perhaps raised to a power, like x^2. The procedure involves taking the power to which x is raised and making it the new coefficient on x then reducing the original power by one. When this is applied to x^2 the result is 2x. The power, 2, is placed in front of the x, forming the coefficient, and the power reduced from 2 to 1:

$$x^2 \text{ becomes } 2x^{2-1} \text{ or simply } 2x$$

This means that for the equation:

$$y = x^2$$

the slope, or the rate at which y changes in response to a unit change in x, is 2x. This is the difference to y that a change in x makes, the differential of the equation, which is represented as dy/dx:

$$y = x^2$$

$$\frac{dy}{dx} = 2x$$

You may find it helpful to associate the process of differentiation as finding such a difference. A more exact definition is that it is the marginal change in y resulting from an infinitely small marginal change in x. Because the differential is derived from the original equation it is also known as the derivative.

If the expression already includes a coefficient for x, like $2x^2$, we multiply the power by the existing coefficient to give us the new coefficient:

$$y = 2x^2 \quad \frac{dy}{dx} = 2 * 2x = 4$$

In this case the differential includes x, so the slope of the equation depends on the size of x; whatever x is, the rate of change in y arising from a change in x is four times the value of x. If we apply the same procedure to 3x, the result is a constant, 3. In carrying out the differentiation of 3x remember that 3x is 3 times x to the power one so the power reduces to zero, and that any quantity raised to the power zero is one:

$$y = 3x^1$$

$$\frac{dy}{dx} = 1 * 3x^{1-1} = 3x^0 = 3$$

In this case the slope is simply 3, and does not depend on the value of x: whether x is small or large the slope will always be 3. The other type of differentiation result that you should know concerns cases where x is raised to a negative power, such as the reciprocal of x, 1/x, which can be written as x^{-1}. The process is the same, take the original power and multiply it by the existing coefficient then reduce the power by one:

$$y = \frac{2}{x^2} = 2x^{-2} \frac{dy}{dx} = (-2) * 2x^{-2-1} = -4x^{-3} = \frac{-4}{x^3}$$

When you differentiate expressions like this the key is to remember that a constant divided by x raised to a positive power is simply the constant times x raised to the negative power. When x is taken above the line the power becomes negative.

Some of the equations you may have to differentiate will consist of several different parts, not necessarily all involving x. For the types of equation we shall look at you need only deal with the parts one at a time to reach the differential.

Example 6

The production cost equation for the car plant in Example 4 was:

$$y = x^2 - 6x + 11$$

where y is the cost per car in thousands of pounds and x is the number of cars produced in millions.

Differentiate this equation.

$$\frac{dy}{dx} = 2x^{2-1} - 6x^{1-1} = 2x - 6$$

Note that in Example 6 the constant of 11 is not represented in the derivative. The derivative tells us how y changes with respect to x. When x changes so will x^2 and 6x but the constant remains to be same as 11.

When an equation has a turning point, a maximum or a minimum, we can use the differential to find the exact position of the turning point. At the turning point the slope is zero, in other words the differential, the rate of change in y with respect to x, is zero. Once we know the differential we can find the value of x at which the slope is zero simply by equating it to zero and solving the resulting equation.

Example 7

Find the location of the turning point of the production cost equation for the car plant in Example

From Example 6 we know that the derivative is:

$$\frac{dy}{dx} = 2x - 6$$

The value of x at which this is equal to zero is the position of the turning point along the horizontal axis:

$$2x - 6 = 0$$

so

$$2x = 6 \text{ and } x = 3$$

The turning point is located above 3 on the horizontal axis. If you look back to Figure 4 you can see that the plotted curve reaches its minimum at that point. We can conclude that the minimum production cost per car will be achieved when 3 million cars are produced.

The cost per car at that level of production is something we can establish by inserting the value of x at the turning point into the original production cost equation:

$$y = x^2 - 6x + 11$$

Minimum cost = $3^2 - 6*3 + 11 = 9 - 18 + 11 = 2$

If 3 million cars are produced the cost per car will be Rs.2000.

In Example 7 we were able to refer back to Figure 4 and see from the graph that the turning point was a minimum. But what if the cost equation had not been plotted, how could we tell that it was a minimum and not a maximum? We take the derivative and differentiate again to produce a second derivative. If the second derivative is positive the turning point is a minimum, if it is negative the turning point is a maximum. It may help to think that after a minimum the only way to go is up, so the second derivative is positive whereas after a maximum the only way to go is down, so the second derivative is negative.

Example 8

Find the second derivative of the production cost equation from Example

The first derivative of the cost equation is:

$$\frac{dy}{dx}=2x-6$$

If we differentiate this again we get 2, which is of course positive, confirming that the turning point is minimum. To distinguish the second from the original or first derivative the notation representing it is:

$$\frac{d^2y}{dx^2}=2$$

The inclusion of the 2s on the left hand side signifies that the process of differentiation has been applied twice in reaching the result.

Example 9

The total revenue for the firm in Example 5 was:

$$y = -x^2 + 4x$$

where y is the total revenue in millions of pounds and x is the price per holiday in thousands of pounds.

Find the first order derivative and use it to locate the turning point. Confirm that the turning point is a maximum by finding the second derivative, and work out the maximum revenue.

The first derivative is:

$$\frac{dy}{dx}=-2+4$$

Turning point location:

$$-2x + 4 - 2x = -4$$

$$x = 2$$

Revenue will be maximized when the price is Rs. 2000. The second derivative is:

$$\frac{d^2y}{dx^2}=-2$$

Since the second derivative is negative, the turning point is a maximum. The revenue when the price is Rs. 2000:

$$y = -(2)^2 + 4 * 2 = -4 + 8 = 4$$

The maximum revenue is Rs.4 million.

THE ECONOMIC ORDER QUANTITY MODEL

An important application of the calculus we looked at in the previous section occurs in a technique companies use to manage inventories, the Economic Order Quantity (EOQ) model. This model was developed to help companies manage stocks of materials and components, specifically by enabling managers to work out the quantity to order each time if they want to minimize costs.

Before we look at the model in detail it is worth reflecting on the reasons companies keep stocks or inventories. Most companies keep some stock of the materials they need for their operations; a bus company will probably have a stock of diesel fuel, a furniture maker will probably have a stock of wood. Such stocks are important because being without the material would disadvantage the company. On the other hand, if a company keeps a large amount of stock the costs of holding it are likely to be very high. The stock would have to be stored somewhere, perhaps under certain temperature or security constraints, and these facilities will have a cost.

For sound business reasons then a company will not want to run out of stock, yet will not want to hold too much. To resolve this, a company might consider placing small, regular orders with their supplier. Whilst this would mean that stock would never be very high, and hence stockholding costs would be modest, it will probably cost money every time an order is made; a requisition may have to be processed, a delivery charge met, a payment authorized. They would find that the more orders they make, the higher the cost of making them.

The dilemma they face is to decide how much material should be ordered each time they place an order, the order quantity, so that the combined costs of making the orders and holding the stock, the total stock cost, is at a minimum. To see how this can be resolved we need to start by examining how the total stock-holding costs and the total order costs vary in relation to the quantity ordered.

We shall concentrate on the simplest Economic Order Quantity model, in which we assume that the rate at which the material is used is constant. The amount used in one week is the same as the amount used in any other week. We also assume that once an order is placed the material will be delivered right away, there is no time lag for delivery.

This latter assumption means that the company can wait until their stock runs out before placing an order for its replenishment.

Taking these assumptions together we can conclude that the highest amount that could be in stock would be the order quantity, which we will refer to as Q, the amount that is ordered every time an order is placed. The lowest level of stock will be zero, since they don't need to order more until they run out. The rate of use is constant, so the fluctuations in the stock level will follow the pattern shown in Figure.

The repeating saw-tooth pattern that you can see in Figure 6 consists of a series of vertical lines each of which represents a delivery of the order quantity, Q. The stock level peaks at Q at the point of each delivery and then declines at a constant rate as the material is taken out of the store and used until the stock level is zero and another delivery comes in.

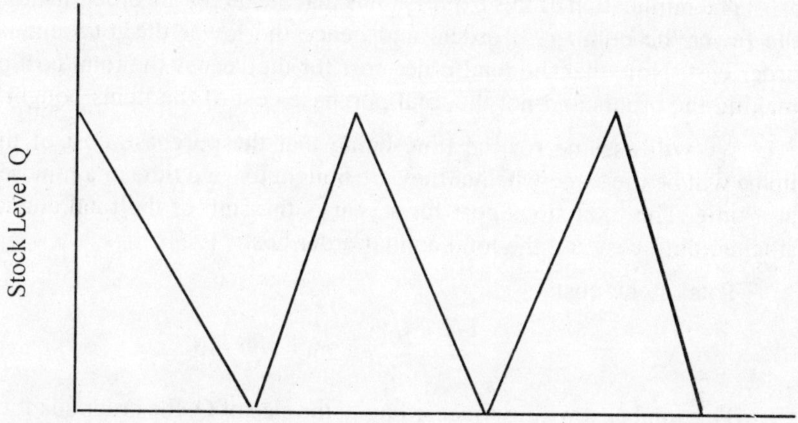

Figure 6: Stock levels over time

The level of stock fluctuates between Q and 0. The even rate of depletion means that the average stock level will be midway between these extremes, half of Q.

If we use S to represent the cost of storing one unit of the material for a year then the cost of storing an average of Q/2 units in stock for a year, the total annual stock-holding cost, is:

$$\frac{SQ}{2}$$

The implication of this expression is that the bigger the order quantity, the larger the average stock and hence the greater the total annual stock cost. The other part of the total stock cost is the total order cost, which again we shall express for a whole year. If we use Y to represent the number of units of the material that are used over a year, then the number of orders made during a year will be Y divided by the amount that is ordered on each occasion, the order quantity:

$$\frac{Y}{Q}$$

If we use C to represent the cost of making an order, the total order cost for a year will be the number of orders multiplied by the order cost:

$$\frac{CY}{Q}$$

The implication of this expression is that the larger the order quantity the fewer the number of orders and hence the lower the total annual order cost. Note that the total order cost for the year is the total cost of making the orders and not the total purchase cost of the items bought.

We will assume for the time being that the purchase cost of the items will be the same whether they are bought ten at a time or a hundred at a time. The total stock cost for a year is the sum of the total annual stockholding cost and the total annual order cost:

Total stock cost:

$$\frac{SQ}{2} = \frac{50Q}{2} = 25Q$$

This total cost will vary according to the size of Q, the order quantity. We assume that in any given context the other factors, the storage cost, annual demand and so on, are fixed, so we can focus on how big the order quantity should be if the total stock cost is to be minimized.

Example 10

The Cheesty Cleaning Company uses 200 gallons of floor cleaner over a year. The company would like to find out how many gallons of floor cleaner they should order at a time to minimize their total stock costs. The cost of storing one gallon of floor cleaner for a year is Rs. 50. We will begin by showing graphically how the total annual stock-holding costs are related to the quantity ordered. Using this expression we can work out the total annual stock-holding cost for a given order quantity, for instance if the order quantity is 5 the total annual stock-holding cost will be Rs.125. The expression is plotted in Figure.

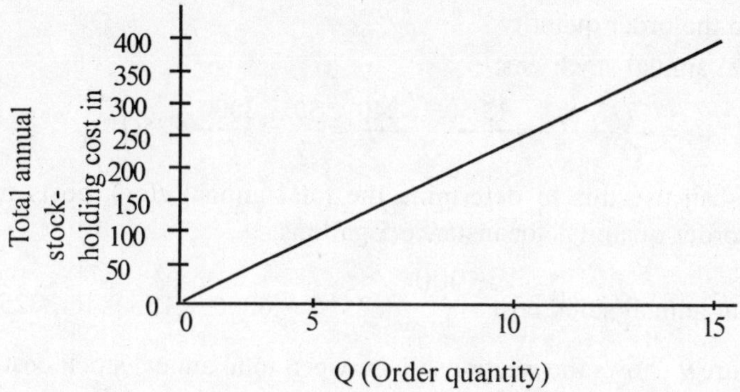

Figure 7: Total annual stock-holding cost in Rs.

The cost of processing an order for a consignment of floor cleaner is Rs.12.50. We can show graphically how the total annual order costs are related to the quantity ordered.

$$\text{Total annual order cost} = \frac{CQ}{Q} = \frac{12.50Q \times 200}{Q} = \frac{2500}{Q}$$

From this we can find the total annual order cost for a given order quantity. If, say, the order quantity is 5 gallons the total annual order cost will be 2500/5, Rs. 500. The expression is plotted in Figure.

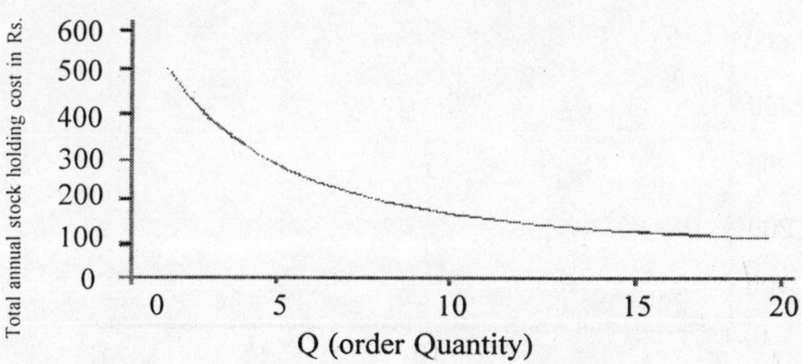

Figure 8: Total annual order cost and order quantity in Example

The company will have both stock-holding and order costs so we need to see how these costs combined, the total annual stock cost, are related to the order quantity.

Total annual stock cost

$$= \frac{CQ}{Q} + \frac{SQ}{2} = \frac{12.50Q \times 240}{Q} = \frac{50}{Q} = \frac{3000}{Q} + 25Q$$

We can use this to determine the total annual stock costs for a specific order quantity, for instance 5 gallons:

$$\text{Total annual stock cost} \frac{3000}{5} + 25*5 = 6000 + 125 = \text{Rs. } 725$$

Figure 9 shows the relationship between total annual stock cost and order quantity. The uppermost line in Figure 9 represents the total annual stock cost. The lower straight line represents the total annual stock holding cost, the lower curve represents the total annual order cost. These lines reflect the fact that as the order quantity is increased the holding costs will rise and the order costs will fall.

If you look carefully at Figure 9 you will see that the curve representing the total annual stock cost does reach a minimum when the order quantity is about 10 gallons.

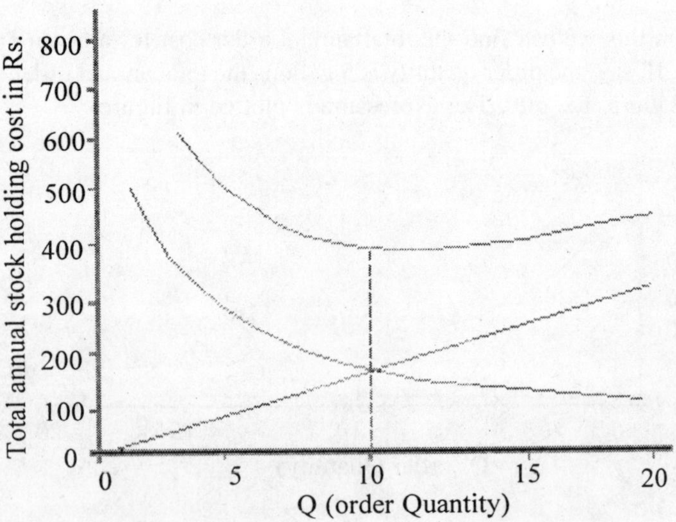

Figure 9: Total annual stock cost and order quantity in Example 10

To ascertain the exact position of the minimum point of the total stock cost equation we can differentiate it:

Total annual stock cost

$$=\frac{CY}{Q}=\frac{SQ}{2}=CYQ^{-1}+\frac{SQ}{2}$$

$$\frac{dCost}{dQ}=-CYQ^{-2}+\frac{S}{2}=\frac{CY}{Q^2}+\frac{S}{2}$$

At the minimum point of the curve this derivative will be equal to zero:

$$-\frac{CY}{Q^2}+\frac{S}{2}=0$$

We can rearrange this to obtain a definition of the least-cost order quantity:

$$\frac{S}{2}=\frac{CY}{Q^2}$$

$$\frac{S}{2CY}=\frac{1}{Q^2}$$

$$\frac{2CY}{S}=Q^2$$

$$\sqrt{\frac{2CY}{S}}=Q$$

So Q, the least cost or economic order quantity is: $Q=\sqrt{\frac{2CY}{S}}$

This is the Economic Order Quantity (EOQ) model. of course, the square root of the expression on the left of the EOQ model can in theory be either positive or negative, but since only a positive order quantity makes practical sense the positive root is the only relevant one.

We can confirm that at this value of Q the total stock cost is at a minimum by finding the second derivative of the total stock cost equation:

$$\frac{d^2Cost}{dQ^2}=(-2)-CYQ^{-3}=\frac{CY}{Q^3}$$

If this is positive it means that the turning point is indeed a minimum. This will be the case because C, the order cost, and Y, the annual demand for the item, and all plausible values of Q will be positive so the second derivative will always have a positive value.

5

Fuelling Quantitative Analysis

In previous chapters we have concentrated on techniques or models involving single values that are known with certainty. Examples of these are break-even analysis and linear programming. In break-even analysis the revenue per unit, the fixed cost and the variable cost per unit are in each case a specified single value. In linear programming we assume that both profit per unit and resource usage are constant amounts. In the Economic Order Quantity model the order cost and the stock-holding cost per unit are each known single values. Because these types of models involve values that are fixed or predetermined they are called deterministic models.

Deterministic models can be useful means of understanding and resolving business problems. Their reliance on known single value inputs makes them relatively easy to use but is their key shortcoming. Companies simply cannot rely on a figure such as the amount of raw material used per unit of production being a single constant value. In practice, such an amount may not be known with certainty, because it is subject to chance variation. Because of this company managers may well need to study the variation and incorporate it within the models they use to guide them.

Models that use input values that are uncertain rather than certain, values that are subject to chance variation rather than known, are called probabilistic models, after the field of probability, which involves the measurement and analysis of chance.

Before you can use probability to reflect the chance variation in business situations you need to know how to get some idea of the variation. To do this we have to start by ascertaining where relevant information might be found. Having identified these sources you need to know how to arrange and present what you find from them in forms that will help you understand and communicate the variation. In order to do this in appropriate ways it is important that you are aware of the different types of data that you may meet.

The purpose of this chapter is therefore to acquaint you with some essential preliminaries for studying variation. We will start with definitions of some key terms, before looking into sources of data and considering the different types of data. Subsequently we shall look at basic methods of arranging data.

SOURCES OF DATA

The data that form the basis of an investigation might be collected at first hand in response to a specific problem. This type of data, collected by direct observation or measurement, is known as primary data. The procedures used to gather primary data are surveys, experiments and observational methods. A survey might involve asking consumers their opinion of a product. A series of experiments might be conducted on products to assess their quality. Observation might be used to ascertain the hazards at building sites.

The advantages of using primary data are that they should match the requirements of those conducting the investigation and they are up-to-date. The disadvantages are that gathering such data is both costly and time-consuming.

An alternative might be to find data that have already been collected by someone else. This is known as secondary data. A company looking for data for a specific study will have access to internal sources of secondary data, but as well as those there are a large number of external sources; government statistical publications, company reports, academic and industry publications, and specialist information services such as the Economist Intelligence Unit. The advantages of using secondary data are that they are usually easier and cheaper to obtain. The disadvantages are that they could be out of date and may not be entirely suitable for the purposes of the investigation.

TYPES OF DATA

Collecting data is usually not an end in itself. When collected the data will be in 'raw' form, a state that might lead someone to refer to it as 'meaningless data'. Once it is collected the next stage is to begin transforming it into information, literally to enable it to inform us about the issue being investigated.

There is a wide range of techniques that you can use to organize, display and represent data. Selecting which ones to use depends on the type of data you have. The nature of the raw material you are working with determines your choice of tools. Scissors are fine for cutting paper but no good for cutting wood. A saw will cut wood but is useless for cutting paper. It is therefore essential that you understand the nature of the data you want to analyse before embarking on the analysis, so in this section we will look at several ways of distinguishing between different types of data.

There are different types of data because there are different ways in which facts are gathered. Some data may exist because specific things have characteristics that have been categorized whereas other data may exist as a result of things being counted, or measured, on some sort of scale.

Example 1

Holders of a certain type of investment account are described as 'wealthy'. To investigate this we could use socio-economic definitions of class to categorize each account holder, or we could count the number of homes owned by each account holder, or we could measure the income of each account holder.

Perhaps the most important way of contrasting data types is on the basis of the scales of measurement used in obtaining them. The acronym NOIR stands for Nominal, Ordinal, Interval, Ratio; the four basic data types. Nominal is the 'lowest' form of data, which contains the least amount of information. Ratio is the 'highest' form of data, which contains the most amount of information.

The word nominal comes from the same Latin root as the word name. Nominal data are data that consist solely of names or labels. These labels might be numeric such as a bank account number, or they might be non-numeric such as gender. Nominal data can be categorized using the labels themselves to establish, for instance the number of males and females. It is possible to represent and analyse nominal data using proportions and modes (the modal category is the one that contains the most observations), but carrying out more sophisticated analysis such as calculating an average is inappropriate; for example, adding a set of telephone numbers together and dividing by the number there are to get an average would be meaningless.

Like nominal data, ordinal or 'order' data consist of labels that can be used to categorize the data, but order data can also be ranked. Examples of ordinal data are academic grades and finishing positions in a horse race. An academic grade is a label (an 'A' grade student) that also belongs to a ranking system ('A' is better than 'B'). Because ordinal data contain more information than nominal data we can use a wider variety of techniques to represent and analyse them. As well as proportions and modes we can also use order statistics, such as identifying the middle or median observation. However, any method involving arithmetic is not suitable for ordinal data because although the data can be ranked the intervals between the ranks are not consistent. For instance, the difference between the horse finishing first in a race and the one finishing second is one place. The difference between the horse finishing third and the one finishing fourth is also one place, but this does not mean that there is the same distance between the third- and fourth-placed horses as there is between the first- and second-placed horses.

Interval data consist of labels and can be ranked, but in addition the intervals are measured in fixed units so the differences between values have meaning. It follows from this that unlike nominal and ordinal, both of which can be either numeric or non-numeric, interval data are always numeric. Because interval data are based on a consistent numerical scale, techniques using arithmetical procedures can be applied to them. Temperatures measured in degrees Fahrenheit are interval data. The difference between 30° and 40° is the same as the difference between 80° and 90°.

What distinguishes interval data from the highest data form, ratio data, is that interval data are measured on a scale that does not have a meaningful zero point to 'anchor' it. The zero point is arbitrary, for instance 0° Fahrenheit does not mean a complete lack of heat, nor is it the same as 0° Celsius. The lack of a meaningful zero also means that ratios between the data are not consistent, for example 40° is not half as hot as 80°. (The Celsius equivalents of these temperatures are 4.4° and 26.7°, the same heat levels yet they have a completely different ratio between them.)

Ratio-type data has all the characteristics of interval data – it consists of labels that can be ranked as well as being measured in fixed amounts on a numerical scale. The difference is that the scale has a meaningful zero and ratios between observations are consistent. Distances are ratio data whether we measure them in miles or kilometres. Zero kilometres and zero miles mean the same – no distance. Ten miles is twice as far as five, and their kilometre equivalents, 16 and 8, have the same ratio between them.

Example 2

Identify the data types of the variables in Example

The socio-economic classes of account holders are ordinal data because they are labels for the account holders and they can be ranked.

The numbers of homes owned by account holders and the incomes of account holders are both ratio data. Four homes are twice as many as two, and Rs.60,000 is twice as much income as Rs.30,000.

Another important distinction you need to make is between qualitative data and quantitative data. Qualitative data consist of categories or types of a characteristic or attribute and are always either nominal or ordinal. The categories form the basis of the analysis of qualitative data. Quantitative data are based on counting 'how many' or measuring 'how much' and are always of interval or ratio type. The numerical scale used to produce the figures forms the basis of the analysis of quantitative data.

There are two different types of quantitative data: discrete and continuous. Discrete data are quantitative data that can take only a limited number of values because they are produced by counting in distinct or 'discrete' steps, or measuring against a scale made up of distinct steps. There are three types of discrete data that you may come across. First, data that can only take certain values because other values simply cannot occur, for example the number of hats sold by a clothing retailer in a day. There could be 12 sold one day and 7 on another, but selling 9.3 hats in a day is not possible because there is no such thing as 0.3 of a hat. Such data are discrete by definition.

Secondly, data that take only certain values because those are the ones that have been established by long-standing custom and practice, for example bars in the UK sell draught beer in whole and half pints. You could try asking for three-quarters of a pint, but the bar staff would no doubt insist that you purchase the smaller or larger quantity. They simply would not have the equipment or pricing information to hand to do otherwise.

There are also data that only take certain values because the people who have provided the data or the analysis have decided, for convenience, to round values that do not have to be discrete. This is what you are doing when you give your age to the last full year. Similarly, the temperatures given in weather reports are rounded to the nearest degree, and the distances on road signs are usually rounded to the nearest mile. These data are discrete by convention rather than by definition. They are really continuous data.

Discrete data often but not always consist of whole number values. The number of visitors to a website will always be a whole number, but shoe sizes include half sizes. In other cases, like the UK standard sizes of women's clothing, only some whole numbers occur.

The important thing to remember about discrete data is that there are gaps between the values that can occur, that is why this type of data is sometimes referred to as discontinuous data. In contrast, continuous data consist of numerical values that are not restricted to specific numbers. Such data are called continuous because there are no gaps between feasible values. This is because measuring on a continuous scale such as distance or temperature yields continuous data.

The precision of continuous data is limited only by how precisely the quantities are measured. For instance, we measure both the length of bus journeys and athletic performances using the scale of time. In the first case a clock or a wristwatch is sufficiently accurate, but in the second case we would use a stopwatch or an even more sophisticated timing device. The terms discrete variable and continuous variable are used in describing data sets. A discrete variable has discrete values whereas a continuous variable has continuous values.

Example 3

A motoring magazine describes cars using the following variables:

Type of vehicle – Hatchback/Estate/MPV/Off-Road/Performance

Number of passengers that can be carried

Fuel type – petrol/diesel

Fuel efficiency in miles per gallon

Which variables are qualitative and which quantitative?

The type of car and fuel type are qualitative; the number of passengers and the fuel efficiency are quantitative.

Which quantitative variables are discrete and which continuous?

The number of passengers is discrete; the fuel efficiency is continuous.

In most of your early work on analysing variation you will probably be using data that consist of observed values of a single variable. However you may need to analyse data that consist of observed values of two variables in order to find out if there is a connection between them. For instance, we might want to ascertain how cab fares are related to journey times.

In dealing with a single variable we apply univariate analysis, whereas in dealing with two variables we apply bivariate analysis. The prefixes uni- and bi- in these words convey the same meanings as they do in other words like unilateral and bilateral. You may also find reference to multivariate analysis, which involves exploring relationships between more than two variables.

You may come across data referred to as either hard or soft. Hard data are facts, measurements or characteristics arising from situations that actually exist or were in existence. Temperatures recorded at a weather station and the nationalities of tourists are examples of hard data. Soft data are about beliefs, attitudes and behaviours. Asking consumers what they know about a product or how they feel about an advertisement will yield soft data. The implication of this distinction is that hard data can be subjected to a wider range of quantitative analysis. Soft data is at best ordinal and therefore offers less scope for quantitative analysis.

A further distinction you need to know is between cross-section and time series data. Cross-section data are data collected at the same point in time or based on the same period of time. Time series data consist of observations collected at regular intervals over time. The volumes of wine produced in European countries in 2002 are cross-section data whereas the volumes of wine produced in Italy in the years 1992 to 2002 are time series data.

ARRANGEMENT OF DATA

Arranging or classifying data in some sort of systematic manner is the vital first stage you should take in transforming the data into information, and hence getting it to 'talk to you'. The way you approach this depends on the type of data you wish to analyse.

ARRANGING QUALITATIVE DATA

Dealing with qualitative data is quite straightforward as long as the number of categories of the characteristic being studied is relatively small. Even if there are a large number of categories, the task can be made easier by merging categories.

The most basic way you can present a set of qualitative data is to tabulate it, to arrange it in the form of a summary table. A summary table consists of two parts, a list of categories of the characteristic, and the number of things that fall into each category, known as the frequency of the category. Compiling such a table is simply a matter of counting how many elements in the study fall into each category.

Example 4

Suppose we want to find how many different types of retail outlet in an area sell trainers. We could tour the area or consult the telephone directory in order to compile a list of outlets, but the list itself may be too crude a form in which to present our results. By listing the types of outlet and the number of each type of outlet we find we can construct a summary table:

Table 1: The number of outlets selling trainers by type of outlet

Type of outlet	*Frequency*	*Relative frequency (%)*
Shoe shops	12	30.8
Sports shops	11	28.2
Department stores	6	15.4
Other	10	25.6
Total number of outlets	39	100.0

In Table 1 the outlet types are qualitative data. The 'Other' category, which might contain several different types of outlet, such as hypermarkets and market stalls, has been created in order to keep the summary table to manageable proportions.

Notice that for each category, the number of outlets as a percentage of the total, the relative frequency of the category, is listed on the right hand side. This is to make it easier to communicate the contents; saying 30.8% of the outlets are shoe shops is more effective than saying 12/39ths of them were shoe shops, although they are different ways of saying the same thing.

You may want to use a summary table to present more than one attribute. Such a two-way tabulation is also known as a contingency table because it enables us to look for connections between the attributes, in other words to find out whether one attribute is contingent upon another.

Example 5

Four large retailers each operate their own loyalty scheme. Customers can apply for loyalty cards and receive points when they present them whilst making purchases. These points are accumulated and can subsequently be used to obtain gifts or discounts.

A survey of usage levels of loyalty cards provided the information in the following table:

Table 2: Number of transactions by loyalty card use

	Transactions		
Retailer	***With card***	***Without card***	***Total***
Aptyeka	236	705	941
Botinky	294	439	733
Crassivy	145	759	904
Total	675	1903	2578

Arranging Quantitative Data

The nature of quantitative data is different to qualitative data and therefore the methods used to arrange quantitative data are rather different. However, the most appropriate way of arranging some quantitative data is the same as the approach we have used to arrange qualitative data.

This applies to the analysis of a discrete quantitative variable that has a very few feasible values. You simply treat the values as you would the categories of a characteristic and tabulate the data to show how often each value occurs. When quantitative data are tabulated, the resulting table is called a frequency distribution because it demonstrates how frequently each value in the distribution occurs.

Example 6

The UREA department store offers free refills when customers purchase hot beverages in its cafe. The numbers of refills taken by 20 customers were:

0	1	3	1	2	0	2	2	0	1
0	3	1	0	1	2	1	1	0	2

These figures can be tabulated as follows:

Table 3: Number of hot beverage refills taken

Number of Refills	***Number of Customers***
0	6
1	7
2	5
3	2
Total number of customers	100

We can present the data in Example 6 in the form of a simple table because there are only a very limited number of values. Unfortunately this is not always the case, even with discrete quantitative data.

For instance, if Example 6 included customers who spent all day in the café and drank 20 or so cups of coffee each then the number of refills might go from none to 30. This would result in a table with far too many rows to be of use.

To get around this problem we can group the data into fewer categories or classes by compiling a grouped frequency distribution. This shows the frequency of observations in each class.

Example 7

The numbers of email messages received by 22 office workers in one day were:

50	14	25	81	03	35	21	24	51	57	59
81	33	15	26	75	17	20	12	64		

Produce a grouped frequency distribution to present these data.

Number of Messages received	*Frequency*
0–19	11
20–39	4
40–59	4
60–79	2
80–99	1
Total Frequency	22

In order to compile a grouped frequency distribution you will need to exercise a little judgement because there are many sets of classes that could be used for a specific set of data. To help you, there are three rules:

1. Don't use classes that overlap.
2. Don't leave gaps between classes.
3. The first class must begin low enough to include the lowest observation and the last class must finish high enough to include the highest observation.

In Example 7 it would be wrong to use the classes 0–20, 20–40, 40–60 and so on because a value on the very edge of the classes like 20 could be put into either one, or even both, of two classes. Although there are numerical gaps between the classes that have been used in Example 7, they are not real gaps because no feasible value could fall into them. The first class finishes on 19 and the second begins on 20, but since the number of messages received is a discrete variable a value like 19.6, which would fall into the gap, simply will not occur. Since there are no observed values lower than zero or higher than 99, the third rule is satisfied.

We could sum up these rules by saying that anyone looking at a grouped frequency distribution should be in no doubt where each feasible value belongs. Every piece of data must have one and only one place for it to be. To avoid any ambiguity whatsoever, you may like to use the phrase 'and under' between the beginning and end of each class. The classes in Example 7 could be rewritten as:

0 and under 20

20 and under 40 … and so on.

It is especially important to apply these rules when you are dealing with continuous quantitative data. Unless you decide to use 'and under' or a similar style of words, it is vital that the beginning and end of each class is specified to at least the same degree of precision as the data.

Example 8

The results of measuring the contents (in millilitres) of a sample of 30 bottles of 'Nogat' náil polish labelled as containing 10 ml were:

10.30	10.05	10.06	9.82	10.09	9.85	9.98	9.97	10.28
0.01	9.92	10.03	10.17	9.95	10.23	9.92	10.05	10.11
10.02	10.06	10.21	10.04	10.12	9.99	10.19	9.89	10.05
10.11	10.00	9.92						

Arrange these figures in a grouped frequency distribution.

Nail polish (ml)	*Frequency*
9.80–9.89	3
9.90–9.99	7
10.00–10.09	11
10.10–10.19	5
10.20–10.29	3
10.30–10.39	1
Total frequency	30

When you construct a grouped frequency distribution you will also need to decide how many classes to use and how wide they are. These are related issues: the fewer the number of classes the wider each one needs to be. It is a question of balance. You should avoid having a very few very wide classes because they will only convey a crude impression of the distribution. On the other hand, if you have very many narrow classes you will be conveying too much detail. So, what is too few and what is too many? As a guide, take the square root of the number of observations in the set of data. In Example 8 there are 30 observations. The square root of 30 is 5.48, so we should round down to 5 or up to 6 because we can only have whole numbers of classes. We have actually used six classes for these data, which according to this guide is about right.

Once you have some idea of the number of classes, the width of the classes has to be decided. It is useful if all the classes have the same width, especially if the frequency distribution is going to be the basis for further work on the data.

The set of classes you use must cover all the observations from lowest to highest, so to help you decide the width of classes, subtract the lowest observation from the highest observation to give you the difference between the two, known as the range of the values. Divide this by the number of classes you want to have and the result will be the minimum class width you must use. If you look back at Example 7 the range of observations is 93 (98 minus 5) which, when divided by 5 gives 18.6. So if we want a set of five classes of equal width to cover the range from 5 to 98, each class must be at least 18.6 wide.

This number, 18.6, is not particularly 'neat', so to make our grouped frequency distribution easier to interpret we can round it up. The most obvious number to take is 20, so 5 classes 20 units wide will be sufficient to cover the range. In fact because these classes will combine to cover a range of 100, whereas the range of our data is 93 we have some flexibility when it comes to deciding where the first class should start.

The first class must begin at or below the lowest observation in the set, in Example 7 this means it must start at 5 or below. Because 5 is a fairly 'neat' round number it would make a perfectly acceptable start for our first class, which would then be '5–24', the second class would be 25–44' and so on. But what if the first observed value was 3 or 7?

Starting a set of classes with such a value would result in a grouped frequency distribution that would look rather ungainly. If we start the classes at a round number lower than the lowest value in the distribution, for instance zero in Example 7, we can guarantee that the resulting set of classes will have 'neat' beginnings.

Grouped frequency distributions are very useful for comparing two or more sets of data because the classes provide a common framework. The best way of using grouped frequency distributions in this way is to calculate the relative frequencies of the number of observations in every class for each set of data.

Example 9

A rival brand of nail polish, Pallyets, also comes in 10 ml bottles. The contents in millilitres of a sample of 26 bottles of this product were:

10.19 9.92 10.22 10.39 9.95 10.15 10.12 10.25 9.94

9.88 9.92 10.23 9.86 10.34 10.37 10.38 10.34 10.08

10.23 10.05 9.86 9.92 10.35 10.07 9.93 10.14

Classify these data using the classes from Example 8 and work out the relative frequencies for both distributions.

Nali polish (ml)	Frequency (nogat)	Relative Frequency (%)Nogat	Frequncy (Pallyets)(%)	Relative frequency (%)
9.80 - 9.89	3	10.0	3	11.5
9.90 - 9.99	7	23.3	6	23.1
10.00-10.09	11	36.7	3	11.5
10.10 - 10.19	5	16.7	4	15.4
10.20 - 10.29	3	10.0	4	15.4
10.30 - 10.39	1	3.3	6	23.1
Total	30	100.0	26	100.0

The use of relative frequencies in Example 9, given in percentages to one place of decimals, makes direct comparison of the two sets of data much easier. Saying for instance that 3.3% of the sample of Nogat and 34.6% of the sample of Pallyets contained 10.3 ml or more is more straightforward than comparing 1/30 with 6/26.

6

Pictorial Presentation of Data

In the previous chapters we looked at arranging and tabulating data, taking the first steps in transforming raw data into information, bringing meaning to the apparently meaningless. In this chapter we will continue this theme by considering various ways of portraying data in visual form. Used appropriately the diagrams and charts you will find here are very effective means of communicating the patterns and meaning contained in data, specifically the patterns and sequences in distributions.

There are techniques that are very common in business documents so being able to understand what they mean is an important skill. There are many different diagrams and charts that can be used to do this, so it is important to know when to use them. The techniques we use depend on the type of data we want to present, in the same way as the suitability of the methods of arranging data featured in the last chapter depended on the type of data. Essentially, the simpler the data, the simpler the presentational tools that can be used to represent them: simple nominal data restricted to a few categories can be shown effectively in the form of a simple bar chart whereas ratio data require the more rigorous scaling of something like a histogram.

DISPLAYING QUALITATIVE DATA

In the last chapter we covered the arrangement of qualitative data in the form of summary tables. As well as being a useful way of displaying qualitative data, a summary table is an essential preliminary task to preparing a diagram to portray the data.

A diagram is usually a much more effective way of communicating data because it is easier for the eye to digest than a table. This will be important when you have to include data in a report or presentation because you want your audience to focus their attention on what you are saying. They can do that more easily if they don't have to work too hard to understand the form in which you have presented your data.

Displaying qualitative data is fairly simple if there are few categories of the attribute or characteristic being investigated. With more categories, the task can be simplified by merging categories.

There are three types of diagram that you can use to show qualitative data: pictographs, pie charts and bar charts. We will deal with them in this section in order of increasing sophistication.

PICTOGRAPHS

A pictograph his little more than a simple extension of a summary table. The categories of the attribute are listed as they are in a summary table, and we use symbols to represent the number of things in each category. The symbols you use in a pictograph should have a simple and direct visual association with the data.

A pictograph can be an effective way of presenting a simple set of qualitative data. The symbols are a simple way of representing the number in each category and have the extra advantage of emphasizing the context of the data.

Pictographs do have some drawbacks that may put you off using them. Unless you are artistically gifted and can create appropriate images by hand, you will probably have to rely on computer software to produce them for you. Creating a pictograph using a PC can be a laborious process. Spreadsheet and statistical packages cannot produce a pictograph for you directly from data, so symbols have to be grafted alongside text in a word processing package.

If you do use pictographs you need to choose the symbols carefully. They should be easy to associate with the context of the data and not so elaborate that the symbols themselves become the focus of attention rather than the data they are supposed to represent.

You may occasionally see a pictograph in academic and business documents; you are more likely to see them on television and in newspapers. The computer graphics software reporters and editors use is much more sophisticated than any that you are likely to have access to during your studies.

PIE CHARTS

The second method of displaying qualitative data that we will look at is the pie chart. Pie charts are used much more than pictographs in part because they can be produced using widely available computer software. A pie chart, like a pictograph, is designed to show how many things belong to each category of an attribute. It does this by representing the entire set of data as a circle or 'pie' and dividing the circle into segments or 'slices'. Each segment represents a category, and the size of the segment reflects the number of things in the category.

Just about every spreadsheet or statistical package can produce a pie chart either from the original data or from a summary table. Pie charts are so widely used and understood that it is very tempting to regard them as an almost universal means of displaying qualitative data. In many cases they are appropriate and effective, but in some situations they are not.

Because the role of a pie chart is to show how different components make up a whole, you should not use one when you cannot or do not want to show the whole. This may be because there are some values missing from the data or perhaps there is an untidy 'Other' category for data that do not fit in the main categories. In leaving out any data, either for administrative or aesthetic reasons, you would not be presenting the whole, which is exactly what pie charts are designed to do.

One reason that people find pie charts accessible is that the analogy of cutting up a pie is quite an obvious one. As long as the pie chart looks like a pie it works. However if you produce a pie chart that has too many categories it can look more like a bicycle wheel than a pie, and confuses rather than clarifies the data. If you have a lot of categories to present, say more than ten, either merge some of the categories in order to reduce the number of segments in the pie chart or consider an alternative way of presenting your data.

BAR CHARTS

Another method of portraying qualitative data is the bar chart. Like pie charts, bar charts are widely used, fairly simple to interpret, and can be produced using spreadsheet and statistical packages. However because there are several different varieties of bar charts, they are more flexible tools. We can use bar charts to portray not only simple categorizations but also two-way classifications.

The basic function of a bar chart is the same as that of a pie chart, and for that matter a pictograph; to show the number or frequency of things in each of a succession of categories of an attribute. It represents the frequencies as a series of bars. The height of each bar is in direct proportion to the frequency of the category; the taller the bar that represents a category, the more things there are in that category.

A component bar chart is particularly useful if you want to emphasize the relative proportions of each category, in other words to show the balance within the categories of one attribute between the categories of another attribute.

If you want to focus on this balance exclusively and are not too concerned about the absolute frequencies in each category you could use a component bar chart in which each bar is subdivided in percentage terms.

DISPLAYING QUANTITATIVE DATA

Quantitative data are more sophisticated data than qualitative data and therefore the methods used to present quantitative data are generally more elaborate. The exception to this is where you want to represent the simplest type of quantitative data, discrete quantitative variables that have very few feasible values. You can treat the values in these data as you would categories in qualitative data, using them to construct a bar chart or pie chart.

HISTOGRAMS

In general quantitative data consist of a rather larger variety of values than the data portrayed we saw how grouped frequency distributions could be used to arrange quantitative data. Here we will look at what is probably the most widely used way of displaying data arranged in a grouped frequency distribution, the histogram. This is a special type of bar chart where each bar or block represents the frequency of a class of values rather than the frequency of a single value. Because they are composed in this way histograms are sometimes called block diagrams.

A histogram is a visual tool that displays the pattern or distribution of observed values of a variable. The larger the size of the block that represents a class, the greater the number of values that has occurred in that class. Because the connection between the size of the blocks and the frequencies of the classes is the key feature of the diagram the scale along the vertical or 'Y' axis must start at zero.

As long as the classes in a grouped frequency distribution are of the same width it is simply the heights of the blocks of the histogram that reflect the frequencies of observed values in the classes. If the classes have different widths it is important that the areas of the blocks are proportional to the frequencies of the classes. The best way of ensuring this is to represent the frequency density rather than the frequency of the classes. The frequency density is the frequency of values in a class divided by the width of the class. It expresses how densely the values are packed in the class to which they belong.

CUMULATIVE FREQUENCY GRAPHS

An alternative method of presenting data arranged in a grouped frequency distribution is the cumulative frequency graph. This diagram shows the way in which the data accumulates through the distribution from the first to the last class in the grouped frequency distribution. It uses the same horizontal axis as you would use to construct a histogram to present the same data, but you have to make sure that the vertical axis, which must begin at zero, extends far enough to cover the total frequency of the distribution.

To plot a cumulative frequency graph you must begin by working out the cumulative frequency of each class in the grouped frequency distribution. The cumulative frequency of a class is the frequency of the class itself added to the cumulative, or combined frequency of all the preceding classes.

The cumulative frequency of the first class is simply the frequency of the first class because it has no preceding classes. The cumulative frequency of the second class is the frequency of the second class added to the frequency of the first class. The cumulative frequency of the third class is the frequency of the third class added to the cumulative frequency of the second class, and so on.

The cumulative frequency figures represent the number of values that have been accumulated by the end of a class. A cumulative frequency graph is a series of single points each of which represents the cumulative frequency of its class plotted above the very end of its class. There should be one plotted point for every class in the distribution.

The final step is to connect the points with straight lines. It may be more convenient to plot a cumulative relative frequency graph, in which the points represent the proportions of the total number of values that occur in and prior to each class. This is particularly useful if the total number of values in the distribution is an awkward number. You will find further discussion of cumulative frequency graphs in the next chapter because they offer an easy way of finding the approximate values of medians, quartiles and other order statistics.

STEM AND LEAF DISPLAYS

Histograms and cumulative frequency graphs are effective and widely used means of presenting quantitative data. Until fairly recently they could be described as unrivalled. However, there is an alternative way of presenting quantitative data in visual form, the stem and leaf display. This is one of a number of newer techniques known collectively as Exploratory Data Analysis (EDA).

The role of a stem and leaf display is the same as the role of a histogram, namely to show the pattern of a distribution. But unlike a histogram, a stem and leaf display is constructed using the actual data as building blocks, so as well as showing the pattern of a distribution it is also a list of the observations that make up that distribution. It is a very useful tool for making an initial investigation of a set of data as it portrays the shape of the distribution, identifies unusual observations and provides the basis for judging the suitability of different types of averages.

The basis of a stem and leaf display is the structure of numbers, the fact that a number is made up of units, tens, hundreds and so on. For instance the number 45 is composed of two digits, the 4 tens and the 5 units. Using the analogy of a plant, the stem of the number 45 is the number on the left-hand side, 4 (the number of tens) and the leaf is the number on the right hand side, 5 (the number of units). A stem on a plant can have different leaves; in the same way the numerical stem 4 can have different numerical leaves. The number 48 has the same stem as the number 45, but a different leaf, 8.

To produce a stem and leaf display for a set of data we have to list the set of stem digits that appear in the data and then record each observation by putting its leaf digit alongside its stem digit. When we have done this for every observed value in the set of data the result is a series of 'stem lines' each of which consists of a stem digit and the leaf digits of all the observations sharing that particular stem. The final stage in the process is to arrange the leaf digits on each stem line in order of magnitude.

Although a stem and leaf display may appear a little strange it is a tool that is well worth learning to use because it has two advantages over a histogram: particular values can be highlighted and two distributions can be shown in one display. A histogram simply cannot do the former because it consists of blocks rather than data. It is possible to plot a histogram showing two distributions but the result is cumbersome and you would do better to plot two separate histograms.

To show two distributions in one stem and leaf display you simply list the leaf digits for one distribution to the left of the list of stem digits and the leaf digits for the other distribution to the right of the stem digits.

PRESENTING BIVARIATE QUANTITATIVE DATA

The techniques for presenting quantitative data that you have met so far in this chapter have one thing in common: they are all designed to portray the observed values of one variable. They are sometimes called tools of univariate analysis.

But what if you want to present values of two variables in one diagram in order to illustrate a connection (or maybe a lack of connection) between them? In that case you need another type of graph, the scatter diagram, which is a tool of bivariate, that is, two-variable, analysis. The word scatter is used because the intention of the diagram is to show how the observed values of one variable are distributed or scattered in relation to the observed values of another variable.

A set of bivariate data consists of two sets of observed values, a pair of values for each item or thing or person that has been studied. A scatter diagram is constructed by plotting a point for each pair of observed values in the set of data. One value in the pair is plotted against the horizontal axis, the other against the vertical axis. The result is a scatter of points that will form some pattern if there is a connection between the variables.

Typically when we plot a scatter diagram we do so because we have a specific notion about the possible connection between the two variables. If we believe that one variable depends in some way on the other variable we refer to one of the variables as the dependent variable whose values we think depend on the values of the other, which is called the independent variable. The dependent variable is known as the Y variable and its observed values are plotted against the Y, or vertical, axis. The independent variable is known as the X variable and its values are plotted against the X, or horizontal, axis.

PRESENTING TIME SERIES DATA

A time series is a set of data that consists of observations collected over a period, usually at regular intervals. It is bivariate data in which one of the variables is time. Businesses of all kinds collect this sort of data as a matter of course – for instance weekly sales, monthly output, annual profit – so presenting time series data is important.

The type of graph used to portray time series data is a time series plot. It is similar to a scatter diagram in that it consists of a set of plotted points each of which represents a pair of values of two variables plotted against a pair of axes.

However there are key differences. In a time series plot the time variable is always plotted on the horizontal, or X, axis which represents the passage of time from left (the first observation) to right (the last observation). The points that represent the data are joined up to emphasize the flow of time, whereas in a scatter diagram they are never joined up. The scale of the vertical, or Y, axis should begin at zero so that the fluctuations over time are not over-emphasized, whereas the scales on the axes of a scatter diagram do not need to start at zero.

7

Summarizing Data

This chapter is about using figures known as summary measures to represent or summarize quantitative data. Because they are used to describe sets of data they are also called descriptive measures. The summary measures that you will come across are very effective and widely used methods of communicating the essence or gist of a set of observations in just one or two figures, particularly when it is important to compare two or more distributions. Knowing when to use them and how to interpret them will enable you to communicate quantitative information effectively.

There are two basic ways of summarizing data. The first is to use a figure to give some idea of what the values within a set of data are like. This is the idea of an average, something you are probably familiar with; you may have achieved an average mark, you may be of average build etc.

The word average suggests a 'middle' or 'typical' level. An average is a representative figure that summarizes a whole set of numbers in a single figure. There are two other names for averages that you will meet. The first is measures of location, used because averages tell us where the data are positioned or located on the numerical scale. The second is measures of central tendency, used because averages provide us with some idea of the centre or middle of a set of data.

The second basic way of summarizing a set of data is to measure how widely the figures are spread out or dispersed. Summary measures that do this are known as measures of spread or measures of dispersion. They are single figures that tell us how broadly a set of observations is scattered.

These two types of summary measures, measures of location and measures of spread, are not alternatives; they are complementary to each other. That is, we don't use either a measure of location or a measure of spread to summarize a set of data. Typically we use both a measure of location and a measure of spread to convey an overall impression of a set of data.

MEASURES OF LOCATION

There are various averages, or measures of location, that you can use to summarize or describe a set of data. The simplest both to apply and to interpret is the mode.

THE MODE

The mode, or modal value, is the most frequently occurring value in a set of observations. You can find the mode of a set of data by simply inspecting the observations.

Example 1

The ages of 15 sales staff at a cell phone shop are:

17 18 21 18 16 19 17 28 16 20
18 17 17 19 17

What is the mode?

The value 17 occurs more often (5 times) than any other value, so 17 is the mode.

If you want an average to represent a set of data that consists of a fairly small number of discrete values in which one value is clearly the most frequent, then the mode is a perfectly good way of describing the data. Looking at the data in Example 1, you can see that using the mode, and describing these workers as having an average age of 17, would give a useful impression of the data.

The mode is much less suitable if the data we want to summarize consist of a larger number of different values, especially if there is more than one value that occurs the same number of times.

Example 2

The ages of 18 sales staff at a car showroom are:

39 33 17 39 44 28 22 32 39 32
45 31 40 31 37 37 31 42

What is the mode?

The values 31 and 39 each occur three times.

The data set in Example 2 is bimodal; that is to say, it has two modes. If another person aged 32 joined the workforce there would be three modes. The more modes there are, the less useful the mode is to use. Ideally we want a single figure as a measure of location to represent a set of data.

If you want to summarize a set of continuous data, using the mode is going to be even more inappropriate; usually continuous data consist of different values so every value would be a mode because it occurs as often as every other value. If two or more observations take precisely the same value it is something of a fluke.

THE MEDIAN

Whereas you can only use the mode for some types of data, the second type of average or measure of location, the median, can be used for any set of data. The median is the middle observation in a set of data. It is called an order statistic because it is chosen on the basis of its order or position within the data. Finding the median of a set of data involves first establishing where it is then what it is. To enable us to do this we must arrange the data in order of magnitude, which means listing the data in order from the lowest to the highest values in what is called an array. The exact position of the median in an array is found by taking the number of observations, represented by the letter n, adding one and then dividing by two.

$$\text{Median position} = (n + 1)/2$$

Example 3

Find the median of the data in Example

Array:

16 16 17 17 17 17 17 18 18 18
19 19 20 21 28

Here there are 15 observations, that is n = 15, so:

$$\text{Median position} = (15 + 1)/2 = 16/2 = 8$$

The median is in the eighth position in the array, in other words the eighth highest value, which is the first 18, shown in bold type. There are seven observations to the left of it in the array, and seven observations to the right of it, making it the middle value.

The median age of these workers is 18.

In Example 3 there are an odd number of observations, 15, so there is one middle value. If you have an even number of observations there is no single middle value, so to get the median you have to identify the middle pair and split the difference between them.

Example 4

Find the median of the data in Example 2.

Array:

17 22 28 31 31 31 32 32 33 37
37 39

39 39 40 42 44 45

In this case there are 18 observations, n + 18, so:

Median position = (18 + 1)/2 = 9.5

Although we can find a ninth observation and a tenth observation there is clearly no 9.5th observation. The position of the median is 9.5th so the median is located half way between the ninth and tenth observations, 33 and 37, which appear in bold type in the array. To find the half way mark between these observations, add them together and divide by two.

Median = (33 + 37)/2 = 35

The median age of this group of workers is 35.

THE ARITHMETIC MEAN

Although you have probably come across averages before, and you may already be familiar with the mode and the median, they may not be the first things to come to mind if you were asked to find the average of a set of data. Faced with such a request you might well think of adding the observations together and then dividing by the number of observations there are.

This is what many people think of as 'the average', although actually it is one of several averages. We have already dealt with two of them, the mode and the median. This third average, or measure of location, is called the mean or more specifically the arithmetic mean in order to distinguish it from other types of mean. Like the median the arithmetic mean can be used with any set of quantitative data.

The procedure for finding the arithmetic mean involves calculation so you may find it more laborious than finding the mode, which involves merely inspecting data, and finding the median, which involves putting data in order. To get the arithmetic mean you first get the sum of the observations and then divide by n, the number of observations in the set of data.

Arithmetic mean £ x/n

The symbol x is used here to represent an observed value of the variable X, so £x represents the sum of the observed values of the variable X. The arithmetic mean of a sample is represented by the symbol x–, 'x-bar'. The arithmetic mean of a population is represented by the Greek letter ¼, 'mu', which is the Greek 'm' (m for mean). Later on we will look at how sample means can be used to estimate population means, so it is important to recognize this difference.

The mean is one of several statistical measures you will meet which have two different symbols, one of which is Greek, to represent them. The Greek symbol is always used to denote the measure for the population. Rarely do we have the time and resources to calculate a measure for a whole population so almost invariably the ones we do calculate are for a sample.

Example 5

In one month the total costs (to the nearest Rs.) of the calls made by 23 male mobile phone owners were:

17 17 14 16 15 24 12 20 17 17
13 21

15 14 14 20 21 9 15 22 19 27
19

Find the mean monthly cost:

The sum of these costs: £x = 21 + 19 + 22 + ... + 5 + 17 = 398

The arithmetic mean: £x/n = 398/23 = Rs.17.30 (to the nearest penny)

CHOOSING WHICH MEASURE OF LOCATION TO USE

The whole point of using a measure of location is that it should convey an impression of a distribution in a single figure. If you want to communicate this it won't help if you quote the mode, median and mean and then leave it to your reader or audience to please themselves which one to pick. It is important to use the right average.

Picking which average to use might depend on a number of factors:

- The type of data we are dealing with.
- Whether the average needs to be easy to find.
- The shape of the distribution.

- Whether the average will be the basis for further work on the data.

As far as the type of data is concerned, unless you are dealing with fairly simple discrete data the mode is redundant. If you do have to analyse such data the mode may be worth considering, particularly if it is important that your measure of location is a feasible value for the variable to take.

Example 6

The numbers of days that 16 office workers were absent through illness were:

1	1	9	0	2	1	1	4	0	2
4	1	4	3	2	1				

Find the mode, median and mean for this set of data.

The modal value is 1, which occurs six times.

Array:

0	0	1	1	1	1	1	1	2	2
2	3	4	4	4	9				

The median position is: (16 + 1)/2 = 8.5th position

The median is: (8th value + 9th value)/2 = (1 + 2)/2 = 1.5

The arithmetic mean = (0 + 0 + 1 + 1 + ... + 4 + 9)/16 = 36/16 = 2.25

In Example 6 it is only the mode that has a value that is both feasible and actually occurs, 1. Although the value of the median, 1.5 may be feasible if the employer recorded half-day absences, it is not one of the observed values. The value of the mean, 2.25 is not feasible and therefore cannot be one of the observed values.

The only other reason you might prefer to use the mode rather than the other measures of location, assuming that you are dealing with discrete data made up of a relatively few different values, is that it is the easiest of the measures of location to find. All you need to do is to look at the data and count how many times the values occur. Often with the sort of simple data that the mode suits it is fairly obvious which value occurs most frequently and there is no need to count the frequency of each value.

There are more reasons for not using the mode than there are for using the mode. First, it is simply not appropriate for some types of data, especially continuous data. Secondly, there is no guarantee that there is only one mode; there may be two or more in a single distribution. Thirdly, only the observations that have the modal value 'count', the rest of the observations in the distribution are not taken into account at all. In contrast, when we calculate a mean we add all the values in the distribution together; none of them is excluded.

In many cases you will find that the choice of average boils down to either the median or the mean. The shape of the distribution is a factor that could well influence your choice. If you have a distribution that is skewed rather than symmetrical, the median is likely to be the more realistic and reliable measure of location to use.

Example 7

Produce a histogram to display the data from Example 6 and comment on the shape of the distribution.

The distribution of days absent is positively skewed, with the majority of the observations occurring to the left of the distribution.

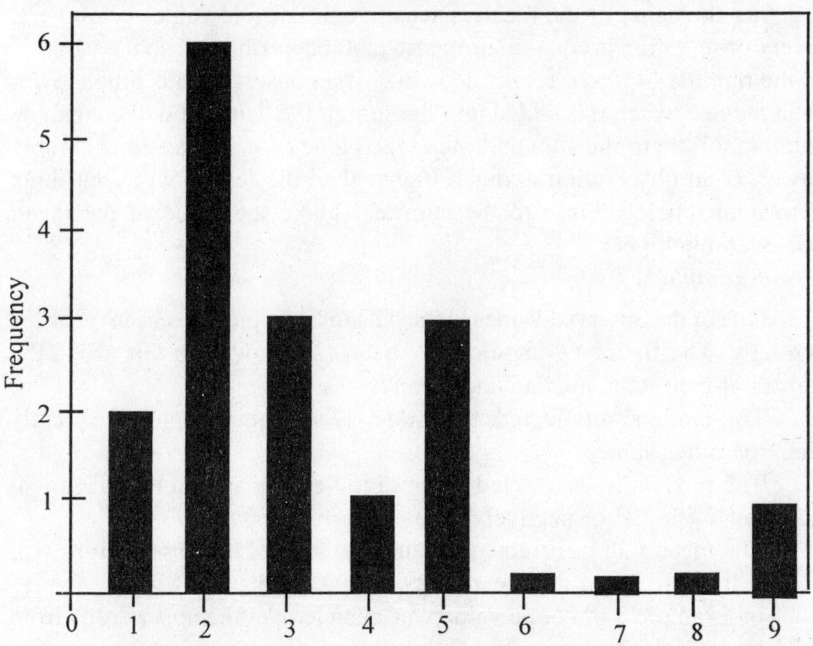

Figure 1: Bar chart of the number of days absent

The median and mean for the data in Example 6 were 1.5 and 2.25 respectively. There is quite a difference between them, especially when you consider that the difference between the lowest and highest values in the distribution is only 9. The difference between the median and the mean arises because the distribution is skewed.

When you find a median you concentrate on the middle of the distribution, you are not concerned with the observations to either side of the middle, so the pattern of the distribution at either end of the distribution does not have any effect on the median. In Example 6 it would not matter if the highest value in the distribution were 99 rather than 9, the median would still be 1.5. The value of the median is determined by how many observations lie to the left and right of it, not the values of those observations.

The mean on the other hand depends entirely on all of the values in the distribution, from the lowest to the highest; they all have to be added together in order to calculate the mean. If the highest value in the distribution were 99 rather than 9 it would make a considerable difference to the value of the mean (in fact it would increase to 7.875).

Because calculating the mean involves adding all the observations together the value of the mean is sensitive to unusual values or outliers. Every observation is equal in the sense that it contributes 1 to the value of n, the number of observations. However if an observation is much lower than the rest, when it is added into the sum of the values it will contribute relatively little to the sum and make the value of the mean considerably lower. If an observation is much higher than the rest, it will contribute disproportionately more to the sum and make the value of the mean considerably higher.

Example 8

One of the observed values in the data in Example 6 has been recorded wrongly. The figure '9' should have been '2'. How does this affect the values of the mode, median and mean?

The mode is unaffected, the value '1' still occurs more frequently than the other values.

The median is unaffected because the eighth and ninth values will still be '1' and '2' respectively.

The mean will be affected because the sum of the observations will reduce by 7 to 29, so the mean is 29/16 = 1.8125.

In Example 8 only one value was changed yet the mean drops from 2.25 to 1.8125.

In a skewed distribution there are typically unusual values so if you use a mean to represent a skewed distribution you should bear in mind that it will be disproportionately influenced or 'distorted' by the relatively extreme values or outliers in the distribution. This is why the median for the data in Example 6 was 1.5 and the mean was 2.25. The higher values in the distribution, the '9' and the '4's, have in effect 'pulled' the mean away from the median.

In general the mean will be higher than the median in positively skewed distributions such as the one shown in Figure 1. In negatively skewed distributions, where the greater accumulation of values is to the right of the distribution, the mean will be lower than the median.

So, should you use the median or the mean to represent a skewed distribution? The answer is that the median is the more representative of the two. Consider the values of the median and mean in relation to Figure 1. The median, 1.5, is by definition in the middle of the distribution, with eight observations below it and 8 observations above it. The mean, 2.25, in contrast has eleven observations below it and only five above it.

If you are dealing with a symmetrical distribution you will find that the mean is not susceptible to distortion because by definition there is roughly as much numerical 'weight' to one side of the distribution as there is to the other. The mean and median of a symmetrical distribution will therefore be close together.

Example 9

Produce a histogram to portray the data in Example 5. Find the median and compare it to the mean.

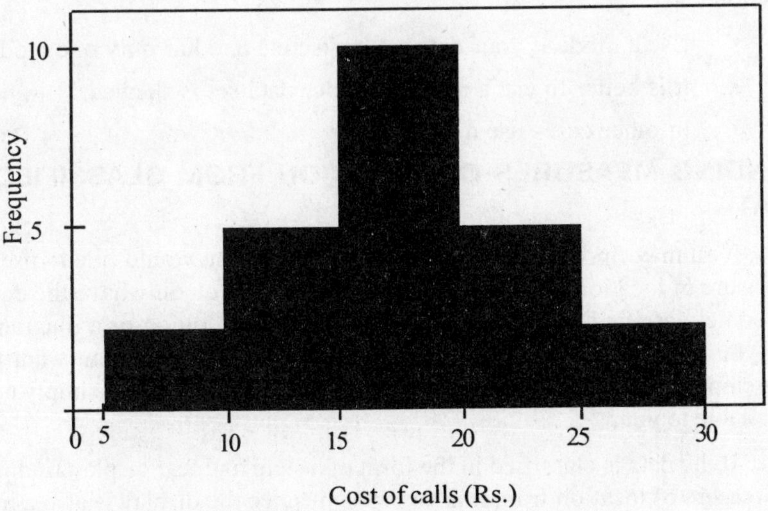

Figure 2 : Histogram of the monthly costs of calls

There are 23 observations so the median is the (23 + 1)/2 = 12th observation.

Array

9 12 13 14 14 14 15 15 15 16 17
17 17 17 19 19 20 20 21 21 22 24
27

The median is 17, which also happens to be the mode as the value 17 occurs four times, and is close to the mean:

(9 + 12 + ... + 24 + 27)/23 = 398/23 = Rs.17.30 (to the nearest penny).

Figure 2 shows a much more symmetrical distribution than the one in Figure 1. This symmetry causes the mean and the median to be close together.

There is one further factor to consider when you need to choose a measure of location, and that is whether you will be using the result as the basis for further statistical analysis. If this were the case you would be well advised to use the mean because it has a more extensive role within statistics as a representative measure than the median.

You will find that choosing the right measure of location is not always straightforward. The conclusions from the discussion in this section are:

- Use a mode if your data set is discrete and has only one mode.
- It is better to use a median if your data set is skewed.
- In other cases use a mean.

FINDING MEASURES OF LOCATION FROM CLASSIFIED DATA

You may find yourself in a situation where you would like to use a measure of location to represent a distribution but you only have the data in some classified form, perhaps a frequency distribution or a diagram. Maybe the original data has been mislaid or discarded, or you want to develop work initiated by someone else and the original data is simply not available to you.

If the data is classified in the form of a stem and leaf display finding a measure of location from it is no problem since the display is also a list of the observed values in the distribution. Each observation is listed, but in a detached form so all you have to do is to put the stems and their leaves back together again to get the original data from which they were derived.

You can find the mode of a distribution from its stem and leaf display by looking for the most frequently occurring leaf digits grouped together on a stem line. Finding the median involves counting down (or up) to the middle value. To get the mean you have to reassemble each observation in order to add them up.

Example 10

Construct a stem and leaf display to show the data in Example 5. Use the display to find the mode, median and mean of the distribution.

Stem and leaf of cost of calls n = 23

0   9

1   2 3 4 4 4

1   5 5 5 6 7 7 7 7 8 9 9

2   0 0 1 1 2 4

2   7

Leaf unit = 1.0

The modal value is 17, the leaf digit '7' appears four times on the lower of the two stem lines for the stem digit '1'.

We know from the calculation (23 + 1)/2 = 12 that the median is the twelfth observation, which is also 17. To find it we can count from the top. The leaf digit on the first stem line, which represents the observed value '9' is the first observed value in the distribution in order of magnitude. The five leaf digits on the next stem line, the first of the two stem lines for the stem digit '1', are the second to the sixth observed values in order of magnitude. The first leaf digit on the third stem line, the second of the two for the stem digit '1', is the seventh observed value, so if we count a further five values along that stem line we come to the twelfth observation, the median value. The leaf digit that represents the median value in the display is shown in bold type.

To get the mean we have to put the observed values back together again and add 9, 12,13, 14, 14 etc. to get the sum of the values, 398, which when divided by 23, the number of values, is Rs.17.30 (to the nearest penny), the same result as we obtained in Example 5.

In Example 10 you can see that we can get the same values for the mode, median and mean as we obtained from the original data because the stem and leaf display is constructed from the parts of the original data. Even if the stem and leaf display were made up of rounded versions of the original data we would get a very close approximation of the real values of the measures of location.

But what if you didn't have a stem and leaf display to work with? If you had a frequency distribution that gave the frequency of every value in the distribution, or a bar chart that depicted the frequency distribution, you could still find the measures of location.

Example 11

Use Figure 1 to find the mode, median and mean of the distribution of days absence through illness.

Figure 1 shows the frequency with which each number of days absence occurs, in the form of a bar. By checking the height of the bar against the vertical axis we can tell exactly how many times that number of days absence has occurred. We can put that information in the form of a frequency distribution:

Number of days absent	Frequency
0	2
1	6
2	3
3	1
4	3
5	0
6	0
7	0
8	0
9	1

We can see that the value '1' has occurred six times, more than any other level of absence, so the mode is 1.

The median position is (16 + 1)/2 = 8.5th. To find the median we have to find the eighth and ninth values and split the difference. We can find these observations by counting down the observations in each category, in the same way as we can with a stem and leaf display. The first row in the table contains two '0's, the first and second observations in the distribution in order of magnitude. The second row contains the third to the eighth observations, so the eighth observation is a '1'. The third row contains the ninth to the eleventh observations, so the ninth observation is a '2'. The median is therefore half way between the eighth value, 1, and the ninth value, 2, which is 1.5.

To find the mean from the frequency distribution we could add each number of days absence into the sum the same number of times as its frequency. We add two '0's, six '1's and so on. There is a much more direct way of doing this involving multiplication, which is after all collective addition. We simply take each number of days absent and multiply it by its frequency, then add the products of this process together. If we use 'x' to represent days absent, and 'f' to represent frequency we can describe this procedure as Sðfx. Another way of representing n, the number of observations, is Sðf, the sum of the frequencies, so the procedure for calculating the mean can be represented as Sðfx/Sðf.

Number of days absent (x)	Frequency (f)	fx
0	2	0
1	6	6
2	3	6
3	1	3
4	3	12
5	0	0
6	0	0
7	0	0
8	0	0
9	1	9
	Sðf = 16	Sðfx = 36

$$\text{The mean} = \frac{\sum fx}{\sum f} = \frac{36}{16} = 2.25\,.$$

You can see that the results obtained in Example 11 are exactly the same as the results found in Example 6 from the original data. This is possible because every value in the distribution is itself a category in the frequency distribution so we can tell exactly how many times it occurs.

But suppose you need to find measures of location for a distribution that is only available to you in the form of a grouped frequency distribution? The categories are not individual values but classes of values. We can't tell from it exactly how many times each value occurs, only the number of times each class of values occurs. From such limited information we can find measures of location but they will be approximations of the true values that we would get from the original data.

Because the data used to construct grouped frequency distributions usually include many different values, hence the need to divide them into classes, finding an approximate value for the mode is a rather arbitrary exercise. It is almost always sufficient to identify the modal class, which is the class that contains most observations.

Example 12

Use Figure 2 to find the modal class of the monthly costs of calls. The grouped frequency distribution used to construct Figure 2 was:

Cost (Rs.)	**Frequency**
5 and under 10	1
10 and under 15	5
15 and under 20	10
20 and under 25	6
25 and under 30	1

The modal class is '15 and under 20' because it contains more values, ten, than any other class.

Since a grouped frequency distribution does not show individual values we cannot use it to find the exact value of the median, only an approximation. To do this we need to identify the median class, the class in which the median is located, but first we must find the median location. Once we have this we can use the fact that, although the values are not listed in order of magnitude the classes that make up the grouped frequency distribution are. So it is a matter of looking for the class that contains the middle value.

When we know which class the median is in we need to establish its likely position within that class. To do this we assume that all the values belonging to the median class are spread out evenly over the width of the class. How far we go through the class to get an approximate value for the median depends on how many values in the distribution are located in the classes before the median class. Subtracting this from the median position gives us the number of values we need to 'go into' the median class to get our approximate median. The distance we need to go into the median class is the median position less the number of values in the earlier classes divided by the number of values in the median class, which we then multiply by the width of the median class.

$$\text{Approximate median} = \text{start of MC}$$
$$\frac{\text{Median position - number of value up to MC}}{\text{Frequency of MC}} * \text{width of MC}$$

Where MC stands for Median Class.

Example 13

Find the approximate value of the median from the grouped frequency distribution in Example 12.

There are 23 observations in the distribution so the median is the (23 + 1)/2 = 12th value in order of magnitude.

The median value does not belong to the first class, '5 and under 10' because it contains only the first observation, the lowest one in the distribution. Neither does it belong to the second class, which contains the second to the sixth values. The median is in the third class, which contains the seventh to the sixteenth values.

The first value in the median class is the seventh value in the distribution. We want to find the twelfth, which will be the sixth observation in the median class. We know it must be at least 15 because that is where the median class starts so all ten observations in it are no lower than 15.

We assume that all ten observations in the median class are distributed evenly through it. If that were the case the median would be 6/10ths the way along the median class. To get the approximate value for the median:

begin at the start of the median class	15
add 6/10ths of the width of the median class 6/10 * 5	3
	18

Alternatively we can apply the procedure:

$$\text{start of MC} + \frac{\text{Median position - number of value up to MC}}{\text{Frequency of MC}}$$

$$* \text{ width of MC}$$

In this case the start of the median class is 15, the median position is 12, there are 6 values in the classes up to the median class, 10 values in the median class and the median class width is 5, so the approximate median is:

$$15+\frac{(12-6)}{10}\times 5=15+\frac{6}{10}\times 5=18$$

This is quite close to the real value we obtained from the original data, 17.

There is an alternative method that you can use to find the approximate value of the median from data presented in the form of a grouped frequency distribution. It is possible to estimate the value of the median from a cumulative frequency graph or a cumulative relative frequency graph of the distribution.

To obtain an approximate value for the median, plot the graph and find the point along the vertical axis that represents half the total frequency. Draw a horizontal line from that point to the line that represents the cumulative frequency and then draw a vertical line from that point to the horizontal axis. The point at which your vertical line meets the horizontal axis is the approximate value of the median.

This approach is easier to apply to a cumulative relative frequency graph as half the total frequency of the distribution is represented by the point '0.5' on the cumulative relative frequency scale along the vertical axis.

To obtain an approximate value for the mean from a grouped frequency distribution we apply the same frequency-based approach as we used in Example 11, where we multiplied each value, x, by the number of times it occurred in the distribution, f, added up these products and divided by the total frequency of values in the distribution:

$$\bar{x}=\frac{\sum fx}{\sum f}$$

The starting point on the left of the horizontal dotted line on the graph in Figure 3 is '0.5' on the vertical axis, midway on the cumulative relative frequency scale. At the point where the horizontal dotted line meets the cumulative relative frequency line, the vertical dotted line drops down to the x axis. The point where this vertical dotted line reaches the horizontal axis is about 17.5, which is the estimate of the median. The graph suggests that half of the values in the distribution are accumulated below 17.5 and half are accumulated above 17.5.

If we have data arranged in a grouped frequency distribution we have to overcome the problem of not knowing the exact values of the observations in the distribution as all the values are in classes. To get around this we assume that all the observations in a class take, on average, the value in the middle of the class, known as the class midpoint. The set of class midpoints is then used as the values of the variables, x, that are contained in the distribution.

MEASURES OF SPREAD

Just as there are several measures of location you can use to convey the central tendency of a distribution, there are several measures of spread to convey the dispersion of a distribution. They are used alongside measures of location in order to give an overall impression of a distribution; where its middle is and how widely scattered the observations are around the middle. Indeed, the two most important ones are closely linked to the median and the mean.

THE RANGE

The simplest measure of spread is the range. The range of a distribution is the difference between the lowest and the highest observations in the distribution, that is:

Range = highest observed value – lowest observed value

The range is very easy to use and understand, and is sometimes a perfectly adequate method of measuring dispersion. However, it is not a wholly reliable or thorough way of assessing spread because it is based on only two observations. If, for instance, you were asked to compare the spread in two different sets of data you may find that the ranges are very similar but the observations are spread out very differently.

Although the ranges for the distributions are identical, the histograms show different levels of dispersion. The figures for Slugar are more widely spread or dispersed than the figures for Rabota. The range is therefore not a wholly reliable way of measuring the spread of data, because it is based on the extreme observations only.

QUARTILES AND THE SEMI-INTERQUARTILE RANGE

The second measure of dispersion at our disposal is the semi-interquartile range, or SIQR for short. It is based on quartiles, which are order statistics like the median.

One way of looking at the median, or middle observation, of a distribution is to regard it as the point that separates the distribution into two equal halves, one consisting of the lower half of the observations and the other consisting of the upper half of the observations. The median, in effect, cuts the distribution in two.

If the median is a single cut that divides a distribution in two, the quartiles are a set of three separate points in a distribution that divide it into four equal quarters. The first, or lower quartile, known as Q1, is the point that separates the lowest quarter of the observations in a distribution from the rest. The second quartile is the median itself; it separates the lower two quarters (i.e. the lower half) of the observations in the distribution from the upper two quarters (i.e. the upper half). The third, or upper quartile, known as Q3, separates the highest quarter of observations in the distribution from the rest.

The median and the quartiles are known as order statistics because their values are based on the order or sequence of observations in a distribution. You may come across other order statistics such as deciles, which divide a distribution into tenths, and percentiles, which divide a distribution into hundredths.

You can find the quartiles of a distribution from an array or a stem and leaf display of the observations in the distribution. The quartile position is half way between the end of the distribution and the median, so it is defined in relation to the median position, which is $(n + 1)/2$, where n is the number of observations. To find the approximate position of the quartiles take the median position, round it down to the nearest whole number if it is not already a whole number, add one and divide by two, that is:

Quartile position = (median position + 1)/2

Once you know the quartile position you can find the lower quartile by counting up to the quartile position from the lowest observation and the upper quartile by counting down to the quartile position from the highest observation.

Example 17

In one month the total costs (to the nearest Rs.) of the calls made by 23 female mobile phone owners were:

14	5	15	6	17	10	22	10	12	17	13
29	7	27	33	16	30	9	15	7	33	28
21										

Find the median and upper and lower quartiles for this distribution.

Array

5	6	7	7	9	10	10	12	13	14	15
15	16	17	17	21	22	27	28	29	30	33
33										

The median position = (23 + 1)/2 = 12th position, so the median value is the value '15'. This suggests that the monthly cost of calls for half the female owners is below Rs.15, and the monthly costs for the other half is above Rs.15.

The quartile position = (12 + 1)/2 = 6.5th position, that is midway between the sixth and seventh observations.

The lower quartile is half way between the observations sixth and seventh from the lowest, which are both 10, so the lower quartile is 10. This suggests that the monthly cost of calls for 25% of the female owners is below Rs.10.

The upper quartile is half way between the observations sixth and seventh from the highest, which are 27 and 22 respectively. The upper quartile is midway between these values, i.e. 24.5, so the monthly cost of calls for 25% of the female owners is above Rs.24.50.

If the upper quartile separates off the top quarter of the distribution and the lower quartile separates off the bottom quarter, the difference between the lower and upper quartiles is the range or span of the middle half of the observations in the distribution. This is called the interquartile range, which is the range between the quartiles. The semi-interquartile range (SIQR) is, as its name suggests, half the interquartile range, that is:

$$SIQR = (Q3 - Q1)/2$$

The semi-interquartile range is a measure of spread. The larger the value of the SIQR, the more dispersed the observations in the distribution are.

Example 19

Find the SIQR of the data in Example 5 and compare this to the SIQR of the data in Example 17.

Array

9 12 13 14 14 14 15 15 15 16 17 17

17 17 19 19 20 20 21 21 22 24 27

There are 23 observations, so the median position is the (23 + 1)/2 12th position.

The quartile position is the (12 + 1)/2 = 6.5th position.

Q1 = (Rs.14 + Rs.15)/2 = Rs.14.5Q3 = (Rs.20 + Rs.20)/2 = Rs.20

SIQR = (Rs.20 – Rs.14.5)/2 = Rs.2.75

The SIQR for the data for the males (Rs.2.75) is far lower than the SIQR for the data for the females (Rs.7.25) indicating that there is more variation in the cost of calls for females.

There is a diagram called a boxplot, which is a very useful way of displaying order statistics. In a boxplot the middle half of the values in a distribution are represented by a box, which has the lower quartile at one end and the upper quartile at the other. A line inside the box represents the median. The top and bottom quarters are represented bystraight lines called 'whiskers' protruding from each end of the box. A boxplot is a particularly useful way of comparing distributions.

A boxplot is particularly useful for identifying outliers, observed values that seem detached from the rest of the distribution. If you have outliers in a distribution it is important to check firstly that they have not been written down wrongly and secondly, assuming that they are accurately recorded, what reasons might explain such an unusual observation.

The semi-interquartile range (SIQR), based like boxplots on quartiles, is a useful way of measuring spread and, together with the median, is often the best way of summarizing skewed distributions. However, just like the range, the SIQR is based on selected observations in a distribution so it cannot always detect dispersion in data.

THE STANDARD DEVIATION

In order to avoid the shortcomings of the range and the SIQR we have to turn to a measure of spread that is based on including every observation rather than selecting just a few. That measure, the most important measure of spread in Statistics, is known as the standard deviation.

As the name suggests, the standard deviation is based on the idea of measuring the typical, or standard, amount of deviation, or difference, in a set of observations. But deviation from what? Deviation from the arithmetic mean.

We can find the standard deviation by first calculating the mean and then finding how far each observation deviates or varies from it.

Example 23

Six newsagents sell the following number of boxes of plain potato crisps in a particular week:

2 5 6 4 3 4

The mean, $\bar{x}$ = 24/6 = 4

Observation(X)	Mean(X-)	Deviation $(x - \bar{x})$
2	4	-2
5	4	1
6	4	2
4	4	0
3	4	-1
4	4	0

To get a single measure of spread from deviation figures like those in Example 23 it would be very convenient to add up the deviations and divide the sum of the deviations by the number of them to get a sort of 'average' deviation. Unfortunately, as you will find out if you try it with the deviations in Example 23, it doesn't work because the deviations add up to zero.

This will always happen because the mean is, in effect, the centre of gravity of a distribution. In the same way that the centre of gravity of an object has as much weight to one side as it does to the other, the mean has as much numerical 'weight' below it as it has above it. The result is that the deviations between the mean and the observations that are lower than the mean, which are always negative, cancel out the deviations between the mean and the observations that are higher than the mean, which are always positive. You can see in Example 23 that the negative deviations (–1 and –2) would be cancelled out by the positive deviations (1 and 2) if we added all the deviations together.

To get around this problem we square the deviations before adding them up, since any number squared is positive. The sum of the squared deviations, Sð $(x-\overline{x})^2$, is the basis of the standard deviation.

Example 24

Find the sum of the squared deviations, Sð $(x-\overline{x})^2$, from the mean for the data in Example 23.

Observation (x)	*Mean (x –)	*Deviation $(x-\overline{x})$	Squared deviation $(x-\overline{x})^2$
2	4	–2	4
5	4	1	1
6	4	2	4
4	4	0	0
3	4	–1	1
4	4	0	0

Sð $(x-\overline{x})^2$ = 4 + 1 + 4 + 0 + 1 + 0 = 10

Now we have a way of measuring total deviation it would be convenient to simply divide by the number of deviations that have been added together, which is the same as n, the number of observations. However, we actually divide the sum of the squared deviations by one less than n instead of n itself.

The reason for this is that any set of data starts off with the same number of degrees of freedom as it has observations, n. The implication is that if you wanted to specify all the figures in the set of data yourself you can do so freely. However, once you have found the mean you could only specify one less than the number of figures freely. The last one would have to be the only figure that combines with the ones you have specified to keep the mean the same, so you have 'lost' a degree of freedom. For instance if we know that the mean of a set of three figures is 5, and we suggest that 2 and 7 are the first two figures in the set, the third value has to be 6 in order that the mean is still 5. Choose any other value for third figure and the mean will be different.

When we calculate a standard deviation we are using the mean and we lose one degree of freedom, so the procedure that we use to calculate the standard deviation, 's', of a sample involves dividing the sum of squared deviations by (n – 1). The only exception is the rare occasion when we need to calculate the population standard deviation, Ã, in which case the sum of squared deviations is divided by n.

You will find that a sample standard deviation can be used as an estimate of a population standard deviation. This can save time and money, but it can only be done if the sample standard deviation is calculated properly.

The final part of the procedure you follow to obtain a sample standard deviation is to take the square root of the sum of squared deviations divided by (n – 1). You have to do this to get a figure that is in the same units as your original data.

We can sum up the procedure that is used to obtain a sample standard deviation in the following expression:

$$(x-\bar{x})^2$$

Example 25

Calculate the standard deviation for the data in Example 23.

The sum of squared deviations is 10 and the number of observations is 6, so the standard deviation of this sample is:

$$s=\sqrt{\frac{10}{5}}=\sqrt{2}=1.414$$

Calculating standard deviations as we have done so far is rather cumbersome, especially for large sets of data, because it involves subtracting the mean from every observation. An alternative way of obtaining a sample standard deviation is to square the observations and add them up to get the sum of the squared observations and then take the sum of the observations and square that. This latter amount is the square of the sum of the observations. We divide it by the number of observations we have and subtract the result from the sum of the squared observations. Finally, multiply by one divided by the number of degrees of freedom and take the square root. We can express the procedure as:

$$s = \sqrt{\frac{1}{n-1}\left(\sum x^2 - \frac{(\sum x)^2}{n}\right)}$$

Example 26

Calculate the standard deviation for the data in Example 23 without subtracting each observation from the mean.

Observation (x)	x^2
2	4
5	25
6	36
4	16
3	9
4	16
Sðx = 24	Sðx² = 106

This is exactly the same as the result we obtained in Example 25 using the original approach.

$$s = \sqrt{\frac{1}{6-1}\left(106 - \frac{(24)^2}{6}\right)} = \sqrt{\left(106 - \frac{576}{6}\right)} = \sqrt{\frac{1}{5}(106-96)}$$

If your data come from an entire population you do not have to worry about degrees of freedom and the procedure you need to apply to find the population standard deviation, sigma (Ã), is:

$$\sigma = \sqrt{\frac{\sum (x-\mu)^2}{n}}$$

Note that to get the population standard deviation you have to subtract the population mean, mð, from every value. The alternative approach, which does not involve subtracting every value from the mean, is:

$$\sigma = \sqrt{\left(\sum x^2 - \frac{(\sum x)^2}{n}\right)}$$

If you use any of these expressions to calculate the standard deviation of a set of data with many observations you will find the experience laborious. It really is a task that should be carried out with the aid of calculator or computer software.

In later quantitative work you may encounter something called a variance. The variance is the square of the standard deviation. The expression for the variance looks like the expression for the standard deviation and in fact the only difference is that finding the variance does not involve taking a square root.

$$\text{The sample variance, } s^2 = \frac{\sum (x - \overline{x})^2}{n-1}$$

$$\text{The population variance, } \sigma^2 = \frac{\sum (x - \mu)^2}{n}$$

The standard deviation is widely used with the mean to provide an overall summary of a distribution. Indeed, for many distributions the mean and the standard deviation are the key defining characteristics or parameters of the distribution.

One of the reasons the standard deviation has become such an important measure of spread is that it is a reliable way of detecting dispersion.

Example 27

Find the mean and the standard deviation of the following.

Rabota: Mean = (0 + 4 + 4 + 5 + 7 + 8 + 10 + 11 + 15)/9 = 7.111

Length of service (x)	x^2
0	0
4	16
4	16

5	25
7	49
8	64
10	100
11	121
15	225
64	616

$$s=\sqrt{\frac{1}{8}(616-\frac{(64)^2}{9})}$$

$$=\sqrt{\frac{1}{6}(616-455.111)}$$

$$=\sqrt{\frac{1}{8}(160.889)}$$

$$=\sqrt{20.111}=4.485$$

Slugar: Mean = (0 + 0 + 4 + 4 + 7 + 10 + 10 + 14 + 15)/9 = 7.111

Length of service (x)	x^2
0	0
0	0
4	16
4	16
7	49
10	100
10	100
14	196
15	225
64	702

$$s = \sqrt{\frac{1}{8}(702 - \frac{(64)^2}{9})}$$

$$= \sqrt{\frac{1}{8}(702 - 455.111)}$$

$$= \sqrt{\frac{1}{8}(246.889)}$$

The means are the same, 7.111, but the standard deviation for Slugar is higher than the standard deviation for Rabota, 5.555 compared to 4.485.

The mean and standard deviation can be used to approximate the overall spread of observations in a distribution. Typically, nearly all the observations will lie between the point three standard deviations below the mean and the point three standard deviations above the mean. Another way of saying this is to say that almost the entire distribution is located within three standard deviations of the mean. Another rule of thumb is that 90% or so of a distribution will be within two standard deviations of the mean.

In further work you will find that the mean and the standard deviation can be used to define the positions of values in a distribution. For instance, if the mean of a set of examination marks is 55 and the standard deviation is 10 a result of 75 marks could be described as being two standard deviations above the mean. A result of 40 could be described as being one and a half standard deviations below the mean.

You may meet the coefficient of variation, which is sometimes used to compare distributions, especially where the units of measurement differ. This is simply the standard deviation as a percentage of the mean:

$$\text{Coefficient of variation (CV)} = \frac{s}{x} * 100$$

FINDING MEASURES OF SPREAD FROM CLASSIFIED DATA

You may need to determine measures of spread for data that are already classified. The ease of doing this and the accuracy of the results depend on the type of data and the form in which they are presented.

If you have a frequency distribution that shows the number of times each one of a small number of discrete values occurs then you will be able to identify all the values in the distribution and carry out the appropriate procedures and calculations on them. Similarly, if you have data in the form of a stem and leaf display you should be able to identify at least the approximate values of the data. In either case the results you obtain should be identical to, or at least very close to the real values.

If, however, the data you have are in the form of a grouped frequency distribution then it is possible to find measures of spread, but these will be approximations. Here we will consider how to find an approximate value of a standard deviation from a grouped frequency distribution and how to find approximate values for quartiles, and hence the semiinterquartile range, from a cumulative relative frequency graph.

A grouped frequency distribution shows how many observed values in the distribution fall into a series of classes. It does not show the actual values of the data. Since calculating a standard deviation does usually require the actual values, we have to find some way of representing the actual values based on the classes to which they belong. In fact the midpoint of each class is used as the approximate value of every value in the class.

The approximate value of the standard deviation is:

$$s = \sqrt{\frac{1}{\sum f - 1}\left[\sum fx^2 - \frac{(\sum fx)^2}{\sum f}\right]}$$

where f represents the frequency of a class and x its midpoint.

You can find the approximate values of the quartiles of a distribution from a cumulative frequency graph or a cumulative relative frequency graph by employing the same approach as we used to find the approximate value of the median. The difference is that to approximate the quartiles we start from points one-quarter and three-quarters the way up the vertical scale.

8

Relationships between Two Variables

This chapter is about techniques that you can use to study relationships between two variables. The types of data set that these techniques are intended to analyse are called bivariate because they consist of observed values of two variables. The techniques themselves are part of what is known as bivariate analysis.

Bivariate analysis is of great importance to business. The results of this sort of analysis have affected many aspects of business considerably. The establishment of the relationship between smoking and health problems transformed the tobacco industry. The analysis of survival rates of micro-organisms and temperature is crucial to the setting of appropriate refrigeration levels by food retailers. Marketing strategies of many organizations are often based on the analysis of consumer expenditure in relation to age or income.

The chapter will introduce you to some of the techniques that companies and other organizations use to analyse bivariate data. The techniques you will meet here are correlation analysis and regression analysis. Suppose you have a set of bivariate data that consist of observations of one variable, X, and the associated observations of another variable, Y, and you want to see if X and Y are related. For instance, the Y variable could be sales of ice cream per day and the X variable the daily temperature, and you want to investigate the connection between temperature and ice cream sales. In such a case correlation analysis enables us to assess whether there is a connection between the two variables and, if so, how strong that connection is.

If correlation analysis tells us there is a connection we can use regression analysis to identify the exact form of the relationship. It is essential to know this if you want to use the relationship to make predictions, for instance if we want to predict the demand for ice cream when the daily temperature is at a particular level.

The assumption that underpins bivariate analysis is that one variable depends on the other. The letter Y is used to represent the dependent variable, the one whose values are believed to depend on the other variable. This other variable, represented by the letter X, is called the independent variable. The Y or dependent variable is sometimes known as the response because it is believed to respond to changes in the value of the X variable. The X variable is also known as the predictor because it might help us to predict the values of Y.

CORRELATION ANALYSIS

Correlation analysis is a way of investigating whether two variables are correlated, or connected with each other. We can study this to some extent by using a scatter diagram to portray the data, but such a diagram can only give us a visual 'feel' for the association between two variables, it doesn't actually measure the strength of the connection. So, although a scatter diagram is the thing you should begin with to carry out bivariate analysis, you need to calculate a correlation coefficient if you want a precise way of assessing how closely the variables are related.

In this section we shall consider two correlation coefficients. The first and more important is Pearson's product moment correlation coefficient, related to which is the coefficient of determination. The second is Spearman's rank correlation coefficient. Pearson's coefficient is suitable for assessing the strength of the connection between quantitative variables, variables whose values are interval or ratio data. Spearman's coefficient is designed for variables whose values are ranked, and is used to assess the connection between two variables, one or both of which have ordinal values.

PEARSON'S PRODUCT MOMENT CORRELATION COEFFICIENT

Pearson's correlation coefficient is similar to the standard deviation in that it is based on the idea of dispersion or spread. The comparison is not complete because bivariate data are spread out in two dimensions; if you look at a scatter diagram you will see that the points representing the data are scattered both vertically and horizontally.

The letter r is used to represent the Pearson correlation coefficient for sample data. Its Greek counterpart, the letter rð ('rho') is used to represent the Pearson correlation coefficient for population data. As is the case with other summary measures, it is very unlikely that you will have to find the value of a population correlation coefficient because of the cost and practical difficulty of studying entire populations.

Pearson's correlation coefficient is a ratio; it compares the co-ordinated scatter to the total scatter. The co-ordinated scatter is the extent to which the observed values of one variable, X, vary in co-ordination with, or 'in step with' the observed values of a second variable, Y. We use the covariance of the values of X and Y, Cov_{XY} to measure the degree of co-ordinated scatter.

To calculate the covariance you have to multiply the amount that each x deviates from the mean of the X values, $\overline{x}$, by the amount that its corresponding y deviates from the mean of the Y values, $\overline{y}$. That is, for every pair of x and y observations you calculate:

$$(x - \overline{x})(y - \overline{y})$$

The result will be positive whenever the x and y values are both bigger than their means, because we will be multiplying two positive deviations together. It will also be positive if both the x and y values are smaller than their means, because both deviations will be negative and the result of multiplying them together will be positive. The result will only be negative if one of the deviations is positive and the other negative.

The covariance is the total of the products from this process divided by n, the number of pairs of observations, minus one. We have to divide by n – 1 because the use of the means in arriving at the deviations results in the loss of a degree of freedom.

$$Cov_{XY} = \text{Sð}\frac{(x-\overline{x})(y-\overline{y})}{(n-1)}$$

The covariance is positive if values of X below $\overline{x}$ tend to be associated with values of Y below $\overline{y}$, and values of X above $\overline{x}$ tend to be associated with values of Y above $\overline{y}$. In other words if high x values occur with high y values and low x values occur with low y values we will have a positive covariance. This suggests that there is a positive or direct relationship between X and Y, that is, if X goes up we would expect Y to go up as well, and vice versa. If you compared the income of a sample of consumers with their expenditure on clothing you would expect to find a positive relationship.

The covariance is negative if values of X below $\overline{x}$ are associated with values of Y above $\overline{y}$, and vice versa. The low values of X occur with the high values of Y, and the high values of X occur with the low values of Y. This is a negative or inverse relationship. If you compared the prices of articles of clothing with demand for them, economic theory suggests you might expect to find an inverse relationship.

Example 1

A Clothing company sells six brands of shower-proof jacket. The prices and the numbers sold in a week are:

Plot a scatter diagram and calculate the covariance.

We are assuming that number sold depends on price rather than the other way round.

Price	18	20	25	27	28	32
Number sold	8	6	5	2	2	1

To calculate the covariance we need to calculate deviations from the mean for every x and y value.

$\overline{x} = (18 + 20 + 25 + 27 + 28 + 32)/6 = 150/5 = 25$

$\overline{y} = (8 + 6 + 5 + 2 + 2 + 1)/6 = 24/6 = 4$

Prince(x)	$\overline{x}$	$(x-\overline{x})$	Numbers sold (y)	$\overline{y}$	$(y-\overline{y})$	$(x-\overline{x})(y-\overline{y})$
18	25	-7	8	4	4	-28
20	25	-5	6	4	2	-10
25	25	0	5	4	1	0
27	25	2	2	4	-2	-4
28	25	3	2	4	-2	-6
32	25	7	1	4	-3	-21

$\sum(x-\overline{x})(y-\overline{y}) = -69$

Covariance = Sð(x − $\overline{x}$)(y − $\overline{y}$)/(n − 1)= − 69/5 = − 13.8

The other input we need to obtain a Pearson correlation coefficient is some measure of total scatter, some way of assessing the horizontal and vertical dispersion. We do this by taking the standard deviation of the x values, which measures the horizontal spread, and multiplying by the standard deviation of the y values, which measures the vertical spread.

The Pearson correlation coefficient, r, is the covariance of the x and y values divided by the product of the two standard deviations.

$$r = \frac{Cov_{XY}}{(s_x * s_y)}$$

There are two important things you should note about r:

- It can be either positive or negative because the covariance can be negative or positive.
- It cannot be larger than 1 or –1 because the co-ordinated scatter, measured by the covariance, cannot be larger than the total scatter, measured by the product of the standard deviations.

Example 2

Calculate the correlation coefficient for the data in Example We need to calculate the sample standard deviation for X and Y.

Price (x)	x	$(x-\bar{x})$	$(x-\bar{x})^2$	Number sold (y)	(y)	$(y-\bar{y})$	$(y-\bar{y})^2$
18	25	– 7	49	8	4	4	16
20	25	–5	25	6	4	2	4
25	25	0	0	5	4	1	1
27	25	2	4	2	4	–2	4
28	25	3	9	2	4	–2	4
32	25	7	49	1	4	–3	9
			136				38

From Example 1: Covariance = – 13.8

Sample standard deviation of X: s_x

$$= \sqrt{\sum (x-\bar{x})^2 / (n-1)} = \sqrt{136/5}$$

Sample standard deviation of Y:

$$s_y = \sqrt{\sum (x-\bar{x})^2 / (n-1)} = \sqrt{38/5} = 2.757$$

Correlation coefficient: r = (– 13.8)/(5.215 * 2.757)

= – 13.8/14.41 = – 0.960

A more direct approach to calculating the value of the Pearson correlation coefficient is to use the following formula, which is derived from the approach we used in Examples 1 and 2:

$$r = \frac{n\sum xy - (\sum x * \sum y)}{\sqrt{(n\sum x^2 - (\sum x)^2) * (n\sum y^2 - (\sum y)^2)}}$$

The advantage of this approach is that there are no subtractions between the observations and their means as it involves simply adding up the observations and their squares.

Example 3

Calculate the Pearson correlation coefficient for the data in Example 1 without subtracting observations from means.

Price (x)	x^2	Number sold (y)	y^2	xy	
18	324	8	64	144	
20	400	6	36	120	
25	625	5	25	125	
27	729	2	4	54	
28	784	2	4	56	
32	1024	1	1	32	
$\Sigma x = 150$	$\Sigma x^2 = 3886$	$\Sigma y = 24$	$\Sigma y^2 = 134$	$\Sigma xy = 531$	$n = 6$

As you can see, calculating a correlation coefficient, even for a fairly simple set of data, is quite laborious. In practice Pearson correlation coefficients are seldom calculated in this way because many calculators and just about all spreadsheet and statistical packages have functions to produce them.

The things to remember about the sample Pearson correlation coefficient, r, are:

- It measures the strength of the connection or association between observed values of two variables.
- It can take any value from – 1 to + 1 inclusive.
- If it is positive it means there is a direct or upward-sloping relationship.
- If it is negative it means there is an inverse or downward-sloping relationship.
- The further it is from zero the stronger the association.
- It only measures the strength of linear relationships.

THE COEFFICIENT OF DETERMINATION

The square of the Pearson correlation coefficient is also used as a way of measuring the connection between variables. Although it is the square of r, the upper case is used in representing it, R^2. It is called the coefficient of determination because it can help you to assess how much the values of one variable are decided or determined by the values of another.

As we saw, the Pearson correlation coefficient is based on the standard deviation. Similarly the square of the correlation coefficient is based on the square of the standard deviation, the variance.

Like the correlation coefficient, the coefficient of determination is a ratio, the ratio of the amount of the variance that can be explained by the relationship between the variables to the total variance in the data. Because it is a ratio it cannot exceed one and because it is a square it is always a positive value. Conventionally it is expressed as a percentage.

Example 4

Calculate the coefficient of determination, R 2, for the data in Example

In Example 2 we calculated that the Pearson correlation coefficient for these data was – 0.960. The square of – 0.960 is 0.922 or 92.2%. This is the value of R^2. It means that 92.2% of the variation in the numbers of jackets sold can be explained by the variation in the prices.

You may find R^2 an easier way to communicate the strength of the relationship between two variables. Its only disadvantage compared to the correlation coefficient is that the figure itself does not convey whether the association is positive or negative. However, there are other ways of showing this, including the scatter diagram.

SPEARMAN'S RANK CORRELATION COEFFICIENT

If you want to investigate links involving ordinal or ranked data you should not use the Pearson correlation coefficient as it is based on the arithmetic measures of location and spread, the mean and the standard deviation. Fortunately there is an alternative, the Spearman rank correlation coefficient.

It is possible to use the Spearman coefficient with interval and ratio data provided the data are ranked. You find the value of the coefficient from the ranked data rather than the original observations you would use to get the Pearson coefficient. This may be a preferable alternative as you may find calculating the Spearman coefficient easier. If your original observations contain extreme values the Pearson coefficient may be distorted by them, just as the mean is sensitive to extreme values, in which case the Spearman coefficient may be more reliable.

To calculate the Spearman coefficient, usually represented by the symbol r_s, subtract the ranks of your y values from the ranks of their corresponding x values to give a difference in rank, d, for each pair of observations. Next square the differences and add them up to get Sðd^2. Multiply the sum of the squared differences by 6 then divide the result by n, the number of pairs of observations, multiplied by the square of n minus one. Finally subtract the result from one to arrive at the coefficient. The procedure can be expressed as follows:

$$r_s = 1 - \frac{6\sum d^2}{n(n^2 - 1)}$$

Example 5

The total annual cost of players' wages for eight football clubs and their final league positions are as follows:

Wages bill (Rs.m)	Final league position
45	1
32	2
41	3
13	4
27	5
15	6
18	7
22	8

Work out the Spearman coefficient for the correlation between the league positions and wages bills of these clubs. One variable, league position, is already ranked, but before we can calculate the coefficient we have to rank the values of the other variable, the wage bill.

Price(x)	Rank(x)	Number sold(y)	Rank(y)	d	d^2
18	1	8	6	1-6=-5	25
20	2	6	5	2-5=-3	9
25	3	5	4	3-4=-1	1
27	4	2	2.5	4-2.5=1.5	2.25
28	5	2	2.5	5-2.5=2.5	6.25
32	6	1	1	6-1=5	25

$\sum d^2 = 68.5 \quad n = 6$

$$r_s = 1 - \frac{6*30}{8(8^2-1)} = 1 - \frac{180}{8(64-1)} = 1 - \frac{180}{8*63}$$

$$= 1 - \frac{180}{504} = 1 - 0.357 = 0.643$$

The interpretation of the Spearman coefficient is the same as we use for the Pearson coefficient. In Example 5 the coefficient is positive, indicating positive correlation and rather less than + 1 suggesting the degree of correlation is modest.

Using the Spearman coefficient with ranked data that contains ties is not quite as straightforward. The ranks for the tied elements need to be adjusted so that they share the ranks they would have had if they were not equal. For instance if two elements are ranked second equal in effect they share the second and third positions. To reflect this we would give them a rank of 2.5 each.

Example 6 Rank the data in Example 1 from lowest to highest and find the Spearman rank correlation coefficient for the prices of the jackets and the number of jackets sold.

Rank of wages bill	League position	d	d^2
1	1	0	0
3	2	+1	1
2	3	+1	1
8	4	+4	16
4	5	-1	1
7	6	+1	1
6	7	-1	1
5	8	-3	9

$\sum d^2 = 30 \quad n = 8$

$$S\delta d^2 = 68.5 \quad n = 6$$

$$r_s = 1 - \frac{6*68.5}{6(6^2-1)} = 1 - \frac{411}{6(36-1)} = 1 - \frac{411}{6*35}$$

In Example 6 the Spearman coefficient for the ranked data is very similar to the value of the Pearson coefficient we obtained in Example 2 for the original observations – 0.960. Both results show that the correlation between prices and sales is strong and negative.

SIMPLE LINEAR REGRESSION ANALYSIS

Measuring correlation tells you how strong the linear relationship between two variables might be but it doesn't tell us exactly what that relationship is. If we need to know about the way in which two variables are related we have to use the other part of basic bivariate analysis, regression analysis.

The simplest form of this technique, simple linear regression (which is often abbreviated to SLR), enables us to find the straight line most appropriate for representing the connection between two sets of observed values. Because the line that we 'fit' to our data can be used to represent the relationship it is rather like an average in two dimensions, it summarizes the link between the variables.

Simple linear regression is called simple because it analyses two variables, it is called linear because it is about finding a straight line, but why is it called regression, which actually means going backwards? The answer is that the technique was first developed by the nineteenth century scientist Sir Francis Galton, who wanted a way of representing how the heights of children were genetically constrained or 'regressed' by the heights of their parents.

In later work you may encounter multiple regression, which is used to analyse relationships between more than two variables, and non-linear regression, which is used to analyse relationships that do not have a straight-line pattern.

You might ask why it is necessary to have a technique to fit a line to a set of data?

The trouble with fitting a line by eye is that it is inconsistent and unreliable. It is inconsistent because the position of the line depends on the judgement of the person drawing the line. Different people will produce different lines for the same data.

For any set of bivariate data there is one line that is the most appropriate, the so-called 'best-fit' line. There is no guarantee that fitting a line by eye will produce the best-fit line, so fitting a line by eye is unreliable. We need a reliable, consistent way of finding the line that best fits a set of plotted points, which is what simple linear regression analysis is. It is a technique that finds the line of best-fit, the line that travels as closely as possible to the plotted points. It identifies the two defining characteristics of that line, its intercept, or starting point, and its slope, or rate of increase or decrease.

We can use these defining characteristics to compose the equation of the line of best fit, which represents the line using symbols. The equation enables us to plot the line itself.

Simple linear regression is based on the idea of minimizing the differences between a line and the points it is intended to represent. Since all the points matter, it is the sum of these differences that needs to be minimized. In other words, the best-fit line is the line that results in a lower sum of differences than any other line would for that set of data.

The task for simple linear regression is a little more complicated because the difference between a point and the line is positive if the point is above the line, and negative if the point is below the line. If we were to add up these differences we would find that the negative and positive differences cancel each other out.

This means the sum of the differences is not a reliable way of judging how well a line fits a set of points. To get around this problem, simple linear regression is based on the squares of the differences because they will always be positive. The best-fit line that simple linear regression finds for us is the line which takes the path that results in there being the least possible sum of squared differences between the points and the line. For this reason the technique is sometimes referred to as least squares regression.

For any given set of data, as you can imagine, there are many lines from which the best-fit line could be chosen. To pick the right one we could plot each of them in turn and measure the differences using a ruler. Fortunately, such a laborious procedure is not necessary. Simple linear regression uses calculus, the area of mathematics that is partly about finding minimum or maximum values, to find the intercept and slope of the line of best fit directly from the data.

The procedure involves using two expressions to find, first, the slope and then the intercept. Since simple linear regression is almost always used to find the line of best fit from a set of sample data the letters used to represent the intercept and the slope are a and b respectively. The equivalent Greek letters, α and β, are used to represent the intercept and slope of the population line of best fit.

According to simple linear regression analysis the slope of the line of best fit:

$$b = \frac{\sum xy - \left(\sum x \times \sum y\right)/n}{\sum x^2 - \left(\sum x\right)^2/n}$$

And the intercept:

$$a = \left(\sum y - b\sum x\right)/n$$

These results can then be combined to give the equation of the line of best fit, which is known as the regression equation:

$$Y = a + bX$$

The expressions for getting the slope and intercept of the line of best fit look daunting, but this need not worry you. If you have to find a best fit line you can use a statistical or a spreadsheet package, or even a calculator with a good statistical facility to do the hard work for you.

The process of finding a best fit line with regression analysis is a laborious procedure, even with a relatively simple set of data. It is best performed using appropriate computer software or two-variable calculator functions.

We can use such an equation to predict values of Y that should occur with values of X. These are known as expected values of Y because they are what the line leads us to expect to be associated with the X values. The symbol $\hat{y}$, 'y-hat', is used to represent a value of Y that is predicted using the regression equation, so that we can distinguish it from an actual y value. That is to say, the regression equation

$$Y = a + bX$$

can be used to predict an individual y value that is expected to occur with an observed x value:

$$\hat{y} = a + bx$$

9

Summarizing Money Variables Over Time

In the last two chapters we have looked at ways of summarizing data. In this chapter and the next we will consider ways of summarizing data relating to different periods of time.

Time-based data consist of numerical observations that can be measured and summarized using the techniques you met in the previous chapters. We could, for instance, collect the price of gold at various points in time and calculate the mean price of gold over the period, or use correlation analysis to measure the association between the price of gold and the price of silver at various points in time. However, often the most important aspect of time-based data is the time factor and the techniques in the previous two chapters would not allow us to bring that out of the data.

In this chapter we will look at techniques to summarize money variables that relate to different time periods. We will start by exploring index numbers and how they can be used to summarize the general movements in prices over time. Then we will look at how such price indices can be used to adjust money amounts for the effects of inflation. Later in the chapter we will consider summarizing amounts of interest accumulated over time and how this approach is used to assess the worth of investment projects.

INDEX NUMBERS

Data collected over time are very important for the successful performance of organizations. For instance, such data can reveal trends in consumer expenditure and taste that companies need to follow.

Businesses use information based on data collected by other agencies over time to help them understand and evaluate the environment in which they operate. Perhaps the most important and widespread example of this is the use of index numbers to monitor general trends in prices and costs. For instance, the Retail Price Index is used as a benchmark figure in the context of wage bargaining, and Share Price Indices are reference points in financial decisions companies face.

Most businesses attach a great deal of importance to changes in the costs of things they buy and the prices of things they sell. During periods of high inflation these changes are more dramatic; in periods of low inflation they are modest. Over recent decades, when the level of inflation has fluctuated, companies have had to track general price and cost movements carefully. To help them do this they use index numbers.

Index numbers can be used to represent movements over time in a series of single figures. A simple index number is the value of something at one point in time, maybe the current value, in relation to its value at another point in time, the base period, multiplied by 100 to give a percentage (although the percent sign, %, is not usually written alongside it).

$$\text{Simple price index} = \frac{\text{Current Price}}{\text{Base Period Price}} \times 100 = \frac{p_c}{p_o} \times 100$$

where p_c represents the price in the current year and p_0 represent the price in the base year (i.e. period zero).

Since businesses usually buy and sell more than a single item, a simple price index is of limited use. Of much greater importance are aggregate indices that summarize price movements of many items in a single figure. We can calculate a simple aggregate price index for a combination of goods by taking the sum of the prices for the goods in the current period and dividing it by the sum of the prices of the same goods in the base period. That is

$$\text{Simple aggregate price index} = \frac{\sum p_c}{\sum p_0} * 100$$

In practice, the importance of the price of an item is a reflection of the quantity that is bought as well as the price itself. To measure changes in movements of prices in a more realistic way we need to weight each price in proportion to the quantity purchased and calculate a weighted aggregate price index.

There are two ways we can do this. The first is to use the quantity figure from the base year, represented by the symbol q_0, to weight the price of each item. This type of index is known as the Laspeyre price index. To calculate it we need to work out the total cost of the base period quantities at current prices, divide that by the total cost of the base period quantities at base period prices, and multiply the result by 100:

$$\text{Laspeyre price index} = \frac{\sum q_0 p_c}{\sum q_0 p_0} * 100$$

The Laspeyre technique uses quantities that are historical. The advantage of this is that such figures are usually readily available. The disadvantage is that they may not accurately reflect the quantities used in the current period. The alternative approach, which is more useful when quantities used have changed considerably, is to use quantity figures from the current period, q. This type of index is known as the Paasche price index. To calculate it you work out the total cost of the current period quantities at current prices, divide that by the total cost of the current period quantities at base period prices, and multiply the result by 100:

$$\text{Paasche price index} = \frac{\sum q_c p_c}{\sum q_c p_0} * 100.$$

The advantage of using a Paasche price index is that the quantity figures used are more up-to-date and therefore realistic. But it is not always possible to get current period quantity figures, particularly when there is a wide range of items and a large number of organizations or consumers that buy them.

The other disadvantage of using the Paasche price index is that new quantity figures must be available for each period we want to compare with the base period. If the garage proprietor wants a Paashce price index for prices in 2004 compared to 2000 you could not provide one until you know both the quantities and the prices used in 2004. By contrast, to calculate a Laspeyre price index for 2004 you only need to know the prices in 2004 because you would use quantities from 2000.

Organizations tend to use index numbers that have already been compiled rather than construct their own. Probably the most common use of index numbers that you will meet is in the adjustment of financial amounts to take into account changes in price levels.

A sum of money in one period is not necessarily the same as the same amount in another period because its purchasing power changes. This means that if we want to compare an amount from one period with an amount from another period we have to make some adjustment for price changes. The most common way of doing this is to use the Retail Price Index (RPI), an index the Government Statistical Service calculates to monitor price changes, changes in the cost of living.

INVESTMENT APPRAISAL

Almost every organization at one time or another has to take decisions about making investments. These decisions may involve something as big as the construction of a new plant or something more mundane like the purchase of a new piece of machinery. One of the main difficulties that managers face when taking these sorts of decisions is that the cost of making the investment is incurred when the plant is built or the machine is purchased, yet the income which it is intended to help generate arises in the future, perhaps over many years.

In this section we will look at techniques that enable managers to appraise, or weigh up, investment in long-lasting assets by relating the initial outlay to the future revenue. These techniques are used by businesses both to assess specific investments and to decide between alternative investments. Companies take these decisions very seriously because they involve large amounts of resources and once made they cannot be reversed.

We will begin with the accounting rate of return method then we will consider the payback period approach, and finally the more sophisticated discounting techniques. Despite the differences between them they all involve the determination of single figures that summarize the financial appeal of an investment project.

THE ACCOUNTING RATE OF RETURN

Generally, a rate of return expresses the return or profit resulting from the use of assets such as machinery or equipment in terms of the expenditure involved in purchasing them, usually in percentage terms. You will find that accountants make extensive use of these types of summary measure; look at a business newspaper or a company report and you will probably find reference to measures like the ROCE (Return on Capital Employed). These measures are used by companies to indicate how effectively they have managed the assets under their control.

The accounting rate of return, often abbreviated to ARR, is the use of this approach to weigh up the attraction of an investment proposal. To apply it we need to establish the average (mean) profit per year and divide that by the average level of investment per year.

To calculate the average profit per year we add up the annual profits and divide by the number of years over which the investment will help generate these revenues. Having said that, the profit figures we use must be profits after allowing for depreciation. Depreciation is the spreading of the cost of an asset over its useful life. The simplest way of doing this is to subtract the residual value of the asset, which is the amount that the company expects to get from the sale of the asset when it is no longer of use, from the purchase cost of the asset and divide by the number of years of useful life the asset is expected to have. This approach is known as straight-line depreciation and it assumes that the usefulness of the asset, in terms of helping to generate profits, is reasonably consistent over its useful life.

To work out the average level of investment, we need to know the cost of the asset and the residual value of the asset. The average investment value is the difference between the initial cost and the residual value divided by two, in other words we split the difference between the highest and lowest values of the asset while it is in use. After dividing the average return by the average investment we multiply by 100 so that we have a percentage result. The accounting rate of return is widely used to evaluate investment projects. It produces a percentage figure which managers can easily compare to interest rates and it is essentially the same approach to future investment as accountants take when working out the ROCE (Return on Capital Employed) to evaluate a company's past performance.

The critical weakness in using the accounting rate of return to appraise investments is that it is completely blind to the timing of the initial expenditure and future income. It ignores what is called the time value of money. The value that an individual or business puts on a sum of money is related to when the money is received; for example if you were offered the choice of a gift of Rs.1000 now or Rs.1000 in two year's time you would most likely prefer the cash now. This may be because you need cash now rather than then, but even if you have sufficient funds now you would still be better off having the money now because you could invest the money in a savings account and receive interest on it.

The other investment appraisal techniques we shall examine have the advantage of bringing the time element into consideration. The other difference between them and the accounting rate of return approach is that they are based on net cash flows into the company, which are essentially net profits before depreciation.

PAYBACK PERIOD

The payback period approach to investment appraisal does take the timing of cash flows into account and is based on a straightforward concept – the time it will take for the net profits earned using the asset to cover the purchase of the asset. We need only accumulate the negative (expenditure) and positive (net profits before depreciation) cash flows relating to the investment over time and ascertain when the cumulative cash flow reaches zero. At this point the initial outlay on the asset will have been paid back.

The payback period is a simple concept for managers to apply and it is particularly appropriate when firms are very sensitive to risk because it indicates the time during which they are exposed to the risk of not recouping their initial outlay. A cautious manager would probably be comfortable with the idea of preferring investment opportunities that have shorter payback periods.

The weakness of the payback approach is that it ignores cash flows that arise in periods beyond the payback period. Where there are two alternative projects it may not suggest the one that performs better overall.

A better approach would be to base our assessment of investments on all of the cash flows involved rather than just the earlier ones, and to bring into our calculations the time value of money. Techniques that allow us to do this adjust or discount cash flows to compensate for the time that passes before they arrive. The first of these techniques that we shall consider is the net present value.

NET PRESENT VALUE

The net present value (NPV) of an investment is a single figure that summarizes all the cash flows arising from an investment, both expenditure and receipts, each of which have been adjusted so that whenever they arise in the future it is their current or present value that is used in the calculation. Adjusting, or discounting them to get their present value means working out how much money would have to be invested now in order to generate that specific amount at that time in the future.To do this we use the same approach as we would to calculate the amount of money accumulating in a savings account. We need to know the rate of interest and the amount of money initially deposited. The amount in the account at the end of one year is the original amount deposited plus the rate of interest, r, applied to the original amount:

Amount at the end of the year = Deposit + (Deposit * r)

We can express this as:

Amount at the end of the year = Deposit * (1 + r)

If the money stays in the account for a second year:

Amount at the end of the second year =

$$\text{Deposit} * (1 + r)*(1 + r) = \text{Deposit} * (1 + r)^2$$

In general if we deposit an amount in an account paying an annual interest rate r for n years, the amount accumulated in the account at the end of the period will be:

$$\text{Deposit} * (1 = r)^n$$

The deposit is, of course, the sum of money we start with, it is the present value (PV) of our investment, so we can express this procedure as:

$$\text{Amount at the end of year n} = PV*(1 = r)^n$$

This expression enables us to work out the future value of a known present value, like the amount we deposit in an account. When we assess investment projects we want to know how much a known (or at least expected) amount to be received in the future is worth now. Instead of knowing the present value and wanting to work out the future, we need to reverse the process and determine the present value of a known future amount. To obtain this we can rearrange the expression we used to work out the amount accumulated at the end of a period:

$$\text{Present value (PV)} = \frac{\text{Amount at the end of year n}}{\left(1+r^2\right)}$$

The interest, or discount, rate a company uses is likely to reflect the opportunity cost, which may be the interest it could earn by investing the money in a bank. It may also reflect the prevailing rate of inflation and the risk of the investment project not working out as planned.

THE INTERNAL RATE OF RETURN

A fourth investment appraisal method widely used by businesses is the internal rate of return (IRR). It is closely related to the net present value approach; indeed the internal rate of return is the discount rate at which the total present value of the cash flows into a business arising from an investment precisely equals the initial outlay. To put it another way, the internal rate of return is the discount rate that would result in a net present value (NPV) of zero for the investment. Because the concept of discounting is at the heart of both NPV and IRR they are known as discounted cash flow (DCF) methods.

Finding the internal rate of return for a project is a rather hit and miss affair. We try out one discount rate and if the result is a positive NPV we try a higher discount rate; if the result is negative, we try a lower discount rate.

In general, the higher the internal rate of return, the more attractive the project. The internal rate of return and the net present value methods of investment appraisal are similar in that they summarize all the cash flows associated with a venture and are therefore superior to the payback method. They also take the time value of money into account and are therefore superior to the accounting rate of return approach.

The drawback of the internal rate of return technique compared to the net present value method is that the IRR is an interest rate, a relative amount, which unlike the NPV gives no idea of the scale of the cash flows involved. Both IRR and NPV are rather laborious to calculate. Companies may well use the fairly basic approach of the payback period as the threshold that any proposed investment must meet, and then use either NPV or IRR to select from those that do.

10

Analysing Time Series Data

Organizations collect time series data, which is data made up of observations taken at regular intervals, as a matter of course. Look at the operations of a company and you will find figures such as daily receipts, weekly staff absences and monthly payroll. If you look at the annual report it produces to present its performance you will find more time series data such as quarterly turnover and annual profit.

The value of time series data to managers is that unlike a single figure relating to one period a time series shows changes over time; maybe improvement in the sales of some products and perhaps deterioration in the sales of others. The single figure is like a photograph that captures a single moment, a time series is like a video recording that shows events unfolding. This sort of record can help managers review the company performance over the period covered by the time series and it offers a basis for predicting future values of the time series.

By portraying time series data in the form of a time series chart it is possible to use the series to both review performance and anticipate future direction. You can use them to look for an overall movement in the series, a trend, and perhaps recurrent fluctuations around the trend. When you inspect a plotted time series the points representing the observations may form a straight line pattern. Typically time series data that businesses need to analyse are seldom this straightforward so we need to consider different methods.

COMPONENTS OF TIME SERIES

Whilst plotting a time series graphically is a good way to get a 'feel' for the way it is behaving, to analyse a time series properly we need to use a more systematic approach. One way of doing this is the decomposition method, which involves breaking down or decomposing the series into different components. This approach is suitable for time series data that has a repeated pattern, which includes many time series that occur in business.

The components of a time series are:

- a trend (T), an underlying longer-term movement in the series that may be upward, downward or constant
- a seasonal element (S), a short-term recurrent component, which may be daily, weekly, monthly as well as seasonal
- a cyclical element (C), a long-term recurrent component that repeats over several years
- an error or random or residual element (E), the amount that isn't part of either the trend or the recurrent components.

The type of 'seasonal' component we find in a time series depends on how regularly the data are collected. We would expect to find daily components in data collected each day, weekly components in data collected each week and so on. Seasonal components are usually a feature of data collected quarterly, whereas cyclical components, patterns that recur over many years, will only feature in data collected annually.

It is possible that a time series includes more than one 'seasonal' component, for instance weekly figures may exhibit a regular monthly fluctuation as well as a weekly one. However, usually the analysis of a time series involves looking for the trend and just one recurrent component.

Neither is it possible to identify error components as these 'leftover' components can only be discerned when the trend and seasonal components have been 'sifted out'. We can do this using classical decomposition analysis.

CLASSICAL DECOMPOSITION OF TIME SERIES DATA

Classical decomposition involves taking apart a time series so that we can identify the components that make it up. The first stage we take in decomposing a time series is to separate out the trend. We can do this by calculating a set of moving averages for the series. Moving averages are sequential; they are means calculated from sequences of values in a time series. A moving average (MA) is the mean of a set of values consisting of one from each time period in the time series.

The second point to note is that, like any other average, we can think of a moving average as being in the middle of the set of data from which it has been calculated. In the case of a moving average we associate it with the middle of the period covered by the observations that we used to calculate it. The first moving average is therefore associated with Thursday of Week 1 because that is the middle day of the first seven days, the days whose observed values were used to calculate it, the second is associated with Friday of Week 1 and so on. The process of positioning moving averages in line with the middle of the observations they summarize is called centring.

The third point to note is that there are fewer moving averages (15) than series values (21). This is because each moving average summarizes seven observations that come from different days.

The process of centring is a little more complicated if you have a time series with an even number of smaller time periods in each larger time period. In quarterly time series data the periodicity is four because there are observations for each of four quarters in every year. For quarterly data you have to use four-point moving averages and to centre them you split the difference between two moving averages because the ones you calculate are 'out of phase' with the time series observations.

Centring moving averages is important because the moving averages are the figures that we need to use as estimates of the trend at specific points in time. We want to be able to compare them directly with observations in order to sift out other components of the time series.

The procedure we use to separate the components of a time series depends on how we assume they are combined in the observations. The simplest case is to assume that the components are added together with each observation, y, being the sum of a set of components:

Y = Trend component (T) + Seasonal component (S)
+ Cyclical component (C) + Error component (E)

Unless the time series data stretch over many years the cyclical component is impossible to distinguish from the trend element as both are long-term movements in a series. We can therefore simplify the model to:

Y = Trend component (T) + Seasonal component (S)
+ Error component (E)

This is called the additive model of a time series. Later we will deal with the multiplicative model. If you want to analyse a time series which you assume is additive, you have to subtract the components from each other to decompose the time series. If you assume it is multiplicative, you have to divide to decompose it.

We begin the process of decomposing a time series assumed to be additive by subtracting the centred moving averages, which are the estimated trend values (T), from the observations they sit alongside (Y). What we are left with are deviations from the trend, a set of figures that contain only the seasonal and error components, that is

$$Y - T = S + E$$

The next stage is to arrange the Y – T results by the quarters of the year and calculate the mean of the deviations from the trend for each quarter. These will be our estimates for the seasonal components for the quarters, the differences we expect between the trend and the observed value in each quarter.

We can take the analysis a stage further by subtracting the seasonal components, S from the Y – T figures to isolate the error components,

E. That is:

$$E = Y - T - S$$

The T components are what the model suggests the trend should be at a particular time and the S components are the deviations from the trend that the model suggests occur in the different quarters, the T and S values combined are the predicted values for the series. The error components are the differences between the actual values (Y) and the predicted values (T + S):

$$E = \text{Actual sales} - \text{Predicted sales} = Y - (T + S)$$

The error components enable us to review the performance over the period. A negative error component such as in the summer quarter of year 1 suggests the store under-performed in that period and might lead them to investigate why that was. A positive error component such as in the spring quarter of year 3 suggests the store performed better than expected and they might look for reasons to explain the success. This type of evaluation should enable the store to improve sales performance because they can counter the factors resulting in poor performances and build on the factors that contribute to good performances.

Occasionally the analysis of a time series results in a very large error component that reflects the influence of some unusual and unexpected external influence such as a fuel shortage or a sudden rise in exchange rates. You can usually spot the impact of such factors by looking for prominent peaks or troughs, sometimes called spikes, when the series is plotted.

The error components terms have another role in time series analysis; they are used to judge how well a time series model fits the data. If the model is appropriate the errors will be small and show no pattern of variation. You can investigate this by plotting them graphically.

There are statistical measures that you can use to summarize the errors; they are called measures of accuracy because they help you to assess how accurately a time series model fits a set of time series data. The most useful one is the mean squared deviation (MSD).

The standard deviation is based on the squared differences between observations and their mean because deviations from the mean can be positive or negative, and can thus cancel each other out. In the same way deviations between actual and predicted time series values can be negative and positive, so in calculating the MSD we square the deviations. The MSD is the sum of the squared deviations divided by the number of deviations (n):

$$MSD = \frac{\sum (Error)^2}{n}$$

There are other measures of accuracy that you may meet. The mean absolute deviation (MAD) is the mean of the absolute values of the errors, which means ignoring any negative signs when you add them up. There is also the mean absolute percentage error (MAPE) which is the mean of the errors as percentages of the actual values they are part of. As with the MSD, the lower the values of these measures, the better the model fits the data.

The model we have applied so far is the additive decomposition model that assumes the components of a time series are added together. This model is appropriate for series that have regular and constant fluctuations around a trend. The alternative form of the decomposition model is the multiplicative model in which we assume that the components of the series are multiplied together. This is appropriate for series that have regular but increasing or decreasing fluctuations around a trend.

To apply the multiplicative model we need exactly the same centred moving averages as we need for the additive model, but instead of subtracting them from the actual series values to help us get to the seasonal components we divide each actual value by its corresponding centred moving average to get a seasonal factor. We then have to find the average seasonal factor for each quarter, adjusting as necessary. Once we have the set of seasonal factors we multiply them by the trend estimates to get the predicted series values, which we can subtract from the actual values to get the errors.

We can use decomposition models to construct forecasts for future periods. There are two stages in doing this. The first is to project the trend into the periods we want to predict, and the second is to add the appropriate seasonal component to each trend projection, if we are using the additive model:

$$\hat{y} = T + S$$

If we are using the multiplicative model we multiply the trend projection by the appropriate seasonal factor:

$$\hat{y} = T * S$$

Here $\hat{y}$ is the estimated future value, and T and S are the trend and seasonal components or factors. You can see there is no error component. The error components are, by definition, unpredictable.

You could produce trend projections by plotting the centred moving averages and fitting a line to them by eye, then simply continuing the line into the future periods you want to predict. An alternative approach that does not involve graphical work is to take the difference between the first and last trend estimates for your series and divide by the number of periods between them; if you have n trend estimates you divide the difference between the first and last of them by n – 1. The result is the mean change in the trend per period. To forecast a value three periods ahead you add three times this amount to the last trend estimate, four periods ahead, add four times this to the last trend estimate and so on.

Another method of projecting the trend is to use regression analysis to get the equation of the line that best fits the moving averages and use the equation to project the trend. The regression equation in this context is called the trend line equation.

EXPONENTIAL SMOOTHING OF TIME SERIES DATA

The decomposition models we considered in the last section are called static models because in using them we assume that the components of the model are fixed over time. They are appropriate for series that have a clear structure. They are not appropriate for series that are more erratic. To produce forecasts for these types of series we can turn to dynamic models such as exponential smoothing which use recent observations in the series to predict the next one.

In exponential smoothing we create a forecast for the next period by taking the forecast we generated for the previous period and adding a proportion of the error in the previous forecast, which is the difference between the actual and forecast values for the previous period. We can represent this as:

New forecast = Previous forecast + að* (Previous actual – Previous forecast)

The symbol að represents the smoothing constant, the proportion of the error we add to the previous forecast to adjust for the error in the previous forecast. Being a proportion, að ðmust be between 0 and 1 inclusive. If it is zero then no proportion of the previous error is added to the previous forecast to get the new forecast, so the forecast for the new period is always the same as the forecast for the previous period. If að ðis one, the entire previous error is added to the previous forecast so the new forecast is always the same as the previous actual value. When we forecast using exponential smoothing every new forecast depends on the previous one, which in turn depends on the one before that and so on. The influence of past forecasts diminishes with time; mathematically the further back the forecast the greater the power or exponent of an expression involving að ðthat is applied to it, hence the term exponential in the name of the technique.

The lower the value of að ðwe use the less the weight we attach to the previous forecast and the greater the weight we give to forecasts before it. The higher the value of að, the greater the weight we attach to the previous forecast relative to forecasts before it. This contrast means that lower values of að produce smoother sequences of forecasts compared to those we get with higher values of að. On the other hand, higher values of að result in forecasts that are more responsive to sudden changes in the time series.

Selecting the appropriate að value for a particular time series is a matter of trial and error. The best að value is the one that results in the lowest values of measures of accuracy like the mean squared deviation (MSD).

Before we can use exponential smoothing we need a forecast for the previous period. The easiest way of doing this is to take the actual value for the first period as the forecast for the second period.

In this chapter we have concentrated on relatively simple methods of analysing time series data. The field of time series analysis is substantial and contains a variety of techniques.

11

Probability

This chapter is intended to introduce you to the subject of probability, the branch of mathematics that is about finding out how likely real events or theoretical results are to happen. The subject originated in gambling, in particular the efforts of two seventeenth-century French mathematical pioneers, Fermat and Pascal, to calculate the odds of certain results in dice games.

Probability may well have remained a historical curiosity within mathematics, little known outside casinos and race-tracks, if it were not for the fact that probability has proved to be invaluable in fields as varied as psychology, economics, physical science, market research and medicine. In these and other fields, probability offers us a way of analysing chance and allowing for risk so that it can be taken into account whether we are investigating a problem or trying to make a decision.

Probability makes the difference between facing uncertainty and coping with risk. Uncertainty is a situation where we know that it is possible that things could turn out in different ways but we simply don't know how probable each result is. Risk, on the other hand, is when we know there are different outcomes but we also have some idea of how likely each one is to occur.

Business organizations operate in conditions that are far from certain. Economic circumstances change, customer tastes shift, employees move to other jobs. New product development and investment projects are usually rather a gamble. As well as these examples of what we might call normal commercial risk, there is the added peril of unforeseen risk. Potential customers in developing markets may be ravaged by disease, an earthquake may destroy a factory, strike action may disrupt transport etc.

The topics you will meet in this chapter will help you to understand how organizations can measure and assess the risks they have to deal with. But there is a second reason why probability is a very important part of your studies: because of the role it plays in future statistical work. Almost every statistical investigation that you are likely to come across during your studies and in your future career, whether it is to research consumer behaviour, employee attitudes, product quality, or any other facet of business, will have one important thing in common; it will involve the collection and analysis of a sample of data.

In almost every case both the people who commission the research and those who carry it out want to know about an entire population. They may want to know the opinions of all customers, the attitudes of all employees, the characteristics of all products, but it would be far too expensive or time-consuming or simply impractical to study every item in a population. The only alternative is to study a sample and use the results to gain some insight into the population.

This can work very well, but only if we have a sample that is random and we take account of the risks associated with sampling. A sample is called a random sample if every item in the population has the same chance of being included in the sample as every other item in the population. If a sample is not random it is of very little use in helping us to understand a population. Taking samples involves risk because we can take different random samples from a single population. These samples will be composed of different items from the population and produce different results.

Some samples will produce results very similar to those that we would get from the population itself if we had the opportunity to study all of it. Other samples will produce results that are not typical of the population as a whole.

To use sample results effectively we need to know how likely they are to be close to the population results even though we don't actually know what the population results are. Assessing this involves the use of probability.

MEASURING PROBABILITY

A probability, represented by capital P, is a measure of the likelihood of a particular result or outcome. It is a number on a scale that runs from zero to one inclusive, and can be expressed as a percentage. If there is a probability of zero that an outcome will occur it means there is literally no chance that it will happen. At the other end of the scale, if there is a probability of one that something will happen, it means that it is absolutely certain to occur. At the half-way mark, a probability of one half means that a result is equally likely to occur as not to occur. This probability literally means there is a fifty-fifty chance of getting the result.

So how do we establish the probability that something happens? The answer is that there are three distinct approaches that can be used to attach a probability to a particular outcome. We can describe these as the judgemental, experimental and theoretical approaches to identifying probabilities.

The judgemental approach means evaluating the chance of something happening on the basis of opinion alone. Usually the something is relatively uncommon, which rules out the use of the experimental approach, and doesn't occur within a context of definable possibilities, which rules out the use of the theoretical approach. The source of the opinion on which the probability is based is usually an expert.

You will often find judgemental probabilities in assessments of political stability and economic conditions, perhaps concerning investment prospects or currency fluctuations. You could, of course, use a judgemental approach to assessing the probability of any outcome even when there are more sophisticated means available. For instance, some people assess the chance that a horse wins a race solely on their opinion of the name of the horse instead of studying the horse's record or 'form'.

If you use the horse's form to work out the chance that it wins a race you would be using an experimental approach, looking into the results of the previous occasions when the 'experiment', in this case the horse entering a race, was conducted. You could work out the number of races the horse has won as a proportion of the total number of races it has entered. This is the relative frequency of wins and can be used to estimate the probability that the horse wins its next race.

A relative frequency based on a limited number of experiments is only an estimate of the probability because it approximates the 'true' probability, which is the relative frequency based on an infinite number of experiments.

There are other situations when we want to establish the probability of a certain result of some process and we could use the experimental approach. If we wanted to advise a car manufacturer whether they should offer a three-year warranty on their cars we might visit their dealers and find out the relative frequency of the cars that needed major repairs before they were three years old. This relative frequency would be an estimate of the probability of a car needing major repair before it is three years old, which the manufacturer would have to pay for under a three-year warranty. We don't need to go to the trouble of using the experimental approach if we can deduce the probability using the theoretical approach. You can deduce the probability of a particular outcome if the process that produces it has a constant, limited and identifiable number of possible outcomes, one of which must occur whenever the process is repeated.

There are many examples of this sort of process in gambling, including those where the number of possible outcomes is very large indeed, such as in bingo and lotteries. Even then, the number of outcomes is finite, the possible outcomes remain the same whenever the process takes places, and they could all be identified if we had the time and patience to do so.

Probabilities of specific results in bingo and lotteries can be deduced because the same number of balls and type of machine are used each time. In contrast, probabilities of horses winning races can't be deduced because horses enter only some races, the length of races varies and so on.

Gambling is a rich source of illustrations of the use of probabilities because it is about games of chance. However, it is by no means the only field where you will find probabilities. Whenever you buy insurance you are buying a product whose price has been decided on the basis of the rigorous and extensive use of the experimental approach to finding probabilities.

THE TYPES OF PROBABILITY

So far the probabilities that you have met in this chapter have been what are known as simple probabilities. Simple probabilities are probabilities of single outcomes. A compound probability is the probability of a compound or combined outcome. To illustrate the different types of compound probability we can apply the experimental approach to bivariate data. We can estimate compound probabilities by finding appropriate relative frequencies from data that have been tabulated by categories of attributes, or classes of values of variables.

Finding the probability of an intersection of two outcomes is quite straightforward if we apply the experimental approach to bivariate data. In other situations, for instance where we only have simple probabilities to go on, we need to use the multiplication rule of probability, which we will discuss later in the chapter.

There is a second type of compound probability, which measures the probability that one out of two or more alternative outcomes occurs. This type of compound probability includes the word 'or' in the description of the outcomes involved.

To get a probability of a union of outcomes from other probabilities, rather than by applying the experimental approach to bivariate data, we use the addition rule of probability.

The third type of compound probability is the conditional probability. Such a probability measures the chance that one outcome occurs given that, or on condition that, another outcome has already occurred.

THE RULES OF PROBABILITY

In situations where we do not have experimental data to use we need to have some method of finding compound probabilities. There are two rules of probability: the addition rule and the multiplication rule.

THE ADDITION RULE

The addition rule of probability specifies the procedure for finding the probability of a union of outcomes, a compound probability that is defined using the word 'or'.

According to the addition rule, the compound probability of one or both of two outcomes, which we will call A and B for convenience, is the simple probability that A occurs added to the simple probability that B occurs. From this total we subtract the compound probability of the intersection of A and B, the probability that both A and B occur.

That is:

$$P(A \text{ or } B) = P(A) + P(B) - P(A \text{ and } B)$$

The addition rule can look more complicated than it actually is because it is called the addition rule yet it includes a subtraction. It may help to represent the situation in the form of a Venn diagram, the sort of diagram used in part of mathematics called set theory. In a Venn diagram the complete set of outcomes that could occur, known as the sample space, is represented by a rectangle. Within the rectangle, circles are used to represent sets of outcomes.

The area covered by both circles represents the probability that a transaction is at Kuriatina or involves a Couple. The area of overlap represents the probability that a transaction is both at Kuriatina and involves a Couple. The area of the rectangle outside the circles contains transactions that are not at Kuriatina and do not involve Couples.

By definition the area of overlap is part of both circles. If you simply add the areas of the two circles together to try to get the area covered by both circles, you will include the area of overlap twice. If you subtract it once from the sum of the areas of the two circles you will only have counted it once.

The addition rule would be simpler if there were no overlap; in other words, there is no chance that the two outcomes can occur together. This is when we are dealing with outcomes that are known as mutually exclusive. The probability that two mutually exclusive outcomes both occur is zero.

In this case we can alter the addition rule:

P(A or B) = P(A) + P(B) – P(A and B)

to P(A or B) = P(A) + P(B)

because P(A and B) = 0.

A footnote to the addition rule is that if we have a set of mutually exclusive and collectively exhaustive outcomes their probabilities must add up to one. A probability of one means certainty, which reflects the fact that in a situation where there are a set of mutually exclusive and collectively exhaustive outcomes, one and only one of them is certain to occur.

This footnote to the addition rule can be used to derive probabilities of one of a set of mutually exclusive and collectively exhaustive outcomes if we know the probabilities of the other outcomes.

THE MULTIPLICATION RULE

The multiplication rule of probability is the procedure for finding the probability of an intersection of outcomes, a compound probability that is defined using the word 'and'.

According to the multiplication rule the compound probability that two outcomes both occur is the simple probability that the first one occurs multiplied by the conditional probability that the second outcome occurs, given that the first outcome has already happened:

$$P(A \text{ and } B) = P(A) * P(B|A)$$

The multiplication rule is what bookmakers use to work out odds for 'accumulator' bets, bets that a sequence of outcomes, like several specific horses winning races, occurs. To win the bet the first horse must win the first race; the second horse must win the second race and so on. The odds of this sort of thing happening are often something like five hundred to one. The numbers, like five hundred, are large because they are obtained by multiplication.

The multiplication rule can look more complex than it actually is because it includes a conditional probability. We use a conditional probability for the second outcome because the chances of it occurring could be influenced by the first outcome. This is called dependency; in other words, one outcome is dependent on the other. You can find out whether two outcomes are dependent by comparing the conditional probability of one outcome given that the other has happened, with the simple probability that it happens. If the two figures are different, the outcomes are dependent.

The multiplication rule can be rearranged to provide us with a way of finding a conditional probability:

if P(A and B) = P(A) * P(B|A)

then if we divide both sides by P(A) we get

$$\frac{P(A \text{ and } B)}{P(A)} = P(B/A)$$

so

$$P(B|A) = \frac{P(A \text{ and } B)}{P(A)}$$

In situations where outcomes are independent, the conditional probabilities of the outcomes are the same as their simple probabilities. This means we can simplify the multiplication rule when we are dealing with independent outcomes. We can replace the conditional probability of the second outcome given that the first outcome has occurred with the simple probability that the second outcome occurs.

That is:

instead of P(A and B) = P(A) * P(B|A)

we can use P(A and B) = P(A) * P(B)

because $P(B) = P(B|A)$.

Conditional probabilities are particularly important if you want to work out the chance of a sequence of outcomes involving a limited number of elements. In these cases the selection of one of the elements alters the probabilities of further selections.

BAYES' RULE

In the last section we looked at how the multiplication rule, which enables us to find the compound probability that both of two outcomes occur, could be rearranged to provide a definition of the conditional probability that the second outcome occurs given that the first outcome had already occurred. That is, if

$$P(A \text{ and } B) = P(A) * P(B|A)$$

then

$$P(B|A) = \frac{P(A \text{ and } B)}{P(A)}$$

In this context we normally assume that outcome A occurs before outcome B, for instance the probability that a person buys a car (B) given that they have test driven it (A).

Thanks to the work of the eighteenth-century clergyman and mathematician Thomas Bayes, we can develop this further to say that:

$$P(B \text{ and } A) = P(B) * P(A|B)$$

So

$$P(A|B) = \frac{P(B \text{ and } A)}{P(B)}$$

This means that we can find the probability that outcome A happened given that we know outcome B has subsequently happened. This is known as a posterior, or 'after-the event' probability. In contrast, the simple probability that outcome A happens is a prior, or 'before-the event' probability.

The compound probability that both A and B occur is the same whether it is described as the probability of A and B or the probability of B and A. That is:

$$P(A \text{ and } B) = P(B \text{ and } A)$$

The multiplication rule tells us that:

$$P(A \text{ and } B) = P(A) * P(B|A)$$

We can therefore express the conditional probability that A has occurred given that we know B has subsequently occurred as:

$$P(A|B) = \frac{P(A) * P(B|A)}{P(B)}$$

This definition of the posterior probability of an outcome is known as Bayes' rule or Bayes' theorem.

APPLYING THE RULES OF PROBABILITY

Although we have dealt separately with different types of probability, rules of probability and so on, when it comes to applying them to solve problems involving sequences of outcomes you may well have to use them together.

TREE DIAGRAMS

If you have to investigate the probabilities of sequences of several outcomes it can be difficult to work out the different combinations of outcomes in your head. It helps if you write down all the different variations, and you may find a Venn diagram a useful way of arranging them in order to work out probabilities of certain types of combinations. But perhaps the best way of sorting out this kind of problem is to use a tree diagram.

A tree diagram, which is sometimes called a probability tree, represents the different sequences of outcomes in the style of a tree that 'grows' from left to right. Each branch of the tree leads to a particular result.

On the right hand side of the diagram, at the end of each branch, we can insert the combination of outcomes that the sequence of branches represents and, using the multiplication rule, the probability that the sequence of outcomes happens.

A tree diagram should include all possible sequences. One way you can check that it does is to add up the probabilities on the right-hand side. Because these outcomes are mutually exclusive and collectively exhaustive their probabilities should add up to one.

There is one field of business where the very definition of the products is probabilities; the betting industry. Whether you want to gamble on a horse race, bet on which player will score first in a game of football, have a punt on a particular tennis player winning a grand slam event, you are buying a chance, a chance which is measured in terms of probability, 'the odds'. Another industry delivering products based on probability is the insurance industry. When you buy insurance you are paying the insurer to meet the financial consequences of any calamity that may be visited upon you. When you buy motor insurance, for example, you are paying for the insurance company to cover the costs you might incur if you have an accident. Clearly the company would be rash to offer you this cover without weighing up the chances of your having an accident, which is why when you apply for insurance you have to provide so much information about yourself and your vehicle. If you don't have an accident the company makes a profit from you, if you do it will lose money. Insurance companies have extensive records of motor accidents. They reference the information you give them, your age and gender, the type of car you use, etc. against their databases to assess the probability of your having an accident and base the cost of your insurance on this probability.

The legal context within which businesses operate places obligations on them to ensure their operations do not endanger the health and safety of their workers, and their products are not harmful to their customers or the wider environment. For this reason companies undertake risk assessments. These assessments typically involve using probability to define the risks that their activities may pose. Boghani (1990) describes how probability has been employed in assessing the risks associated with transporting hazardous materials on special trains. North (1990) explains how the process of judgemental evaluation was used to ascertain probabilities of potential damage to forestry production and fish stocks in the lakes of Wisconsin from sulphur dioxide emissions. In the same paper North shows how experimental data were used to assess the health risks arising from the use of a particular solvent in dry-cleaning.

12

Analysing Decisions

In the previous chapter we looked at how probability can be used to assess risk. In this chapter we will consider how probability is used in the analysis of decisions. We will begin with expectation, the process of multiplying probabilities by the tangible results of the outcomes whose chances they measure to obtain expected values of the process or situation under investigation. We will move on to examine various quantitative approaches to taking decisions, including decision trees.

EXPECTATION

A probability assesses the chance of a certain outcome in general. Expectation is using a probability to produce a predicted or expected value of the outcome. To produce an expected value we have to apply the probability to something specific. If the probability refers to a process that is repeated, we can predict how many times a certain outcome will occur if the process happens a specific number of times by multiplying the probability by the number of times the process happens.

In many business situations outcomes are associated with specific financial results. In these cases the probabilities can be applied to the monetary consequences of the outcomes to produce a prediction of the average amount of money income or expenditure. These types of prediction are called expected monetary values (EMVs).

DECISION RULES

From time to time companies are faced with decisions that are pivotal to their future. These involve developing new products, building new facilities, introducing new working practices and so on. In most cases the managers who take these decisions will not know whether they have made the right choices for many months or years to come. They have to take these decisions against a background of either uncertainty, where they cannot attach a probability to each of the outcomes, or risk, where they can put a probability to each of the outcomes.

In this section we will look at decision rules, techniques available to managers taking decisions under conditions of both uncertainty and risk. All of these techniques assist managers by helping them analyse the decisions and the possible outcomes in a systematic way. The starting point is the pay-off table in which the results or pay-offs of the different possibilities or strategies that could be chosen are arranged according to the conditions or states of nature affecting the pay-off that might prevail.

THE MAXIMAX RULE

According to the maximax rule the best strategy is the one that offers the highest pay-off irrespective of other possibilities. We apply the maximax rule by identifying the best pay-off for each strategy and choosing the strategy that has the best among the best, or maximum among the maximum, pay-offs.

The attitude of the decision-maker has a bearing on the suitability of decision rules. The maximax rule is appropriate for decision-makers who are risk-seekers; those who are prepared to accept the chance of losing money in gambling on the biggest possible pay-off. However, we should add that the attitude of the decision-maker may well be influenced by the financial state of the business. If it is cash-rich, the maximax approach would make more sense than if it were strapped for cash. In the former case it would have the resources to cushion the losses that may result in choosing the strategy with the highest pay-off.

THE MAXIMIN RULE

If maximax is the rule for the optimists and the gamblers, maximin is for the pessimists and the risk-avoiders. The maximin rule is to pick the strategy that offers the best of the worst returns for each strategy, the maximum of the minimum pay-offs.

This approach would be appropriate for a business that does not have large cash resources and would therefore be especially vulnerable to taking a loss. It would therefore make sense to pass up the opportunity to gain a large pay-off if it carries with it a risk of a loss and settle for more modest prospects without the chance of losses.

THE MINIMAX REGRET RULE

This rule is a compromise between the optimistic maximax and the pessimistic maximin. It involves working out the opportunity loss or regret you would incur if you selected any but the best strategy for the conditions that come about. To apply it you have to identify the best strategy for each state of nature. You then allocate a regret of zero to each of these strategies, as you would have no regret if you had picked them and it turned out to be the best thing for that state of nature, and work out how much worse off you would be under that state of nature had you chosen another strategy. Finally look for the largest regret figure for each strategy and choose the strategy with the lowest of these figures, in doing so you are selecting the strategy with the minimum of the maximum regrets.

THE EQUAL LIKELIHOOD DECISION RULE

In decision-making under uncertainty there is insufficient information available to assign probabilities to the different states of nature. The equal likelihood approach involves assigning probabilities to the states of nature on the basis that, in the absence of any evidence to the contrary, each state of nature is as likely to prevail as any other state of nature; for instance if there are two possible states of nature we give each of them a probability of 0.5. We then use these probabilities to work out the expected monetary value (EMV) of each strategy and select the strategy with the highest EMV.

DECISION TREES

The decision rules we examined in the previous section help to deal with situations where there is uncertainty about the states of nature and no probabilities are available to represent the chances of their happening. If we do have probabilities for the different states of nature we can use these probabilities to determine expected monetary values (EMVs) for each strategy. This approach is at the heart of decision trees.

As their name implies, decision trees depict the different sequences of outcomes and decisions in the style of a tree, extending from left to right. Each branch of the tree represents an outcome or a decision. The junctions, or points at which branches separate, are called nodes. If the branches that stem from a node represent outcomes, the node is called a chance node and depicted using a small circle. If the branches represent different decisions that could be made at that point, the node is a decision node and depicted using a small square.

All the paths in a decision tree should lead to a specific monetary result that may be positive (an income or a profit) or negative (a cost or a loss). The probability that each outcome occurs is written alongside the branch that represents the outcome. We use the probabilities and the monetary results to work out the expected monetary value (EMV) of each possible decision. The final task is to select the decision, or series of decisions if there is more than one stage of decision-making, that yields the highest EMV.

Once we have come to a recommendation for the later course of action we assume that the decision-maker would follow our advice at that stage and hence we need only incorporate the preferred strategy in the subsequent analysis. We work out the EMV of each decision open to the decision-maker at the earlier stage and recommend the one with the highest EMV.

The probabilities used in decision trees are often little more than educated guesses, yet they are an integral part of the analysis. It is therefore useful to see how the recommendation might change if the probabilities of the relevant outcomes are altered, in other words to see how sensitive the recommendation is to changes in these probabilities. Sensitivity analysis involves finding out by how much the probabilities would have to change for a different decision to be recommended.

Although decision trees can be a useful approach to weighing up decisions, they do have some shortcomings as techniques for taking decisions. Their first weakness is that they are only as good as the information that you put into them. If the probabilities and monetary figures are not reliable then the conclusion is also unreliable.

The second shortcoming is that they take no account of the attitude that the people making the decision have towards risk.

The third drawback is that it is difficult to introduce factors that are non-quantifiable or difficult to quantify into the process.

Despite these weaknesses decision trees can help to investigate decisions and their consequences, especially when we are interested in the effects of altering some of the figures to see whether the conclusion changes.

13

Discrete Probability Distributions and Simulation

In this chapter we will bring together two key concepts from earlier chapters. The first of these is the idea of a frequency distribution, which shows the frequency or regularity with which the values of a variable occur, in other words how they are distributed across their range. Here we will be looking at probability distributions which portray not the frequency with which values of a distribution actually occur but the probability with which we predict they will occur.

Probability distributions are very important tools for modelling or representing processes that occur at random, such as customers visiting a website or accidents on a building site. These are examples of discrete random variables as they vary in a random fashion and can have only certain values, whole numbers in both cases; we cannot conceive of half a customer visiting a website or 0.3 of an accident happening. We use discrete probability distributions to model these sorts of variables.

In studying probability distributions we will look at how they can be derived and how we can model or represent the chances of different combinations of outcomes using the same sort of approach as we use to arrange data into frequency distributions. Following that we will examine two standard discrete probability distributions; the binomial and the Poisson. Lastly we will look at how random numbers and discrete probability distributions can be used to simulate the operation of random business processes.

SIMPLE PROBABILITY DISTRIBUTIONS

A probability distribution is very similar to a frequency distribution. Like a frequency distribution, a probability distribution has a series of categories, but instead of categories of values it has categories of types of outcomes. The other difference is that each category has a probability instead of a frequency.

In the same way as a frequency distribution tells us how frequently each type of value occurs, a probability distribution tells us how probable each type of outcome is. We can use the mean and standard deviation to summarize distributions of probabilities.

Just as we needed a set of data to construct a frequency distribution, we need to identify a set of compound outcomes in order to create a probability distribution. We also need the probabilities of the simple outcomes that make up the combinations of outcomes.

The symbol 'P(x)' represents the probability that the variable X takes a particular value, x. For instance, we can represent the probability that the number of females is one, as

$$P(X = 1) = 0.243$$

We can find summary measures to represent this distribution, in the same way as we could use summary measures to represent distributions of data. However, as we don't have a set of data to use to get our summary measures we use the probabilities to 'weight' the values of X, just as we would use frequencies to obtain the mean from a frequency distribution. You work out the mean of a probability distribution by multiplying each value of x by its probability and then adding up the products:

mð = SðxP(x)

Notice that we use the Greek symbol mð ðto represent the mean of the distribution. The mean of a probability distribution is a population mean because we are dealing with a distribution that represents the probabilities of all possible values of the variable.

Once we have found the mean we can proceed to find the variance and standard deviation. We can obtain the variance, Ã^2, by squaring each x value, multiplying the square of it by its probability and adding the products. From this sum we subtract the square of the mean.

Ã^2 = Sðx^2 P(x) – ¼^2

The standard deviation, Ã, is simply the square root of the variance.

Again you can see that we use a Greek letter in representing the variance and the standard deviation because they are population measures.

The mean of a probability distribution is sometimes referred to as the expected value of the distribution. Unlike the mean of a set of data, which is based on what the observed values of a variable actually were, the mean of a probability distribution tells us what the values of the variable are likely, or expected to be.

We may need to know the probability that a discrete random variable takes a particular value or a lower value. This is known as a cumulative probability because in order to get it we have to add up or accumulate other probabilities. You can calculate cumulative probabilities directly from a probability distribution.

We can use the same cumulative probabilities if we manipulate them using our knowledge of the addition rule of probability. If, for instance, we want to know the probability that a variable is more than two, we can find it by taking the probability that it is two or less away from one.

P(X > 2) = 1 – P(X d” 2)

We can do this because the two outcomes (X being greater than two and X being less than or equal to two) are mutually exclusive and collectively exhaustive. One and only one of them must occur. There are no other possibilities so it is certain that one of them happens.

In the expression P(X > 2), which represents the probability that X is greater than two, we use the symbol '>' to represent 'greater than'. (It may help you to recognize this symbol if you remember that the larger end of it is pointing to the X and the smaller end is pointing to the 2, implying than X is bigger than 2.)

Imagine that you had to use the same approach to produce a probability distribution if there were five or six condoms in a packet instead of just three. We had to be careful enough in identifying the three different ways in which there could be two defectives in a packet of three. If the packets contained five condoms, identifying the different ways that there could be say two defectives in a packet would be far more tedious.

Fortunately there are methods of analysing such situations that do not involve strenuous mental gymnastics. These involve using a type of probability distribution known as the binomial distribution.

THE BINOMIAL DISTRIBUTION

The binomial distribution is the first of a series of 'model' statistical distributions that you will meet in this chapter and the two that follow it.

The distribution was first derived theoretically but is widely used in dealing with practical situations. It is particularly useful because it enables you not only to answer a specific question but also to explore the consequences of altering the situation without actually doing it.

You can use the binomial distribution to solve problems that have what is called a binomial structure. These types of problems arise in situations where a series of finite, or limited number of 'experiments', or 'trials' take place repeatedly. Each trial has the same two mutually exclusive and collectively exhaustive outcomes, as the bi in the word binomial might suggest. By convention one of these outcomes is referred to as 'success'; the other as 'failure'.

To analyse a problem using the binomial distribution you have to know the probability of each outcome and it must be the same for every trial. In other words, the results of the trials must be independent of each other. Words like 'experiment' and 'trial' are used to describe binomial situations because of the origins and widespread use of the binomial distribution in science. Although the distribution has become widely used in many other fields, these scientific terms have stuck.

We will use the symbol X to represent the number of 'successes' in a certain number of trials, n. X is what is called a binomial random variable. The probability of success in any one trial is represented by the letter p. The probability that there are x successes in n trials is:

$$P(X = x) = \frac{n!}{x!(n-x)!} = p^*(1-p)^{n-x}$$

You will see that an exclamation mark is used several times in the equation. It represents a factorial, which is a number multiplied by one less than itself then multiplied by two less itself and so on until we get to one. For instance four factorial, 4!, is four times three times two times one, 4 * 3 * 2 * 1, which comes to 24.

THE POISSON DISTRIBUTION

Some types of business problem involve the analysis of incidents that are unpredictable. Usually they are things that can happen over a period of time, such as the number of telephone calls coming through to an office worker. However, it could be a number of things over an area, such as the number of stains in a carpet.

The Poisson distribution describes the behaviour of variables like the number of calls per hour or the number of stains per square metre. It enables us to find the probability that a specific number of incidents happen over a particular period. The distribution is named after the French mathematician Simeon Poisson, who outlined the idea in 1837, but the credit for demonstrating its usefulness belongs to the Russian statistician Vladislav Bortkiewicz, who applied it to a variety of situations including famously the incidence of deaths by horse kicks amongst soldiers of the Prussian army.

Using the Poisson distribution is quite straightforward. In fact you may find it easier than using the binomial distribution because we need to know fewer things about the situation. To identify which binomial distribution to use we had to specify the number of trials and the probability of success; these were the two defining characteristics, or parameters of the binomial distribution. In contrast, the Poisson distribution is a single parameter distribution, the one parameter being the mean.

The probability that the number of incidents, X, takes a particular value, x, is:

$$P(X = x) = \frac{e^{-\mu} * \mu^{x}}{x!}$$

The letter e is the mathematical constant known as Euler's number. The value of this, to 4 places of decimals, is 2.7183, so we can put this in the formula:

$$P(X = x) = \frac{2.7183^{-\mu} * \mu^{x}}{x!}$$

The symbol ¼ represents the mean of the distribution and x is the value of X whose probability we want to know.

SIMULATING BUSINESS PROCESSES

Most businesses conduct operations that involve random variables; the numbers of customers booking a vehicle service at a garage, the number of products damaged in transit, the number of workers off sick etc. The managers of these businesses can use probability distributions to represent and analyse these variables. They can take this approach a stage further and use the probability distributions that best represent the random processes in their operations to simulate the effects of the variation on those operations.

Simulation is particularly useful where a major investment such as a garage building another service bay is under consideration. It is possible to simulate the operations of the vehicle servicing operation with another service bay so that the benefits of building the extra bay in terms of increased customer satisfaction and higher turnover can be explored before the resources are committed to the investment.

There are two stages in simulating a business process; the first is setting up the structure or framework of the process, the second is using random numbers to simulate the operation of the process. The first stage involves identifying the possible outcomes of the process, finding the probabilities for these outcomes and then allocating bands of random numbers to each of the outcomes in keeping with their probabilities. In making such allocations we are saying that whenever a random number used in the simulation falls within the allocation for a certain outcome, for the purposes of the simulation that outcome is deemed to have occurred. Simulation allows us to investigate the consequences of making changes.

In practice, simulations are performed on computers and the runs are much longer than the ones we have conducted in this section, and in practice there would be many runs carried out. Much of the work in using simulation involves testing the appropriateness or validity of the model; only when the model is demonstrated to be reasonably close to the real process can it be of any use. For more on simulation try Brooks and Robinson (2001) and Oakshott (1997).

14

Continuous Probability Distributions and Basic Queuing Theory

In the previous chapter we looked at how two different types of theoretical probability distributions, the binomial and Poisson distributions, can be used to model or simulate the behaviour of discrete random variables. These types of variable can only have a limited or finite number of values, typically only whole numbers like the number of defective products in a pack or the number of telephone calls received over a period of time.

Discrete random variables are not the only type of random variable. You will also come across continuous random variables, variables whose possible values are not confined to a limited range. In the same way as we used discrete probability distributions to help us investigate the behaviour of discrete random variables we use continuous probability distributions to help us investigate the behaviour of continuous random variables. Continuous probability distributions can also be used to investigate the behaviour of discrete variables that can have many different values.

The most important continuous probability distribution in Statistics is the normal distribution. As the name suggests, this distribution represents the pattern of many 'typical' or 'normal' variables. You may find the distribution referred to as the Gaussian distribution after the German mathematician Carl Friedrich Gauss (1777–1855) who developed it to model observation errors that arose in surveying and astronomy measurements.

The normal distribution has a very special place in Statistics because as well as helping us to model variables that behave in the way that the normal distribution portrays, it is used to model the way in which results from samples vary. This is of great importance when we want to use sample results to make predictions about entire populations.

THE NORMAL DISTRIBUTION

Just as we saw that there are different versions of the binomial distribution that describe the patterns of values of binomial variables, and different versions of the Poisson distribution that describe the behaviour of Poisson variables, there are many different versions of the normal distributions that display the patterns of values of normal variables.

Each version of the binomial distribution is defined by n, the number of trials, and p, the probability of success in any one trial. Each version of the Poisson distribution is defined by its mean. In the same way, each version of the normal distribution is identified by two defining characteristics or parameters: its mean and its standard deviation.

The normal distribution has three distinguishing features:

- It is unimodal, in other words there is a single peak.
- It is symmetrical, one side is the mirror image of the other.
- It is asymptotic, that is, it tails off very gradually on each side but the line representing the distribution never quite meets the horizontal axis.

Because the normal distribution is a symmetrical distribution with a single peak, the mean, median and mode all coincide at the middle of the distribution. For this reason we only need to use the mean as the measure of location for the normal distribution. Since the average we use is the mean, the measure of spread that we use for the normal distribution is the standard deviation.

Calculating the probabilities that make up discrete distributions is tedious but not impossible, especially if the number of outcomes involved is quite small. The nature of the variables concerned, the fact that they can only take a limited number of values, restricts the number of calculations involved.

In contrast, calculating the probabilities in continuous distributions can be daunting. The variables, being continuous, can have an infinite number of different values and the distribution consists of a smooth curve rather than a collection of detached blocks. This makes the mathematics involved very much more difficult and puts the task beyond many people. Because it was so difficult to calculate normal distribution probabilities, tables were the only viable means of using the normal distribution. However, the number of versions of the normal distribution is literally infinite, so it was impossible to publish tables of all the versions of the normal distribution.

The solution to this problem was the production of tables describing a benchmark normal distribution known as the Standard Normal Distribution. The advantage of this was that you could analyse any version of the normal distribution by comparing points in it with equivalent points in the Standard Normal Distribution. Once you had these equivalent points you could use published Standard Normal Distribution tables to assist you with your analysis.

Although modern software means that the Standard Normal Distribution is not as indispensable as it once was, it is important that you know something about it. Not only is it useful in case you do not have access to appropriate software, but more importantly, there are many aspects of further statistical work you will meet that are easier to understand if you are aware of the Standard Normal Distribution.

THE STANDARD NORMAL DISTRIBUTION

The Standard Normal Distribution describes the behaviour of the variable Z, which is normally distributed with a mean of zero and a standard deviation of one. Z is sometimes known as the Standard Normal Variable and the Standard Normal Distribution is known as the Z Distribution.

Sometimes we need to use the Standard Normal Distribution in a rather different way. Instead of starting with a value of Z and finding a probability, we may have a probability and need to know the value of Z associated with it.

USING THE STANDARD NORMAL DISTRIBUTION

To use the Standard Normal Distribution to analyse other versions of the normal distribution we need to be able to express any value of the normal distribution that we want to investigate as a value of Z. This is sometimes known as finding its Z-equivalent or Z score. The Z-equivalent of a particular value, x, of a normal variable, X, is the difference between x and the mean of X, ¼, divided by the standard deviation of X, Ã.

$$Z = \frac{x - \mu}{\sigma}$$

Because we are dividing the difference between the value, x, and the mean of the distribution it belongs to, ¼, by the standard deviation of the distribution, Ã, to get it, the Z-equivalent of a value is really just the number of standard deviations the value is away from the mean. Once we have found the Z-equivalent of a value of a normal distribution we can refer to the Standard Normal Distribution table.

In some situations you may need to find a specific point in the normal distribution that cuts off a particular tail area. To do this, you first have to select the value of Z that cuts off the same area in the Standard Normal Distribution. Once you have established this z value, find the point that number of standard deviations away from the mean. If the z value is positive, add that number of standard deviations to the mean, if it is negative, take them away.

The normal distribution is an important statistical distribution because it enables us to investigate the very many continuous variables that occur in business and many other fields, whose values are distributed in a normal pattern. What makes the normal distribution especially important, perhaps the most important distributions in Statistics, is that it enables us to understand how sample results vary. This is because many sampling distributions have a normal pattern.

THE EXPONENTIAL DISTRIBUTION

The importance of the normal distribution and the attention rightly devoted to it in quantitative methods programmes often obscures the fact that it is not the only continuous probability distribution. The normal distribution is a symmetrical distribution and is therefore an entirely appropriate model for continuous random variables that vary in a symmetrical pattern. But not all continuous random variables that crop up in business analysis exhibit this characteristic.

Many business operations involve queues or waiting-lines; you have probably waited in a queue to pay for groceries, you may have waited in a queue for access to a telephone help-line. These are fairly obvious examples, but there are many others; you may have taken a flight in an aircraft that has had to wait in a queue in the airspace above an airport before it can land, when you post a letter in effect it joins a queue to be sorted by the postal service.

In the next section we shall consider a basic queuing model, but before we do so we will look at the exponential distribution. This is a continuous probability distribution that is important for analysing, among other things, service times in queuing processes.

The exponential distribution differs from the normal distribution in two respects; it describes variables whose variables can only be positive, and it is asymmetrical around its mean. The probability that an exponential random variable takes a particular value can be worked out using the formula:

$$P(X = x) = \frac{e^{-x/\mu}}{\mu}$$

where ¼ is the mean of the distribution and x is the value of interest. The letter e represents Euler's number, 2.7183 to four decimal places. Because the exponential distribution is a continuous probability distribution we are almost always interested in a cumulative probability such as the probability that the variable is greater than a particular value, which we can find using:

$$P(X > x) = e^{-x/\mu}$$

Or the probability that the variable is less than a particular value, which is:

$$P(X > x) = 1 - e^{-x/\mu}$$

To use these expressions for any specific distribution you need to know only the mean of the distribution and the specific value of interest.

A SIMPLE QUEUING MODEL

Queues are quite complex processes because they usually depend on the behaviour of random variables – the number of arrivals per unit of time and the time taken to deal with the people or things concerned. They can be difficult to manage because if for instance customers wait too long they may take their business elsewhere yet devoting too many staff to provide the service may result in their being unoccupied for significant periods of time.

Because of the importance of queuing systems in business operations, queuing theory is a substantial subject. Here we will look at one of the simpler models.

The point of any queuing theory model is to provide us with information about the operation of the queuing system it represents, specifically the average waiting time and the average length of the queue.

If we make certain assumptions about the behaviour of individuals in the queue and know the patterns of arrivals and service times we can do this.

The behaviour assumptions underlying the model we will consider are that having joined the queue an individual will stay in it until they have been served and that individuals in the queue are served on a FIFO (First In First Out) basis, in other words, first come first served. We will further assume that individuals join the queue according to the Poisson distribution with a mean of », and that service times are exponentially distributed according to the exponential distribution with a mean of ¼.

The symbol », lambda, is the Greek letter l, which we will use to distinguish the mean of the Poisson arrivals distribution from the mean of the exponential service times distribution in keeping with the conventions of notation in queuing theory. Both means need to be expressed in the same style so we define », the mean of the arrivals distribution, as the mean arrival rate, and ¼, the mean of the service times, as the mean service rate.

In queuing theory models are identified by the distributions of arrivals and service times, with M used to represent the Poisson and exponential distributions. In the simple model we shall study we assume there is just one service point. This model is known as the M/M/1, indicating Poisson arrivals, exponential service times and one server.

The ratio between the mean arrival rate and the mean service rate, » / ¼ is the traffic intensity in the queuing system, represented by the Greek letter rho, rð, the Greek r. For a queuing system to be viable the traffic intensity must be less than 1, in other words the mean arrival rate must be less than the mean service rate, otherwise the queue would simply continue to grow and the system would 'explode'.

By means of mathematical derivations involving probability and differentiation it is possible to determine a number of operating measures of an M/M/1 queuing system including:

The probability that the server is idle = 1 –rð.

The probability that there are more than r individuals in the queue = rð$^{r+2}$

The mean number in the queue, L_q = rð^2/(1 – rð)

The mean waiting time in the queue, W_q = rð/(¼ – »)

15

Project Planning Using Networks

Many business operations involve planning and coordinating a project – a series of interlinked tasks or activities all of which have to be performed in the correct sequence and within the least amount of time in order to achieve a successful conclusion to the venture. This is not only typical of large-scale projects such as you would find in industries like construction and shipbuilding, but also occurs on a more modest basis in administrative processes such as organizing events like conferences and concerts.

To help plan and execute projects successfully managers can turn to network analysis, a system of representing and linking the activities involved in a project. Once they have designed a network they can use critical path analysis (CPA) to establish the minimum duration of the project by identifying those tasks whose completion on time is essential, the critical activities. Beyond this they can bring into consideration the probability distributions that reflect the chances of the activities being completed by specific times using the program evaluation and review technique (PERT). In this chapter we will look at these techniques.

NETWORK ANALYSIS

We can apply network analysis to any project that consists of series of distinct activities provided that we know which activities must be completed before other activities can commence. This is called the precedence of the activities because it involves identifying the activities that must precede each activity. These are crucial because the point of a network diagram is to show how the activities in a project are linked.

The diagrams used for network analysis are built up using a single arrow for each activity. The arrow begins at a circle representing the point in time at which the activity begins and finishes at another circle that represents the completion of the activity. These circles are known as event nodes. We would represent a single activity as shown in Figure 1.

$$\boxed{1}\xrightarrow{A}\boxed{2}$$

Figure 1: A single activity

In Figure 1 the direction of the arrow tells us that the event node on the right marks the completion of the activity. The activity is labelled using a letter and the events nodes are numbered. Network diagrams consist of many arrows and many event nodes, so logical layout and labelling is important.

Networks should be set out so that the beginning of the project is represented by the event node on the extreme left of the diagram and the completion by the event node on the extreme right. In compiling them you should try to ensure that the event nodes are labelled sequentially from left to right from event number 1, the start of the project.

All the arrows should point from left to right either directly or at angle and certainly not from right to left. This is usually straightforward because the purpose of an arrow in a network is to represent the position of the activity in relation to other activities and not its duration. A network diagram is not intended to be to scale.

Both types of dummy activity serve only to clarify the network and avoid ambiguity. The important distinction between real and dummy activities is that the latter do not take time or use resources. Compiling network diagrams often brings an understanding of the way in which activities that make up a project fit together. It enables you to clarify uncertainties about the planning of the project. This is something usually achieved by constructing drafts of the network before producing the final version.

Whilst an understanding of the sequence is important, there is much more to successful project planning. Ascertaining the minimum time in which the project can be completed and scheduling the activities over time are typically the central issues. The technique that enables us to do this is critical path analysis.

CRITICAL PATH ANALYSIS

If we know the duration of each activity we can use a network diagram to find out the least amount of time it will take to finish the project. A network diagram shows the way that activities are linked; in effect it portrays the project as a series of paths of activities. Since every activity must be finished for the project to be completed, the minimum duration of the project is the length of time required to carry out the most time-consuming path of activities. This path is known as the critical path since any delay in the completion of activities along it will prolong the entire project. Finishing those activities on the critical path on time is therefore critical for the project; they are known as critical activities.

Critical path analysis involves increasing the amount of information in the network by enhancing the role of the event nodes. In drawing a network diagram the event nodes are in effect the punctuation marks in the diagram; they bring order to the sequence of arrows. In critical path analysis they become distinct points in time. For each event node we assign an earliest event time (EET) and a latest event time (LET).

To work out the earliest and latest times for the events in a network we use the activity durations. Starting with the event node at the beginning of the network and working through the network from left to right we write in the earliest time that each event node in the network can occur. This is referred to as making a forward pass through the network.

When doing this you need to remember that where there are two or more activities leading to the same event node it is the duration of the longest of the activities that determines the earliest time for the event since all the activities must be completed before the event is reached. We write the earliest event times in the lower left-hand side of the event nodes.

By definition the critical activities in a network have no slack or float, but other activities will. A project manager is likely to be very interested in the float available for these activities, as it indicates the degree of latitude available in scheduling them.

To work out the total float for an activity we need to know the latest event time for the event that marks its completion, its finishing event, and the earliest event time for the event that represents its beginning, its starting event. If we subtract the duration of the activity from the difference between these times what is left over is the total float for the activity. We can summarize this procedure as:

Total float = Latest event time (finishing event) – earliest event time (starting event) – activity duration

Using abbreviations:

$$TF = LET (F) - EET (S) - AD$$

THE PROGRAM EVALUATION AND REVIEW TECHNIQUE (PERT)

So far we have assumed that the activities making up a project each have fixed durations. In reality this is unlikely to be the case. In the ground servicing project introduced factors such as the state of equipment, the time of the day or night, and weather conditions will influence the time it takes to complete the activities. Rather than being fixed, activity durations are more likely to be variable. PERT allows us to take this into account.

In using PERT we assume that the duration of an activity is a continuous variable that follows a continuous probability distribution. We looked at continuous probability distributions like the normal distribution. The distribution used in PERT as the model for activity durations is the beta distribution. Like the normal distribution it is continuous, but unlike the normal distribution it can be skewed or symmetrical and it has a minimum and a maximum value. The key characteristics or parameters of the beta distribution are the minimum or optimistic duration, a, the maximum or pessimistic duration, b, and the most likely duration, m.

The mean duration of an entire project is the sum of the mean durations of the activities that are on the critical path, the critical activities. The variance of the project duration is the sum of the variances of the critical activities and the standard deviation of the project duration is the square root of its variance. Note that you cannot get the standard deviation of the project duration by adding together the standard deviations of the durations of the critical activities; it is the variances that sum, not the standard deviations.

Unless there is clear evidence that the distributions of the durations of the individual activities are consistently skewed, we can assume that the distribution of the project duration is approximately normal. This means we can use the Standard Normal Distribution to work out the probability that the project is completed within a certain timescale or beyond a certain timescale.

We can also work out the timescale within which a certain proportion of ground operations should be completed using the Z distribution.

COST ANALYSIS: CRASHING THE PROJECT DURATION

PERT is designed to allow for random fluctuations in the duration of activities. These are by definition in large part difficult or impossible to anticipate, yet they can have a substantial impact on the duration of a project. In contrast, it may be possible to reduce the project duration by cutting activity durations by intent. Typically this involves incurring extra cost, defined as the cost of crashing the duration of an activity below its anticipated duration.

In most projects there are at least some activities that can be performed more quickly, perhaps by providing more or better equipment, perhaps by allocating more staff, perhaps by hiring a sub-contractor. These contingencies will come at an additional cost, the crash cost, the cost of carrying out the activity in its crash duration rather than its normal duration.

Although there may be several activities in a project that can be crashed, it may not be worthwhile crashing all of them. The project duration is the critical path, the path of critical activities, whose completion on schedule is crucial for the minimum duration of the project to be achieved. If an activity is not on the critical path it is not worth crashing, or at least not until it might have become critical following the crashing of one or more critical activities. Crashing a non-critical activity will not reduce the duration of the critical path, but crashing a critical activity will always reduce the duration of the critical path. Having said that, there is a limit. Once the critical path activities have been crashed to the point that another path loses its float and becomes critical it is not worth crashing critical activities any further. Any further project reduction has to involve further crashing of the activities on the original critical path as well as crashing activities that have become critical after the initial crashing of the critical path activities.

There may be several critical activities than can be crashed. If this is the case the activities to be crashed should be selected on the basis of cost, with the cheapest options implemented first.

16

Unconstrained Optimization

FUNCTIONS OF ONE VARIABLE

This topic reviews basic results about functions of one variable, including the notice of derivative, extremum and convexity. it also describes a numerical method for finding x such f(x)= 0 known as known as "binary search"

DERIVATIVES

It is important to know the following differentation formulas:

Function	Derivative
$f(x)+g(x)$	$f'(x)+g'(x)$
$af(x)$	$af'(x)$
$f(x)g(x)$	$f'(x)g(x)+g'(x)$
$f(x)/g(x)$	$[g(x)f'(x)g'(x)]/g^2(x)$
$f(g(x))$	$f'(g(x))g'(x)$
x^a	ax^{a-1}
e^x	e^x

In x $(x>0)$ Where In x = log, x 1/x

Exercise: Compute the derivatives of the following functions :

$(a)\ x^3-3x+1$

$(b)\ In(1+x^2)$

$(c)\ In(1+x)^{*}$

$(d)\ (3-2x)e^{x^2}$

For a function f of one variable x, recall that the derivative f (x) is equal to the slope of a tangent line at point x. So if the function has a positive derivative at point x then the function is increasing, and if it has a negative derivative, it is decreasing. Since the function and its tangent line are close around point x, the following formula can be used Δ when is small.

$$f(x+\Delta) \approx f(x)+\Delta f'(x)$$

Example: Suppose that the demand for gasoline at price x (in dollar) is $ae^{-0.2x}$ Gallons, where a is a constant. Suppose the Price of gas rises by 10 cents. by how much does demand fall?

Let $f(x)ae^{-0.2x}$ denote the demand for gas at price x. The rate of change is given by the derivative $f'(x) = 0.2f(x)$.

Since $\Delta = 0.10$ we get

$$f(x+0.10) \approx f(x)+0.10(-0.2f(x)) = 0.98f(x).$$

So demand drops by 2%. The factor relating change in demand to change in price is known as "price elasticity of demand" in economics. Here $f(x) = 0.2f(x)$, so price elasticity of demand is -0.2.

Exercise: Suppose thet, if x dollars are spent on advertising for a product during a given year, $f(x) = k(1-e^{-cx})$ customers will purchase the product (k > 0 and c > 0 are two constants).

(a) As x grows large the number of customers purchasing the product approaches a limit. Find this limit. Can you give an imterpretation for the constant k?

(b) The sales response from a dollar of advertising is $f(x+1)-f(x)$. Using the formula for small changes, show that sales response from a dollar of advertising is proportional to the number of potentia! customers who are not purchasing the product at present.

MAXIMUM AND MUNIMUM

Let f be a function of one variable defined for all x in same domain D. A global maximum of f is a point x_0 in D such that $f(x) \le f(x_0)$ for all x in D

For a constant $\Delta > 0$, the neighborhood $N_\Delta(x_0)$ of a point is x_0 the set of all points x such that $x_0 - \Delta < x < x_0 + \Delta$. A point x_0 is a local maximum of f if there exists $\Delta > 0$ such that $f(x) \le f(x_0)$ for all x in $N_\Delta(x_0)$ where f(x) is defined

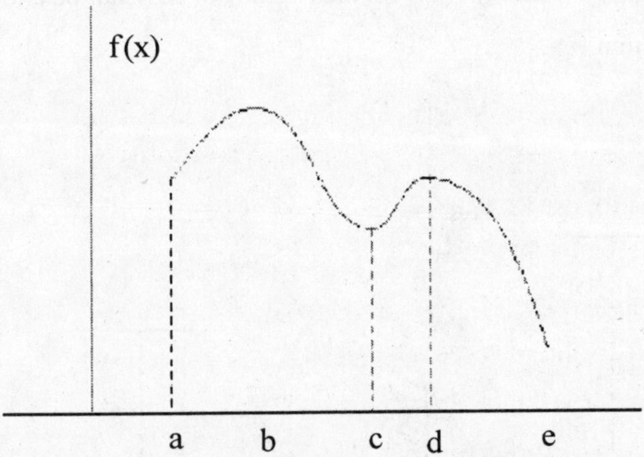

Figure 1: local maximum and minima

Similarly one can difine local and global minima. In Figure 1, the function f is defined for x in domain [a,e].Points b and d are local maxima and b is a global maximum, wheres a,c, and e are local minima and e is a global minimum.

Finding extrema

Extrema whether they are local or global, can occur in three places:

1. at the boundary of the domain,

2. at a point without a derivative, or

3. at a point x_0 with $f'(x_0) = 0$

The last case is particularly important. So we discuss it further. Let f be differentiable in a neithborgood of x_0..If x_0 is a local extremum of f, then $f'(x_0)=0$ Conversely, if $f'(x_0)=0$, three possibilities may arise: x_0 is a local maximum x_0 is a local minimum, or neither. To decide between these three possibilities, one may use the second derivative. Let f be twice differentiable in a neithborhood of x_0

- If $f'(x_0)=0$ and $f''(x_0)>0$ then x_0 is a local minimum.
- If $f'(x_0)=0$ and $f''(x_0)>0$ then x_0 is a local minimum.
- If $f'(x_0)=0$ and $f''(x_0)=0$ then x_0 may or may not be a local extermum

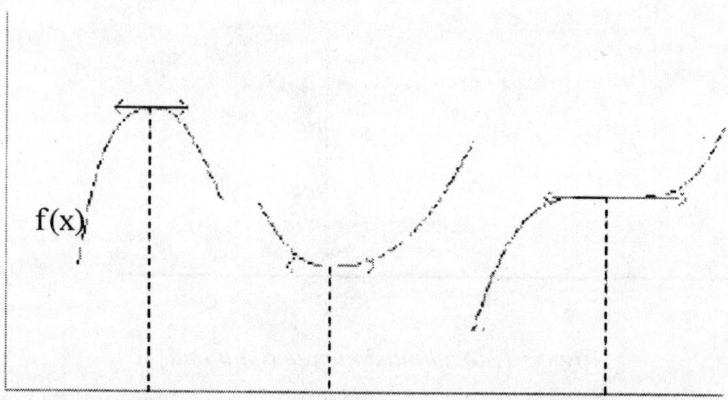

Figure 2: $f''(x_0)>0$ $f''(x_0)<0$ *and one of the possibilities with* $f''(x_0)=0$

Example: Suppose an oil cartel can price gasoline as it wishes. How will it maximize revenue, given that demand for gasoline at price x is

$$f(x)=ae^{-0.2x}$$

The revenue at price x is

$$g(x)=xf(x).$$

We compute the derivative of g and set it to 0.

$$g'(x) = f(x) + x(-0.2f(x) = (1-0.2x)f(x)$$

Since f(x): SP Mgt:0 for all x, setting g'(x) implies 1-0.2 x = 0, So x = 5. This is the only possible local optimum. To determine whether it is a maximum or a minimum, we compute the second derivative.

$$g'(x) = 2(-0.2f(x)) + x(-0.2)^2 f(x) = -0.2(2-0.2x)f(x)$$

Putting in x = 5 shows g" (x). SP Mlt; 0, so this is a maximum: the oil cartel maximizes its revenue by pricing gasoline at $65 Per gallon.

Example: We want to keep paper towels on hand at all times. The cost of stockpiling towels is $ h per case per week, including the cost of space, the cost of tying up capital in inventory, etc. The time and paperwork involved in ordering towels costs $ K per order (this is in addition to the cost of the towels themselves, which is not relevant here becouse we are supposing that there are no price discount for large orders.) Towels are used at a rate of d cases per week. What quantity Q should are at a time, to minimize cost?

We must first calculate the holding cost (cost of stockpiling). If each order period begins with Q cases and ends with zero cases, and if usage is more or less constant, then the average stock level is Q/2. This means that the average holding cost is h Q/2.

Since each order of Q cases lasts Q ld weeks, the average ordering cost per week is $\frac{K}{Q/d} = \frac{Kd}{Q}$ Thus the average tolat cost per week is

$$\frac{hQ}{2} = \frac{Kd}{Q},$$

To find Q that minimizes cost, we set to zero the derivative with respect Q.

$$\frac{h}{2} - \frac{Kd}{Q} = 0,$$

This implies that the optimal order quantity is

$$Q = \sqrt{\frac{2Kd}{h}}.$$

This is the classical economic order quantity (EOQ) model for inventory management.

Exercise: Find the local maxima, and minima, if any of the following functions.

$(a)\ x^3 - 3x + 1$

$(b)\ x^3 - 3x^2 + 3x - 1$

$(c)\ (3 - 2x)ex^2$

Exercise: We want to design a conc- shaped paper drinking cup of volume V that requires a minimum of paper to make. That is, we want to minimize its surface area $\pi r\sqrt{r^2 + h}$, where r is the radius of the open end and h the height. Since $V = V = \frac{\pi}{3} r^2 h$, we can solve for h to get $h = 3V/(\pi r^2)$, . Thus the area in terms of r is

$$A(r) = \pi r \left(r^2 9 \frac{V^2}{\pi^2 r^4} \right)^{1/2} = \left(\pi^2 r^4 + 9 \frac{V^2}{r^2} \right)^{1/2},$$

(a) Compute the derivative A'(r).

(b) Find the radius r at which A (r) is minimzed (the solution you get is in fact a minimum).

(c) What is the retio h/r when r has the optimal value?

Exercise: An air courier company operates a single depot in a large city and wants to decentralize by establishing several depots, each covering the same delivery redius r. The total area to be covered is A, and the area covered by each depot is πr^2 Thus if n depots are installed, we must have $A = n\pi r^2$, so that n= $A/\pi r^2$). Expenses and revenues break down as follows.

Trucking expenses. The number of trucks required at each depot is $a\pi r^3$ so that the total number of trucks required is $na\pi r^3 = (A/\pi r^2)$ $a\pi r^3 = Aar$ Each truck costs $K per day, so that total expense for trucks is \$K A ar. Overhead. Each depot incurs an overhead (fixed expense of \$F, for a total overhead of $nF = FA/(\pi r^2)$

Revenue from customers. Since the total area is fixed, the total revenue from customers is independent of the delivery redius.

Since the total revenue is fixed, we can simply minimize costs:

$$\min \; K\ A\, or + \frac{FA}{\pi r^2}$$

Your solution should indecate that the optimal delivery redius is proportional to the cube root (the 1/3 power) of the fixed cost. Thus if the fixed cost increases eightfold (and other costs were constant), the optimal delivery redius would only double. This is fortunate, since it mean that the rent and other fixed costs must rise substantially (relative to other costs) before they justify relocating depots.

BINARY SEARCH

Binary search is a very simple idea for solving numerically f(x) = 0 it requires:

(i) The function f to be continuous,

(ii) Values (a,b) such that f(a); SP Mgt; 0 and f(b) ; SPMlt ;0

Then a desired value x_0 such that $f(x_0) = 0$ can be found between the value *a* and *b*

The method consists in computing f(c) for $c = \frac{a+b}{2}$

If f(c); SPMgt; 0, the procedure is repeated with the value (a,b) replaced by the value (c, b,).

If f(c).SPMlt; Zero, the procedure is repeated with the values (a,b) replaced by (a, c,).

If f(c)= 0, the procedure terminates as c is the value we are looking for.

This method is easy to program and converges rapidly (20 iterations will give you x_0 with 5 significant figures).

Example: Binary search can be used to compute the internal rate of return of an investment. The internal rate of return of an investment is the interest rate r that makes the present value of the cash flows from the investment equal to the cost of the investment. Mathematically, r is the interest rate that satisfies the equation:

$$\frac{F_1}{1+r}+\frac{F_2}{(1+r)^2}+\frac{F_3}{(1+r)^3}+....+\frac{F_N}{(1+r)^N}-C=0$$

where

F_t = Cash flow in year t

N = Number of years

C = Cost of the investment

For a bond, the internal rate of return r is known as the yield to maturity or simply yield. Let us consider the case of a noncallable bond, i,e, a bond thet the issuer cannot retire prior to its stated maturity date. For such a bond, the cash flows consist of periodic interest payments to the maturity date and the par value paid at maturity. As an example, consider a 4-year noncallable bond with a 10% coupon rate paid annually and a par value of \$ 1000. Such a bond has the following cash flows :

t Year from now	F
1	\$100
2	100
3	100
4	1100

Suppose this bond is now selling for \$900. Compute the yield of this bond.

The yield r of bond is given by the equation

$$\frac{1000}{1+r}+\frac{100}{(1+r)^2}+\frac{1000}{(1+r)^3}+\frac{1100}{(1+r)^4}-900=0$$

Let us denote by f(r) the left hand side of this equation. We find r such that f(r) = 0 using binary search.

We start by finding values (a,b) such that f(a) ;SPMlt; 0 and f(b) ; SPMlt; 0. In this case, we expect r to be between 0 and 1. Since F(0) = 500 and f (1) = - 743.75, we have our starting values.

Next, we let c= 0.5 (the midpoint) and calculate f(c). Since f(0.5) = -541.975, we replace our renge with a = 0 and b= 0.5 and repeat. When we continue, we get the following table of values:

Itcr.	a	c	b	f(a)	f(c)	f(b)
1	0	0.5	1	500	-541.975	-743.75
2	0	0.25	0.5	500	-254.24	-541.975
3	0	0.125	0.25	500	24.85902	-254.24
4	0.125	0.1875	0.25	24.85902	-131.989	-254.24
5	0.125	0.15625	0.1875	24.85902	-58.5833	-131.989
6	0.125	0.140625	0.15625	24.85902	-18.2181	-58.5833
7	0.125	0.132813	0.140625	24.85902	2.967767	-18.2181
8	0.132813	0.136719	0.140625	2.967767	-7.71156	-18.2181
9	0.132813	0.134766	0.136719	2.967767	-2.39372	-7.71156
10	0.132813	0.133789	0.134766	2.967767	0.281543	-2.39372
11	0.133789	0.134277	0.134766	0.281543	-1.05745	-2.39372
12	0.133789	0.134033	0.134277	0.281543	-0.3883	-1.05745

So the yield of the bond is r = 13.4 %.

GOLDEN SECTION SEARCH

Golden section serch is similar in spirit to binary search. It is used to compute the maximum of a function f(x) defined on an interval [a,b].

It assumes that

(i) f is continuous

(ii) f has a unique local maximum in the interval [a,b].

The golden search method consists in computing f(c) andf(d) for a ; SPMlt ; d ; SPMlt ;c ;SPMlt ;b

- If f(c); SPMgy; f(d), the procedure is repeated with the interval (a,b) replaced by (d,b).
- If f(c) ; SPMlt, f(d), the procedure is repeated with the interval (a,b) replaced by (a,c).

Note:- The name "golden section" comes from a certain choice of c and d that yields fast convergence, namely c = a + r (b-a) and d = b+(a-b), where $r = \sqrt{\dfrac{5-1}{2}} = .618034$ ...... This is the golden ratio, already known to the ancient Greeks.

Example: Find the maximum of the function $x^5 - 10x^2 + 2x$ in the internal [0,1].

In this case, we begain with a = 0 and b = 1. Using golden section search, that gives d = 0.382 and c = 0.618. The function value are f (x) = 0, f(d) = - 0.687, f(c) = - 2.493, and f(b) = -7. Since f(c); SPMlt ; f(d), our new renge is a = 0, b = 618, Recalculating from the new range gives d = .236, c = .382 (note that our current c was our previous d : it is this reuse of calculated values that gives golden section serch its speed). We repeat this process to get the following table:

I tcr.	a	d	c	b	f(a)	f(d)	f(c)	f(b)
1	0	0.382	0.618	1	0	-0.6869	-2.4934	-7
2	0	0.2361	0.382	0.618	0	-0.0844	-0.6869	-2.4934
3	0	0.1459	0.2361	0.382	0	0.079	-0.0844	-0.6869
4	0	0.0902	0.1459	0.2361	0	0.099	0.079	-0.0844
5	0	0.0557	0.0902	0.1459	0	0.0804	0.099	0.079
6	0.0557	0.0902	0.1115	0.1459	0.0804	0.099	0.0987	0.079
7	0.0557	0.077	0.0902	0.1115	0.0804	0.0947	0.099	0.0987
8	0.077	0.0902	0.0983	0.1115	0.0947	0.099	0.1	0.0987
9	0.0902	0.0983	0.1033	0.1115	0.099	0.1	0.0999	0.0987
10	0.0902	0.0952	0.0983	0.1033	0.099	0.0998	0.1	0.0999
11	0.0952	0.0983	0.1002	0.1033	0.0998	0.1	0.1	0.0999
12	0.0983	0.1002	0.1014	0.1033	0.1	0.1	0.1	0.0999
13	0.0983	0.0995	0.1002	0.1014	0.1	0.1	0.1	0.1
14	0.0995	0.1002	0.1007	0.1014	0.1	0.1	0.1	0.1
15	0.0995	0.0999	0.1002	0.1007	0.1	0.1	0.1	0.1
16	0.0995	0.0998	0.0999	0.1002	0.1	0.1	0.1	0.1
17	0.0998	0.0999	0.1	0.1002	0.1	0.1	0.1	0.1
18	0.0999	0.1	0.1001	0.1002	0.1	0.1	0.1	0.1
19	0.0999	0.1	0.1	0.1001	0.1	0.1	0.1	0.1
20	0.0999	0.1	0.1	0.1	0.1	0.1	0.1	0.1
21	0.1	0.1	0.1	0.1	0.1	0.1	0.1	0.1

CONVEXITY

Finding global exterma and checking that we have actually found one is harder than finding local extrema, in general. There is one nice case : that of convex and concave functions. A convex function is one where the line segment connectiong two points (x,f(x)) and (y, f(y)) lines above the function. Mathematically, a function f is convex if, for all x,y and all $0 < \alpha < 1$

$$f(ax+(1-\alpha)y) \leq \alpha f(x)+(1-\alpha)f(y).$$

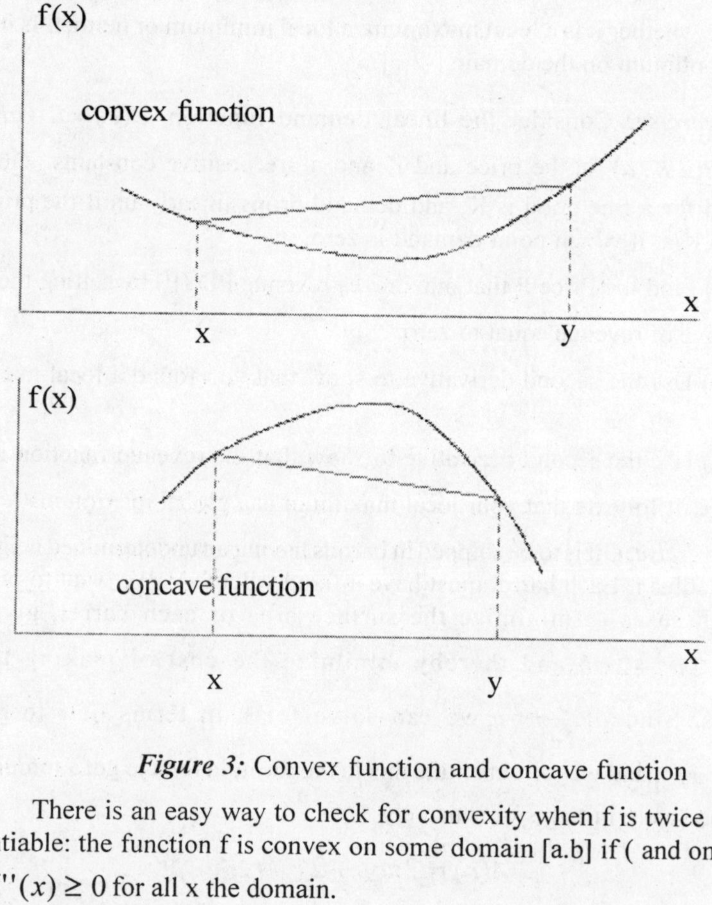

Figure 3: Convex function and concave function

There is an easy way to check for convexity when f is twice differentiable: the function f is convex on some domain [a.b] if (and only if) $f''(x) \geq 0$ for all x the domain.

Similarly,f is concave on some domain [a,b] if (and only if) $f''(x) \leq 0$ for all x in the domain

If f(x) is convex, then any local minimum is also a global minimum

If f(x) is convex, then any local maximum is also a global maximum.

Exercise: Find whether the follwong functions are concave, convex or neither.

$(a)\, x^4 - 4x^3 + 6x^2 + 3x + 1$

$(b) - e^{x^2}$

Exercise: Find a local extermum of the function $f(x) = xe^{-x,}$. Indicate whether it is a local maximum, a local minimum or neither. Is it a global optimum on the domain [-2,2]?

Exercise: Consider the linear demand function $D(P) = K - aP$, where $P(\le K / a)$ is the price and K and a are positive constants. Thus demand for a free good is K, and demand drops linearly until the price reaches K/a, it which point demand is zero.

(a) Find the Price P that maximizes revenue PD (P) by setting the derivative of revenue equal to zero.

(b) Use the second derivative to show that you found a local maximum.

(c) Use the second derivative to show that the revenue function is concave. It follows that your local maximum is a global maximum.

Exercise: Oil is to be shipped in barrels having an undotermined height h and radius r. Each barrel must have a fixed valume V. We want to pick r and h so as to minimize the surface area of each barrel, given by $A = 2\pi r^2 + 2\pi rh,$ and thereby minimize the cost of making the barrels. Since $V = \pi r^2 h,$ we can solve for h in terms of r to get $h = V / \pi r^2$, and we can substitute this in the formula for a to get a fomulae for area solely in terms of r, namely,

$$A(r) = 2\pi r^2 + 2V / r,$$

(a) Compute $A'(r), A''(r)$ and show that the function A is convex.

(b) Find the radius at which A(r) has its global minimum. Explain how you know the minimum is global.

(c) What is the retio h/r when r has the optimal value you just derived?

FUNCTIONS OF SEVERAL VARIABLES

GRADIENT

Given a function f of n variables $x_1, x_2, ...x_n,$ we difine the partial derivative ralative to variable x_i written as $\frac{\theta f}{\theta x_i}$, to be the derivative of f with respect to x_i treating all variables except x_i as constant

Example: Compute the partial derivatives of

$$f(x_1, x_2) = (x_1 - 2)^2 + 2(x_2 - 1)^2,$$

The answer is $\frac{\theta f}{\theta f_{x_1}}(x_1, x_2) = 2(x_1 - 2)$, $\frac{\theta f}{\theta f_{x_2}}(x_1, x_2) = 4(x_2 - 1)$,

Let x denote the vector $(x_1, x_2 ...., x_n)$ With this notation, $f(x) = f(x_1, x_2, ..., x_n)$, $\frac{\theta f}{\theta x_i}(x) = \frac{\theta f}{\theta x_i}(x_1, x_2, ..., x_n)$ etc. The gradient of f at x written $\nabla f(x)$, is the vector $\begin{pmatrix} \frac{\theta f}{\theta x 1}(x) \\ \frac{\theta f}{\theta x 2}(x) \\ \text{M} \\ \frac{\theta f}{\theta x n}(x) \end{pmatrix}$

The gradient vector $\nabla f(x)$, gives the direction of steepest ascent of the function f at point x. The gradient acts like the derivative in that small changes around a given point x^*

$$f(x^* + \Delta) \approx f(x^*) + \Delta \nabla f(x^*)$$

where $\Delta = (\Delta_1 .... \Delta \nabla_n)$ denotes the vector of changes.

Example: If *If* $f(x_1, x_2) = x_1^2 - 3x_{1_2} x_2 + x_2^2$,

Then $f(1,1) = -1$. What is $(1.01, 1.01)$?

In this case $x^* = (1,1)$ and $\Delta = (0.01, 0.01)$.

$$\frac{\theta rf}{\theta x_1}(x_1 x_2) = 2x_1 - 3x_2 \quad \text{and}$$

$$\frac{\theta rf}{\theta x_1}(x_1 x_2) = -3x_1 + 2x_2 \quad \text{we get}$$

$$\nabla f(1,1) = \begin{pmatrix} -1 \\ -1 \end{pmatrix}$$

So

$$f(1.01,1.01) = f(1,1) + (1,1) + (0.01,0.01) \approx f(1,1) + (0.01,0.01)\nabla f(1,1)$$

$$= -1 + (0.01,0.01)\begin{pmatrix} -1 \\ -1 \end{pmatrix} = -1.02$$

Example: Suppose that we want to put away a fishing pole in a closet having dimensions 3 by 5 by feet. If the ends of the pole are placed at opposite corners, there is room for a pole of length

$$f(x_1, x_2 x_3) = f(3,5,1) = \sqrt{x_1^2 + x_2^2 + x_3^2} = 5.9\ ft.$$

It turns out that the actual dimensions of the closet are $3+\Delta_1, 5+\Delta_2$ and $1+\Delta_3$ feet, where Δ_1, Δ_2 and Δ_3 are small correction terms. What is the change is pole lenght, taking into account those corrections?

By the formula for small changes, the change in pole length is

$$f(3+\Delta_1, 5+\Delta_2\ 1+\Delta_3) - f(3,5,1) \approx (\Delta_1 \Delta_2 \Delta_3)\Delta f(3,5,1).$$

So, we need to compute the partial derivatives of f. For i = 1,2,3

$$\frac{\partial}{\partial x_i} f(x_1, x_2, x_3) = \frac{x_i}{\sqrt{x_1^2 + x_2^2 + x_3^2}}$$

Now we get,

$$(\Delta_1\Delta_2\Delta_3)\nabla(3,5,1) = (\Delta_1\Delta_2\Delta_3)\begin{pmatrix}0.51\\0.85\\0.17\end{pmatrix} = 0.51\Delta_1 + 0.85\Delta_2 + 0.17\Delta_{3,}$$

Exercise: Consider the function $f(x_1, x_2) = x_1\, In x_2,$

(a) Compute the gradient of f.

(b) Give the value of the function f and give its gradient at the point (3.1).

(c) Use the formula for small change to obtain an approximate value of the function at the point (2.99,1.05).

Exercise: Consider a conical drinking cup with height h and radius r at the open end. The volume of the cup is $V(r,h) = \frac{\pi}{3}r^2h$

(a) Suppose the cone is now 5 cm high with radius 2 cm. Compute its valume.

(b) Compute the partial derivatives $\partial V / \partial r \; and \; \partial V / \partial h$ at the current height and radius.

(c) By about what fraction (i.e., percentage) would the valume change if the cone were lengthened 10 % ?(Use the partial derivatives.)

(d) It the radius were increased 5%?

(e) If both were done simultaneously?

Hessian matrix

Second partials $\frac{\theta^2 f}{\theta x_i \theta x_j}(x)$ are obtained from f(x) by taking the derivative relative to x_1 (this yields the first partial $\frac{\theta f}{\theta x_i}(x)$ and then by taking the derivative of $\frac{\theta f}{\theta x_i}(x)$ relative to x_j So we can compute $\frac{\theta^2 f}{\theta x_i \theta x_j}(x) = \frac{\theta^2 f}{\theta x_j \theta x_i}(x)$ and soon. These values are arranged into the

Hessian matrix

$$H(x)=\begin{pmatrix} \frac{\theta^2 f}{\theta x_1 \theta x_1}(x) & \frac{\theta^2 f}{\theta x_1 \theta x_2}(x) & \cdots & \frac{\theta^2 f}{\theta x_1 \theta x_n}(x) \\ \frac{\theta^2 f}{\theta x_2 \theta x_1}(x) & \frac{\theta^2 f}{\theta x_2 \theta x_2}(x) & \cdots & \frac{\theta^2 f}{\theta x_2 \theta x_n}(x) \\ \vdots & \vdots & \ddots & \vdots \\ \frac{\theta^2 f}{\theta x_n \theta x_1}(x) & \frac{\theta^2 f}{\theta x_n \theta x_2}(x) & \cdots & \frac{\theta^2 f}{\theta x_n \theta x_n}(x) \end{pmatrix}$$

The Hessian matrix is a symmetric matix, that is $\frac{\theta^2 f}{\theta x_i \theta x_j}(x) = \frac{\theta^2 f}{\theta x_j \theta x_i}(x)$

Example: Find the Hessian matrix of

$$f(x_1, x_2) = (x_1 - 2)^2 + 2(x_2 - 1)^2,$$

The answer is $H(x) = \begin{pmatrix} 2 & 0 \\ 0 & 4 \end{pmatrix}$,

MAXIMUM AND MINIMUM

Optima can occur in three places:

1. at the boundary of the domain,
2. at a nondifferentiable point, or
3. at a point x^* with $\nabla f(x^*) = 0$

We will identify the first type of point with Kuhn- Tucker conditions

The second type is found only by ad hoc methods. The third type of point can be found by solving the gradient equations.

In the remainder of this chapter, we discuss the important case where $\nabla f(x^*) = 0$ .To identify if a point x^* with zero gradient is a local maximum or local minimum, check the Hession

- If $H(x^*)$ is positive definite then x^* is local minimum.
- If $H(x^*)$ is negative definite, then x^* is a local maximum.

Remember that these properties can be chaked by computing the determinats of the principal minors.

Example: Find the local extrema of

$$f(x_1, x_2) = x_1^3 + x_3^3 - 3x_1x_2$$

This function is everywhere differentiable, so extrema can only occur at point x^* such that $\nabla f(x^*) = 0$

$$\nabla f(x) = \begin{pmatrix} 3x_1^2 & - & 3x_2 \\ 3x_2^2 & - & 3x_1 \end{pmatrix}$$

This equals 0 iff $(x_1, x_2) = (0,0)$ or $(1,1)$. The Hessian is

$$H(x) = \begin{pmatrix} 6x_1 & -3 \\ -3 & 6x_2 \end{pmatrix}$$

So

$$H(0,0) = \begin{pmatrix} 0 & -3 \\ -3 & 0 \end{pmatrix}$$

Let H_1 denote the first principal minor of H(0,0) and let H_2 denote its second principal minor. Then det $(H_1) = 0$ and det $(H_2) = -9$ Therefore H(0,0) is neither positive nor negative definite.

$$H(1,1) = \begin{pmatrix} 6 & -3 \\ -3 & 6 \end{pmatrix}$$

Its first principal minor has det $(H1) = 6 > 0$ and its second principal minor has det $(Hl)=36-9=25>0$ Therefore H(1,1) is positive definite, which implies that (1,1) is a local minimum.

Example: Jone and Jim invested \$20,000 in the design and development of a new product. They can manufacture it for \$2per unit. For the next step, they hired marketing consultants XYZ. In a nutshell, XYZ's conclusions are the following : if Jone and Jim spend \$a advertizing and sell the product at price p (per unit), they will sell

$$2{,}000 + 4\sqrt{a} - 20p \text{ Unit}$$

Using this figure, express the profit the Jone and Jim will make as a function of a and p. What price and level of advertising will maximize their profits?

The revenue from sales is $(2{,}000 + 4\sqrt{a} - 20p)p$

The production costs are $(2{,}000 + 4\sqrt{a} - 20p)2$ the development cost is \$20,000 and the cost of advertizing is a.

Therefore, Jone and Jim's profit is

$$f(p,a) = (2{,}000 + 4\sqrt{a} - 20p)(p-2) - a - 20{,}000$$

To find the maximum profit, we compute the partial derivatives of f and set them to 0:

$$\frac{\theta f}{\theta p}(p,a) = 2{,}040 + 4\sqrt{a} - 40p = 0,$$

$$\frac{\theta f}{\theta p}(p,a) = 2(p-2)/\sqrt{a} - 1 = 0,$$

Solving this system of two equations yields

p = 63.25 a = 15,006.25

We varify that this is a maximum by computing the Hessian.

$$H(x) = \begin{pmatrix} -40 & 2/\sqrt{a} \\ 2/\sqrt{a} & -(P-2)/a\sqrt{a} \end{pmatrix}$$

det $(H_1) = -40 < 0$ and det $(H_2) = 40(p-2)/a\sqrt{a} - 4/a > 0$

at the point p = 63.25, a = 15,006.25. So indeed, this solution maximizes profit.

Example: Find the local extrema of

$$f(x_1 x_2 x_3) = x_1^2 + (x_1 + x_2)^2 + (x_1 + x_3)^2$$

$$\frac{\theta f}{\theta x_1}(x) = 2x_1 + 2(x_1 + x_2) + 2(x_1 + x_3)$$

$$\frac{\theta f}{\theta x_1}(x) = 2(x_1 + x_2)$$

$$\frac{\theta f}{\theta x_5}(x) = 2(x_1 + x_3)$$

Setting these partial derivatives to 0 yields the unique solution $x_1 = x_2 = x_3 = 0$. The Hessian matrix is $H(0,0,0) = \begin{pmatrix} 6 & 2 & 2 \\ 2 & 2 & 0 \\ 2 & 0 & 2 \end{pmatrix}$

The determinants of the principal minors are det $(H_1) = 6 > 0$, det $(H_2) = 12 - 4 = 8 > 0$ and det $(H_3) = 24 - 8 - 8 = 8 > 0$. So H(0,0,0) is possitive definite and the solution $x_1 = x_2 = x_3 = 0$ is a minimum

Exercise: Find maxima or minima of the following functions when possible

$$(a)\, f(x_1, x_2, x_3) = -x_1^2 - 3x_2^2 - 10x_3^2 + 4x_1 + 24x_2 + 20x_3$$

$$(b)\, f(x_1, x_2, x_3) = x_1 x_2 + x_1 x_3 + x_3 x_1 - 2x_1 - 2x_2 - 2x_3$$

Exercise: Consider the function of three variables given by

$$f(x_1, x_2, x_3) = x_1^2 - x_1 - x_1 x_2 + x_2^2 - x_2 + x_3^4 - 4x_3,$$

(a) Compute the gradient $\nabla f(x_1, x_2, x_3)$

(b) Compute the Hessian matrix $H(x_1, x_2, x_3)$

(c) Use the gradient to find a local extremum of f.

Hints if $if\ x_3^3 = then\, x_3 = 1$

(d) Compute the three principal minors of the Hassion matrix and use them to identify this extremum as a local minimum or a local maximum.

GLOBAL OPTIMA

Finding global maxima and minima is harder. There is one case thar is of interest.

We say that a domain is convex if every line drawn between two points in the domain lies within the domain.

We say that a function f is convex if the line connecting any two points lies above the function. That is for all xy in the domain and $0 < \alpha < 1$ we have $f(\alpha x + (1-\alpha) \leq \alpha f(x) + (1-\alpha) f(y)$ as before

- If a function is convex on a convex domain, then any local mini mum is a global minimum.
- If funcrion is concave on a convex domain, then any local maxi mum is a global maximum.

To check that a function as convex on a domain, check that its Hessian matrix *H(x)* is positive semidefinite for every point *x* in the domain. To check that a function is concave, check that its Hessian is negative semidefinite for every point in the domain.

Example: Show that the function

$f(x_1, x_2, x_3) = x_1^4 + (x_1 + x_2)^2 + (x_1 + x_3)^2$ is conver over K^3

$$\frac{\theta f}{\theta r_1}(x) = 4x_1^3 + 2(x_1 + x_2) + 2(x_1 + x_3)$$

$$\frac{\theta f}{\theta r_2}(x) = 2(x_1 + x_2)$$

$$\frac{\theta f}{\theta r_5}(x) = 2(x_1 + x_3)$$

$$H(x_1, x_2, x_3) = \begin{pmatrix} 12x_1^2 + 4 & 2 & 2 \\ 2 & 2 & 0 \\ 2 & 0 & 2 \end{pmatrix}$$

The determinants of the principal minors are det $(H_1) = 12x_1^2 + 4 > 0$, det $(H_2) = 12x_1^2 \geq 0$ and det $(H_3) = 48x_1^2 \geq 0$. So $(H) = (x_1, x_2, x_3)$ is positive semidefinite for all $(x_1, x_2 x_3)$ in K^3.This implies that f is convex over K^3

Exercise: For each of the following, determine whether the function is convex, concave, or neither over K^3

$(a)\ f(x) = x_1 + x_2 - x_1^2 - x_2^2$

$(b)\ f(x) = 10x_1 + 20x_2$

$(c)\ f(x) = x_1^4 + x_1 x_2$

$(d)\ f(x) = x_1^2 - x_1 x_2 - 2x_2^2$

Exercise: Let the following function be defined for all points (x, y) in the plane $f(x, y) = 2xy - x^4 - x^2 - y^2$

(a) Write the gradient of the function f.

(b) Write the Hessian matrix of f.

(c) Is the function f convex, concave or neither?

(d) Use the gradient to find a local extremum of f.

(e) Identify this extremum as a minimum, a maximum or neiher.

17

Constrained Optimization

In constraint satisfaction, constraint optimization (also called constrained optimization) seeks for a solution maximizing or minimizing a cost function. A constraint optimization problem can be defined as a regular constraint satisfaction problem in which constraints are weighted and the goal is to find a solution maximizing the weight of satisfied constraints. Alternatively, a constraint optimization problem can be defined as a regular constraint satisfaction problem augumented with a number of "local" cost function. The aim of constraint optimization is find a solution to the problem whose cost, evaluated as the sum of the cost fuctions, while the cost functions are called soft constraints. These names illustrate that hard constraints are to be necessarily satisfied, while soft constraints only express a preference of some solutions (those having a high or low cost) over other ones (those haveng lower / higher cost).

Constraint optimization can be solved by branch and bound algorithms. These are backtracking algorithms storing the cost of the best solution found during execution and use it for avoiding part of the search. More precisely, whenever the algorithm encounters a partial solution that cannot be extended to form a solution of better cost than the stored best cost, the algorithm backtracks, instead of trying to extend this solution.

Assuming that cost is to be maximized, the efficiency of these algorithms depends on how the cost that can be obtained from extending a partial solution is evaluated. Indeed, if the algorithm can backtrack from a partial solution is evaluated. Indeed, if the algorithm can backtrack from a partial solution, part of the search is skipped. The lower the estimated cost, the better the algorithm, as a lower estimated cost is more likely to be lower than the best cost of solution found so far.

On the other hand, this estimated cost cannot be lower than tha effective cost that can be obtained by extending the solution, as otherwise the algorithm could backtrack while a solution better than the best found so far exists. As a result, the algorithm requires an upper bound on the cost that can be obtained from extending a partial solution, and this upper bound should as small as possible.

EQUALITY CONSTRAINTS

Suppose we have a problem:

Maximize

$$5-(x_{1-2})^2-2(x_2-1)^2$$

subject to

$$x_1+4x_2=3$$

If we ignore the constraint, we get the solution $x_1 = 2, x_2 = 1$ which is too a large for the constraint. Let us penalize oveselves λ for making the constraint too big. We end up with a function

$$L(x_1, x_2 \lambda) = 5-(x_1-x_2)^2-2(x_2-1)^2+\lambda(3-x_1-4x_2)$$

This function is called the Lagrangian the problem. The main idea is to adjust λ so thawe use exactly the right amout of the resouce.

$\lambda = 0$ leads to (2,1)

$\lambda = 1$ leads to (3/2,0)which uses too little of the resource.

$\lambda = 2/3$ gives (5/3,1/3) and the constraint is satisfied exactly.

We now expore this idea more formally. Given a nonlinear program (P) with equality constraints:

Minimize (or maximize)f(x)

subject to $g_1(x) = b_1$

$g_2(x) = b_2$

$g_m(x) = b_m$

a solution can be found using the Lagrngian:

$$L(x_i\lambda) = f(x) + \sum_{i=1}^{m} \lambda_i \big(b_i - g_i(x)\big)$$

(Note :- this can also be weitten)

$$f(x) - \sum_{i=1}^{m} \lambda_i (g_i(x) - b_i)$$

Each λ_i gives the proce associated with constraints

The reason L is of interest is the following :

Assume $x = (x_1^*, x_2^*, ...x_3^*)$ maximizes or minimizes f(x) subject to the constraints $g_i(x) = b_i$, for $i = 1,2,.........m$. Then either

(i) the vectors $\nabla g_1(x^*), \nabla g_2(x^*), ...\nabla g_m(x^*)$ are linearly dependent

or

(ii) there exists a vector $\lambda^* = (\lambda_1^*, \lambda_2^*, ..., \lambda_m^*)$ such that

$\nabla L(x^*, \lambda^*) = 0.$

L,c

$$\frac{\partial L}{\partial x_1}(x^*, \lambda^*) = \frac{\partial L}{\partial x_2}(x^*, \lambda^*) = \cdots = \frac{\partial L}{\partial x_n}(x^*, \lambda^*) = 0$$

and $\dfrac{\partial L}{\partial \lambda_1}(x^*, \lambda^*) = \cdots = \dfrac{\partial L}{\partial \lambda_m}(x^* \lambda^*) = 0$

Of course, Case (i) above cannot occur when there is only one constraint. The following example shows how it might occur.

Example 1:

Minimize $x_1 + x_2 + x_3^2$

subject to

$$x_1 = 1$$

$$x_1^2 + x_2^2 = 1$$

It is easy to check directly that the minimum is acheived at $(x_1 + x_2 + x_3) = (1,0,0)$. The associated Lagdangian is

$$L(x_1, x_2, x_3, \lambda_1, \lambda_2) = x_1 + x_2 + x_3^2 + \lambda_2 (1 - x_1^2 - x_2^2,)$$

Observe that $\frac{\partial L}{\partial x_2}(1,0,0,\lambda_1,\lambda_2) = 1$ for all λ_1, λ_2 and consequently $\frac{\theta L}{\theta r_2}$ does not vanish at the optimal solution. The reason for this is the following Let $g_1(x_1 + x_2 + x_3) = x_1$ and $g_2(x_1 + x_2 + x_3) = x_1^2 + x_2^2$ denote the left hand sides of the constraints. Then $\nabla g_1(x1,0,0) = (1,0,0)$ and $\nabla g_2(1,0,0) = (2,0,0)$ are linearly ependent vectors. So Case (i) occurs here!

Nevertheless, Case (i) will not concern us this course. When solving optimization problems with equality constraints, we will only look for solutions x^* that satisfy Case

(ii) Note that the equation

$$\frac{\partial L}{\partial \lambda_1}(x^*, \lambda^*) = 0$$

is nothing more than

$$b_i - g_i(x^*) = 0 \qquad or \qquad g_i(x^*) = b_i$$

In other word, taking the partials with respect to λ does nothing more than return the orginal constraints.

Once we have found candidate solutions x^* it is not always easy to figure out whether they correspond to a minimum, a maximum or neither. The following situation is one when we can conclude. If f(x) is concave and all of the $g_i(x)$ are linear, then any feasible x^* with a corresponding λ^* making $\nabla L(x^*, \lambda^*) = 0$ maximizes f(x) subject to the cibstraints. Similarly, if f(x) convex and each $g_i(x)$ is linear, then any x^* with a λ^* making $\nabla L(x^*, \lambda^*) = 0$ minimizes f(x) subject to the constraints.

Example 2:

Minimize $2x_1^2 + x_2^2$

Subject to

$x_1 + x_2 = 1$

$L(x_1, x_2, \lambda) = 2x_1^2 + x_2^2 + \lambda_1(1 - x_1 - x_2)$

$$\frac{\partial L}{\partial x_1}(x_1^*, x_2^*, \lambda^*) = 4x_1^* - \lambda_1^* = 0$$

$$\frac{\partial L}{\partial x_2}(x_1^*, x_2^*, \lambda^*) = 2x_2^* - \lambda_1^* = 0$$

$$\frac{\partial L}{\partial x_1}(x_1^*, x_2^*, \lambda^*) = 1 - x_1^* - x_1^* = 0$$

Now, the first two equations imply $2x_1^* = x_2^*$ Substituting into the final equation gives the solution $x_1^* = 1/3\, x_2^* = 2/3$ and $\lambda^* = 4/3$ with function value 2/3.

Since $f(x_1, x_2)$ in convex (its Hessian matrix $H(x_1, x_2) = \begin{pmatrix} 4 & 0 \\ 0 & 2 \end{pmatrix}$ is positive definite) and $g(x_1, x_2) = x_1, x_2$ is a linear function, the above solution minimizes $f(x_1, x_2)$ subject to the constraint.

GEOMETRIC INTERPRETATION

There is a geometric interpreatation of the conditions an optimal solution must satisfy. If we graph above Example 2, we get a picture like that in Figure 1.

Now, examine the gradients of f and g at the optimum point. They must point in the same direction, through they may have defferent lengths. This implies:

$$\nabla f(x^*) = \lambda \nabla g(x^*)$$

which along with the feasibility of x^* is exactly the condition $\nabla L(x^*, \lambda^*) = 0$ of case

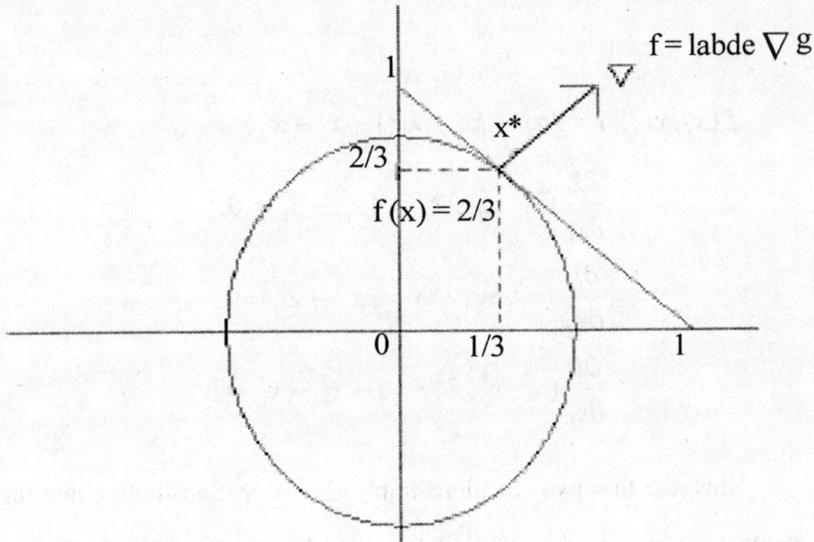

Figure 1

ECONOMIC INTERPRETATION

The values λ_i^* have an important economics interpretation: If the right hand side b_i of Constraint i is increased by Δ then the optimum objective value increases by approximately $\lambda_i^* \Delta$

In particular, consider the problem

Maximize p(x)

subject to

g(x) = b

where p(x) is a profit to maximize and b is a limited amount of resource. Then, the optimum Lagrange multiplier λ^* is the marginal value of the resource. Equivalently, if b were increased by Δ profit would increase by $\lambda^*\Delta$ This is an important result to remember. It will be used repeatedly in your Mangerial Economics course.

Similarly, if

Minimize c(x)

subject to

d(x) =b,

represent the minimum cost c(x) of meeting some demand b, the optimum Lagrange multiplier λ^* is themarginal cost of meeting the demand.

In Example 2.

Minimize $2x_1^2 + x_2^2$

subject to

$x_1 + x_2 = 1$

if we change the right hand side from 1 to 0.5 $(i.e.\Delta = 0.5)$ then the optimum objective function value goes from $\frac{2}{3}$ to roughly

$$\frac{2}{3}+\frac{4}{3}(0.05)=\frac{2.2}{3}.$$

If instead the righ hand side became 0.98, out estimate of the optimum objective function value would be

$$\frac{2}{3}+\frac{4}{3}(0.02)=\frac{1.92}{3},$$

***Example** 3*. Suppose we have a refinery that must ship funished goods to some storage tanks. Suppose further that there are two popelines, A and B to do the shipping. The cost of shipping x units Δ on ax^2 ; is the cost of shipping y units on B is by^2 where a > 0 are given. How can we ship Q units while minimizing cost? What happens to the cost if Q increases by r%?

Minimize $ax^2 + by^2 = Q$

Subject to

$$x + y = Q$$

$$L(x, y, \lambda) = ax^2 + by^2 + \lambda(Q - x - y)$$

$$\frac{\partial L}{\partial x}(x^*, y^*, \lambda^*) = 2ax^* - \lambda^* = 0$$

$$\frac{\partial L}{\partial y}(x^*, y^*, \lambda^*) = 2by^* - \lambda^* = 0$$

$$\frac{\partial L}{\partial \lambda}(x^*, y^*, \lambda^*) = Q - x^* - y^* = 0$$

The first two constraints give $x^* \frac{a}{b} y^*$ which leads to

$x^* = \dfrac{bQ}{a+b}$, $y^* = \dfrac{aQ}{a+b}$, $\lambda^* = \dfrac{2abQ}{a+b}$ and cost of $\dfrac{abQ^2}{a+b}$ The Hessian matrix $H(x_1, x_2) = \begin{pmatrix} 2a & 0 \\ 0 & 2b \end{pmatrix}$ is positive definite since a SPMgt; 0 and b; SPMgt ; So this solution minimize cost, given a,b,Q.

If Q increases by r % then the RHS of the constraint increases by $\Delta = rQ$ and the minimum cost increases by $\lambda * \Delta \dfrac{2abQ^2}{a+b}$ That is the minimum cost increases by 2 r%

Example 4 How should one divide his / her savings between three mutual founds with expected returns 10%, 10% and 15% repectively, so as to minimize risk while achiewig an expected return of 12%. We measure riskk as the varianceof the return on the investment (you will learn more about measuring risk in 45-733): when a fraction x of the savings is invested in Fund 1, y in Fond 2 and z in Fond 3, where x + y + z = 1, the variance of the return has been calculated to be

$$400x^2 + 800y^2 + 200xy + 1600z^2 + 400yz$$

So your problem is

$$\begin{aligned} \min \quad & 400x^2 + 800y^2 + 200xy + 1600z^2 + 400yz \\ s.t. \quad & x + y + 1.5z = 1.2 \\ & x + y + z = 1 \end{aligned}$$

using the Lagrangian method, the follwing optimal solution was obtained

$$x = 0.5 \quad y = 0.1 \quad z = 0.4 \quad \lambda_1 = 1800 \quad \lambda_2 = -1380$$

where λ_1 is the Langrange multiplier associated with the first constraint and λ_2 with the second constraint. The corresponding objective function value (i, e the varance on the return) is 390. If an expected return of 12.5% was desired (instead of 2 %), what would be (approximatcly) the correcponding variance of the return ?

Since $\Delta = 0.05$,The variance would increase by

$$\Delta\lambda_1 = 0.05 \times 1800 = 90$$

So the answer is 390 + 90 = 480.

Example : Record'm Records needs to produce 100 records at one or more of its three studies. The cost of producing x records at studio 1 is 10 x ; the cost of producing y records at studio 2 is $2y^2$ the cost of producing z records at studio 3 is $z^2 + 8z$

(a) Formulate the nonlincar program of producing the 100 records at minimum cost .

(b) What is the Lagrangian associated with your formulation is (a)?

(c) Solve this lagrangian. What is the optimal production plan ?

(d) What is the marginal cost of producing one extra gold record ?

(e) Union regulation require that exactly 60 hours of work be done at studios 2 and 3 combined. Each gold record requires 4 hours at studio 2 and 2 hours at studio 3. Formulate the problem of finding the optimal production plan. It is not necessary to actually solve the equations.

Exercise: (a) Solve the problem

Max $2x + y$

Subject $4x^2 + y^2 = 8$

(b) Estimate the change in the optimal objective function value when the right hand side increases by 5%, i,e. the right hand side increases from 8 to 8.4.

Exercise: (a) Solve the following constrained optimization problem using the method of Lagrange multipliers.

Max $In\ x + 2\ In\ ny + 3\ Inz$

Subject $x + y + z = 60$

(b) Estimate the change in the optimal objective function value if the right hand side of the constraint increases from 60 to 65.

EQUALITY AND INEQUALITY CONSTRAINTS

How do we handle both eqaulity and inequality constraints in (P)? Let (P) be:

Maximize f(x)

Subject to $g_1(x) = b_1$

$\vdots$

$g_m(x) = b_m$

$h_1(x) \leq b_1$

$\vdots$

$h_p(x) \leq h_p$

If you have a program with $\geq$ constraints convert it into $\leq$ by multiplying by - 1 Also convert a minimiztion.

The Lagrangian is

$$L(x,\lambda,\mu) = f(x) + \sum_{i=1}^{m} \lambda_i (b_i - g_i(x)) + \sum_{j=1}^{p} \mu j (d_j - h_j(x))$$

The fundamental result is the following:

Assume $x^* = (x_1^*, x_1^*, \ldots\ldots x_n^*)$ maximizes f(x) subject to the constraints $g_i(x) = b_j$, for $i = 1, 2, \ldots\ldots\ldots, m$ and $h_j(x) \le d_j$ for $j = 1, 2\ldots.., p$, Then either

(i) the vectors $\nabla g_1(x^*), \ldots\ldots, \nabla gm(x^*), \nabla h_1(x^*), \ldots\ldots,$ $\nabla h_p(x^*)$ are linearly dependent, or

(ii) there exists vectors $\lambda^*, = (\lambda_1^*, \ldots\ldots\ldots \lambda_m^*)$ and $\mu^* = (\mu_1^*, \ldots\ldots, \mu_p^*)$ such that

$$\nabla f(x^*) - \sum_{j-1}^{m} \lambda_i^* \nabla g_i(x^*) - \sum_{j=1}^{p} \mu_j^* \nabla h_j(x^*) = 0$$

$$\mu_j^i (h_j(x^*) - d_j) = 0 \text{ (Complementarity)}$$

$$\mu_1^* \ge 0$$

In this course, we will not concern ourselves with Case (i). We will only look for candidate solutions x^* for which we can find λ^* and μ^* satisfying equations in Case (ii) above.

In general, to solve these equations, you begin with complementarity and note that either μ_j^i must be zero or $h_j(x^*) - d_j = 0$. Based on the various possibilities, you come up with one or more candidate solutions. If there is an optimal solution, then one of your candidates will be it.

The above conditions are called the Kuhn- Tucker (or Karush - Kuhn-Tucker) conditions. Why do they make sense ?

For x^* optimal, some of the inequalities will be tight add some not. These not tight can be ignored (and will have corresponding price

$\mu_j^* = 0$). These that are tight can be treated as equalities which leads to the previous Lagrangian stuff. So

$$\mu_j^* = (h_j(x^*) - d_j) = 0 \text{ (Complementarity)}$$

forces either the price μ_j^* to be 0 or the constraint to be tight

Example 1

Maximize $x^3 - 3x$

Subject to $x \leq 2$

The Lagrangian is

$$L = x^3 - 3x + \mu(2 - x)$$

So we need

$$3x^3 - 3x - \mu = 0$$

$$x \leq 2$$

$$\mu(2 - x) = 0$$

$$\mu \geq= 0$$

Typically, at this point we mist break the analysis into cases depending on the complementarity conditions.

If $\mu = 0$ then $3x^3 - 3 = 0$ so $x = 1$ *or* $x = -1$, Both are feasible $f(1) = -2, f(-1) = 2$

If $x = 2$ then $\mu = 9$ which again is fessible. Since $f(2) = 2$ we have two solutions: $x = -1$ and $x = 2$

Example 2

Minimize $(x - 2)^2 + 2(y - 1)^2$

Subject to

$x + 4y \leq 3$

$x \geq y$

First we convert to standerd from, to get

Maximize $(x-2)^2 - 2(y-1)^2$

Subject to

$x - 4y \le 3$

$-x + y \le 0$

$$L(x, y, \mu_{1,}\mu_2) = -(x-2)^2 - 2(y-1)^2$$

$$+\mu_1(3-x-4y)+\mu_2(0+x-y)$$

which gives optimality conditions

$$-2(x-2) - \mu_1 + \mu_2 = 0$$
$$-4(y-1) - 4\mu_1 - \mu_2 = 0$$
$$\mu_1(3 - x - 4y) = 0$$
$$\mu_1(x - y) = 0$$
$$x + 4y \le 3$$
$$-x + y \le$$
$$\mu_1, \mu_2 \ge 0$$

Since there are two complementarity conditions, there are four cases to check :

$\mu_1 = 0, \mu_2 = 0$: gives $x = 2, y = 1$ which is not feasible

$\mu_1 = 0, x - y = 0$: gives $x = 4/3, y = 4/3, \mu_2 = -4/3$ which is not feasible.

$\mu_1 = 0, 3 - x - 4y = 0$: gives $x = 5/3, y = 1/3, \mu_2 = 2/3$ which is O.K.

$3 - x - 4y = 0 x - y = 0$ gives $x = 3/5, y = 3/5, \mu_1 = 22/25, \mu_1 = -48/25$ which is not feasible.

Since it is clear that there is an optimal solution, $x = 5/3, y = 1/3$ is it.

ECONOMIC INTERPRETATION

The economic interpretation is essentially the same as the equality case. If the right hand side of a constraint is chaged by a small amount Δ then the optimal objective changes by $\mu^* \Delta$ where μ^* is the optimal Lagrange multiplier corresponding to that contraint.

Note that if the constraint is not tight then the objective does not change (since then $\mu^* = 0$).

HANDLING NONNEGATIVITY

A special type of constraint is nonnegativity. If you have a constraint $x_k \geq o$ you can write this as $-x_k \leq o$ and use the above result. This constraint would get a Lagrange multiplier of its own, and would be treated just like every other constraint.

An alternative is to treat nonnegativity implicitly. If x_k must be non-negative:

1. Change the equality associated with its partial to a less than or equal to zero: x_k =0

$$\frac{\partial f(x)}{\partial x_k} - \sum_i \lambda_i \frac{\partial h_j(x)}{\partial x_k} - \sum_j \mu_j \frac{\partial h_j(x)}{\partial x_k} \leq 0$$

2. Add a new complementarity constraint:

$$\frac{\partial f(x)}{\partial x_k} - \sum_i \lambda_i \frac{\partial h_i(x)}{\partial x_k} - \sum_j \mu_j \frac{\partial h_j(x)}{\partial x_k} x_k = 0$$

3. Don't forget that $x_k \geq 0$ for x to be feasible.

SUFFICIENCY OF CONDITIONS

The Karush-Kuhn-Tucker conditions give us candidate optimal solutions x^* When are these conditions sufficient for optimality? That is, given x^* with λ^* and μ^* satisfying the KKT conditions, when can we be certain that it is an optimal solution?

The most general condition available is:

1. f(x) is concave, and

2. the feasible region forms a convex region.

While it is straightforward to determine if the objective is concave by computing its Hessian matrix, it is not so easy to tell if the feasible region is convex. A useful condition is as follows:

The feasible region is convex if all of the $g_i(x)$ are linear and all of the $h_j(x)$ are convex

If this condition is satisfied, then any point the satisfies the KKT conditions gives a point that maximizes f(x) subject to the constraints.

Example 4. 2.3 Suppose we can buy a chemical for $ 10 per ounce. There are only 17.25 oz available. We can transform this chemical into two products: A and B. Transforming to costs $3 per oz, while transforming to B costs $5 per oz. If x_1 oz of A are produced, the price we command for A is $30 - x_1 oz of B are produced, the price we get for B is $50 - x_2 How much chemical should we buy, and what should we transform it to ?

There are many ways to model this. Let's let x_3 be the amount of chemical we purchase. Here is one model:

Maximize $x_1(30 - x_1) + x_2(50 - 2x_2) - 3x_1 - 5x_2 - 10x_3$

Subject to $x_1 + x_2 - x_3 \le 0$

$x_3 \le 17.25$

The KKT conditions are the above feasibility constraints along with:

$$30 - 2x_1 - 3 - \mu_1 = 0$$

$$50 - 4x_2 - 5 - \mu_1 = 0$$

$$-10 + \mu_1 - \mu_2 = 0$$

$$\mu_1(-x_1 - x_2 + x_3) = 0$$

$$\mu_1(17.25 - x_3) = 0$$

$$\mu_1, \mu_2 > 0$$

There are four cases to check:

$\mu_1 = 0, \mu_2 = 0$ This gives us -10=0 is the third constraint, so is infeasible.

$\mu_1 = 0, x_3 = 17.25$ This gives $\mu_2 = -10$ so is infeasible.

$-x_1 - x_2 + x_3 = 0,\ \mu_2 = 0,$ This gives $\mu_1 = 10, x_1 = 8.5,$ $x_2 = 8.75, x_3 = 17.25$ which is feasible.

Since the objective is concave and the constraints are linear, this must be an optimal solution. So There is no point is going through the last case $(-x_1 - x_2 + x_3 = 0, x_3 = 17.25)$. We are done with $x_1 = 8.5$, $x_2 = 8.75$ and $x_3 = 17.25$

What is the value of being able to purchase 1 more unit of chemical ?

This questions is equivalent to increasing the right hand side of the constraint $x_3 \le 17.25$ by 1 unit. Since the corresponding lagrangian value is 0, there is no value in increasing the right hand side.

Review of Optimality Conditions:

The following reviews what we have learned so far:

Single Variable (Unconstrained)

Solve f(x) = 0 to get candidate x^*

If $f''(x^*) > 0$ then x^* is a local min $f''(x^*) < 0$ then x^* is a local max

If f(x) convex then a local min is a global min.

f(x) is concave then a local max is a global max

Multiple Variable (Unconstrained)

Solve $\nabla f(x) = 0$ to get candidate x^*

If $H(x^*)$ is positive difinite then x^* is a local min. $H(x^*)$ is negative definite x^* is a local max.

If f(x) is convex then a local min is a global min.

f(x) is convex then a local max is a global max.

Multiple Variable (Equality constrained) Form lagrangian

$$L(x,\lambda) = f(x) + \sum_i \lambda_i (b_i - g_i(x))$$

Solve $\nabla L(x,\lambda) = 0$ to get dandidate x^* (and λ^*)

Best x^* is optimum of optimum exists.

Multiple Variable (Equality and Inequality constrained)

Put into standard form (maximize and $\leq$ constraints)

Form Lagrangian

$$L(x,\lambda) = f(x) + \sum_i \lambda_i (b_i - g_i(x)) + \sum_j \mu_j (d_i - h_i(x))$$

Solve

$$\nabla f(x) - \sum_i \lambda_i \nabla g_i(x) - \sum_j \mu_j \nabla h_i(x) = 0$$

$$g_i(x) = b_i$$

$$h_j(x) \leq d_j$$

$$\mu_j(d_j - h_j(x) = 0$$

$$\mu_j \geq 0$$

to get candidates x^*(and $\lambda *^{\mu^*}$)

Best x^* is optimum if optimum exists.

Any x^* is optimum if f(x) concave $g_i(x)$ Convex, $h_j(x)$ linear.

18

Modelling with Linear Programming

INTRODUCTION

Sil Computers makes quarterly decisions about their product mix. While their full product line includes hundreds of products, we will consider a simpler problem with just two products: notebook computers and desktop computers. Sil Computers would like to know how many of each product to produce in order to maximize profit for the quarter.

There are a number of limits on what Sil Computers can produce. The major constraintsare as follows:

1. Each computer (either notebook or desktop) requires a Processing Chip. Due to tightness in the market, our supplier has allocated 10,000 such chips to us.

2. Each computer requires memory. Memory comes in 16MB chip sets. A notebook computer has 16MB memory installed (so needs 1 chip set) while a desktop computer has 32MB (so requires 2 chip sets). We received a great deal on chip sets, so have a stock of 15,000 chip sets to use over the next quarter.

3. Each computer requires as assembly time. Due to tight toler ances, a notebook computer takes more time to assemble: 4 minutes versus 3 minutes for a desktop. There are 25,000 minutes of assembly time available in the next quarter.

Given current market conditions, material cost, and our production system, each notebook computer produced generate $750 profit, and each desktop produces $1000 profit.

There are many questions Sil Computer might ask. The most obvious are such things as "How many of each type a computer should SilComputer produce in the next quarter?" "What is the maximum profit SilComputer can make?" Less obvious, but perhaps of more managerial interest are "How mich should Sil Computer be willing to pay for an extra memory chip set?" "What is the effect of losing 1,000 munutes of assembly time due to an unexpected machine failure?" " How much profit would we need to make on a 32MB notebook computer to justify its production?"

Linear programming gives us a muchanism, for answering all of thesr questions queckly and easily. There are three steps in applying linear programming : modeling, solving and interpreting.

MODELING

We begin by modeling this problem. Modeling a problem using linear programming involves writing it in the language of linear programming. There are rules about what you can and cannot do within linear programming. These rules are in place to make certain that the remaining steps of the process (solving and interpreting) can be successful. Key to a linear program are the decision variables, objective and constraints.

Decision Variables. The decision variables represent (unknown) decisions to be made. This is in contrast to problem data, which are values that are either given or can be simply calculated from what is given. For this problem, the decision variables are the number of notebooks to produce and the number of desktops to produce. We will represent these unknown values by x_1 and x_2 respectively. To make the numbers more manageable, we will let x_1 be the number of 1000 notebook produced (so $x_1 = 5$ means a decision to produce 5000 notebooks) and x_2 be the number of 1000desktops, Note that a value like the quarterly profit is not(in this model) a decision variable: it is an outcome of decisions x_1 and x_2 .

Objective. Every linear program has an objective. This objective is to be either minimized or maximized. This objective has to be linear in the decision variables, which means it must be the sum of constants times decision variables. $3x_1 - 10x_2$ is a linear function. $x_1 x_2$ is not a linear function, In this case, our objective is to maximize the function $750x_1 + 1000x_2$ (what units is this in?)

Constraints:- Every linear program also has constraints limiting feasible decisions. Here we have four types of constraints: Processing Chips, Memory Sets, Assembly, and Nonnegativety.

In order to satisty the limit on the number of chips available, it is necessary that $x_1 + x_2 \le 10$ If this were not the case (say $x_1 = x_2 = 6$), the decisions would not be implementable (12,000 chips would be required, though we only have 10,000). Linear programming cannot handle arbitrary restrictions: once again, the restrictions have to be linear. This means that a linear function of the decidion variables must be related to a constant, where related can mean less than or equal to, greater than or equal to, or equal to. So $3x_1 - 2x_2 \geq 10$ is a linear constraint, as is $-x_1 + x_3 = 6x_1x_2 \leq 10$ is not a linear constraint, nor is $x_1 + 3x_2 < 3$ Our constraint for Processing Chips $x_1 + x_2 \leq 10$ is a linear constraint,

The constraint for memory clip sets is $x_1 + 2x_2 \leq 15$ a linear constraint,Our constraint on assembly can be written $4x_1 + 3x_2 \leq 25$ again a linear constraint

Finally. we do not want to cosider decisions like $x_1 = -5$ where production is negatove. We add the linear constraints $x_1 \geq 0 x_2 \geq 0$ to enforce nonnegativity of production.

Final Model. This gives us the complete model of this problem:

Maximize $700x_1 + 1000x_2$

Subject to
$$\begin{aligned} x_1 + x_2 &\leq 10 \\ x_1 + 2x_2 &\leq 15 \\ 4x_1 + 3x_2 &\leq 25 \\ x_1 &\geq 0 \\ x_2 &\geq 0 \end{aligned}$$

Formulating a problem as a linear program means going through the above process to clearly define the decision variables, objective, and constraints.

SOLVING THE MODEL

Models are useful in their own right: they allow for a formal difinition of a problem and can be useful in thinking about a problem. Linear programming models are particularly useful, however, because it is easy to have a computer solve for the optimal decision values.

For a model with only two variables, it is possible to solve the problem without a computer by drawing the feasible region and determining how the objective is optimized on the region. We go through that process here. The purpose of this exercise is to give you intuition and understanding of linear programming models and their solution. In any real application, you would use a computer to solve even two variable problems.

We can represent a modet with teo variables by labeling the axes of a graph with each of the variables. The entire graph then represents possible decisions. Constraints are represented by lines on the graph, with the feasible region lying on one side of the line.

The follwing figure illustrates this with the constraint $x_1 + x_2 \leq 10$

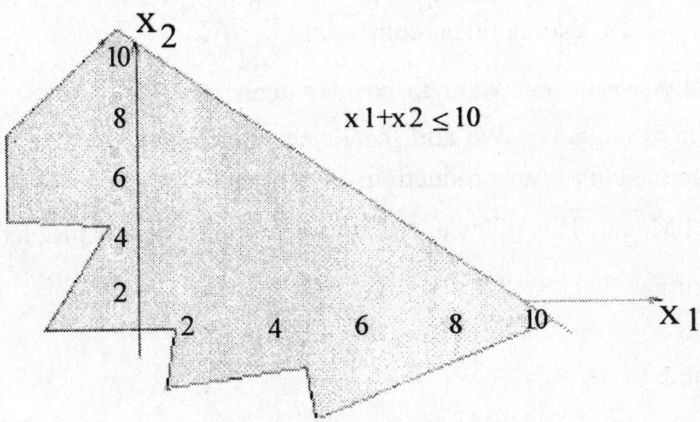

Figure 1: Single Constraint

We can continue this process and add in all of the constraints. Since every constraint must be satisfied, the resulting feasible region is the intersection of the feasible region for each constraint. This is shown in the following fugure2.

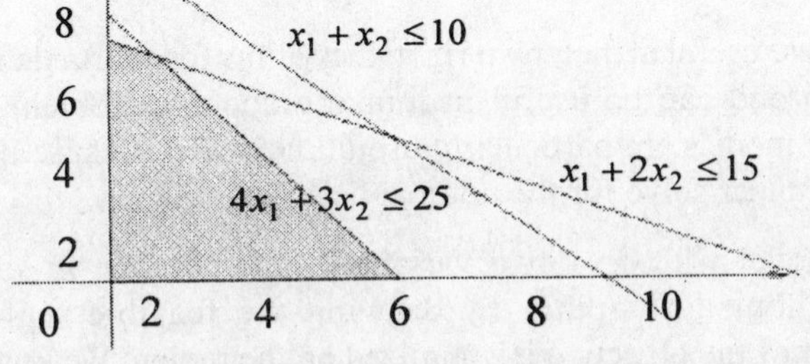

Figure 2: All Constraints

Note the just graphing the model gives us information we did not have before. It seems that the Chip constraint ($x_1 + x_2 \leq 10$) plays little role in this model. This constraint is dominated by other constraints.

Now, how can we find the optimal solution? We can include the objective function on this diagram by drawing iso-profit lines: lines along which the profit is the same. Since our goal is to maximize the profit, we can push the isoprofit line out unitil moving it any further would result in no feasible point. Clearly the optimal profit occuts to point X.

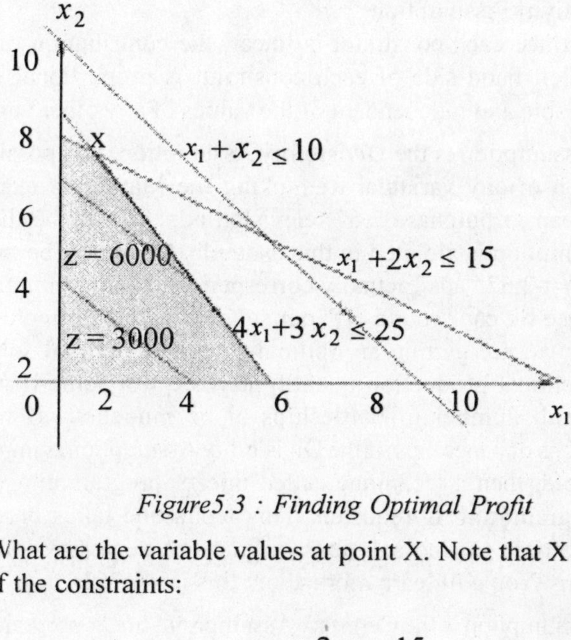

Figure5.3 : Finding Optimal Profit

What are the variable values at point X. Note that X is the intersection of the constraints:

$$x_1 + 2x_2 = 15$$
$$4x_1 + 3x_2 = 25$$

We discussed in the previous section how to solve such equations:the solution here is $x_1 = 1$ and $x_2 = 7$. The optimal decision is to produce 1.000 notebooks and 7,000 desktops, for a profit or $7,750,000.

COMMON FEATURE

Hidden in our models of these problems are a number of assumptions. The usefulness of a model is directly related to how close reality matches up with these assumptions.

The first assumption is due to the linear form or our functions. Since the objective is linear, the contribution to the objective of any decision variable is proportional to the value of the decision variable. Producing twice as much of a product produces twice as much profit; buying twice as many pages of ads costs twice as much. This is the Proportionality Assumption.

Furthermore, the contribution of a variable to the objective is independent of the values of the other variables. One notebook computer is worth $750, independent of how many desktop computers we produce. This is the Additivity Assumption.

Similarly, since each constraint is linear, the contribution of each variable to the left hand side of each constraint is proportional to the value of the variable and independent of the values of any other variable.

The next assumption is the Divisibility Assumption: it is possible to take any fraction of any variable. Rethinking the Marketing example, what does it mean to purchase 2.67 television ads? It may be that the divisibility assumption is violated in this example. Or, it may be that the units are such that 2.67 "ads" actually corresponds to 2666.7 minutes of ads, in which case we can "round off" our solution to 2667 minutes with little doubt that we are getting an optimal or nearly optimal solution. Similarly, a fractional production quantity may be worisome if we are producing a small number of battleships or be innocuous if we are producting millions of paperclips. If the Divisibility Assumption is important and does not hold, then a technique called integer programming rather than linear programming is required. This technique takes orders of magnitude more time to find solutions but may be necessary to create realistic solutions. You will learn more about this in 45-761.

The final assumption is the Certainty Assumption: linear programming allows for no uncertainty about the numbers. An ad will reach the given number of people; the number of assembly hours we give will certainly be avilable.

It is very rare that a problem will meet all of the assumptions exactly. That does not negate the usefulness of a model. A model can still give useful managerial insight even if reality differs slightly from the rigorous requirements of the model. For instance, the knowledge that our chip inventory is more than sufficient holds in our first model even if the proportionality assumptions are not satisfied completly.

LINEAR PROGRAMMING MODELS

Linear programming models are found in almost every field of business. The next sections go through a number of problems, showing how to model them by the appropriate choice of decision variables, objective, and constraints. In all cases, we will describe the problem and give a model.

DIET PROBLEM

What is the perfect diet?An ideal diet would meet or exceed basic nutritional requirements, be inexpensive, have variety, and be "pleasing to the palate". How can we find such a diet?

Suppose the only foods in the worlds are as follows:

Food	Serving Size	Energy (keal)	Proteim (g)	Caleuim (mg)	Price (ceats/serving)	Limit (serving/day)
Oatmeal	28g	110	4	2	3	4
Chicken	100g	205	32	12	24	3
Eggs	2 Large	160	13	54	13	2
While Milk	237cc	160	8	285	9	8
Cherry Pic	170g	420	4	22	20	2
Pork & Beans	260g	260	14	80	19	2

After consulting with nutitionists, we decree that a satisfactory diet has at least 2000 kcal of energy, 55 g of protein, and 800 mg of calcium (vitamins and iron are supplied by pills). While some of us would be happy to subsist on 10 servings of pork and beans, we have decided to impose variety by having a limit on the number of servings/day for each or our six foods. What is the least cost satisfactory diet?

First we decide on decision variables. Let us label the foods 1,2.............6, and let x_i represent the number of servings of food i in the diet.

Our objective is to minimize cost, which can be written

$$3x_1 + 24x_2 + 13x_3 + 9x_4 + 20x_5 + 19x_6$$

We have constraints for energy, protein calcuim, and for each serving/day limit. This gives the formilation.

Minimize $3x_1 + 24x_2 + 13x_3 + 9x_4 + 20x_5 + 19x_6$

Subject to

$$110x_1 + 205x_2 + 160x_3 + 160x_4 + 420x_5 + 260x_6 \geq 2000$$
$$x_1 + 32x_2 + 13x_3 + 8x_4 + 4x_5 + 14x_6 \geq 55$$
$$2x_1 + 12x_2 + 54x_3 + 285x_4 + 22x_5 + 80x_6 \geq 800$$
$$x_1 \leq 4$$
$$x_2 \leq 3$$
$$x_3 \leq 2$$
$$x_4 \leq 8$$
$$x_5 \leq 2$$
$$x_6 \leq 2$$
$$x_i \geq 0$$
for all i

The creation of optimal diets was one of the first uses of linear programming. Some difficulties with linear programming include difficulties in formulating "palatability" requirements, and issues of divisibility (no one wants to eat half a green bean). These linear programming models do give an idea on how much these palatability requirements are costing.

WORKFORCE PLANNING

Consider a restaurant tht is open senen days a week. Based on past experience, the number of workers needed on a particular day is given as follows:

Day	Mon	Tue	Wed	Thu	Fri	Sat	Sun
Number	14	13	15	16	19	18	11

Every worker works five consecutive days, and then takes two days off , repeating this pattern indefinitely. How can we minimize the number of workers that staff the restaurant?

A natural first attempt at this problem is to let x_i be the number of people working on day i. Note that such a variable definition does not match up with what we need to find. It does us no good to know that 15 people work Monday, 13 people Tuesday, and so on because it does not tell us how many workers are needed. Some workers will work both

Monday and Tuesday, some only one day, some niether of those workers will work both Monday and and Tuesday, some only one day, some neither of those days. Instead, let the days be numbers 1 through 7 and let x_i be the number of workers who begin their five day shift on day i. Our objective is clearly:

$$x_1 + x_2 + x_3 + x_4 + x_5 + x_6 + x_7$$

Consider the constraint for Monday's staffing level of 14. Who works on Monday? Clearly those Who start their shift on Monday (x_1) Those who start on Tuesday(x_2) do not work on Monday, nor do these who start on Wednesday (x_3) Those who start on Thursday (x_4) do work on Monday, as do those on Friday, Saturday and Sunday. This gives the constraint:

Similar arguments give a total formulation of :

$$x_1 + x_4 + x_5 + x_6 + x_7 \geq 14$$

Minimize $\sum_i x_i$

Subject to
$$x_1 + x_4 + x_5 + x_6 + x_7 \geq 14$$
$$x_1 + x_2 + x_5 + x_6 + x_7 \geq 13$$
$$x_1 + x_2 + x_3 + x_6 + x_7 \geq 15$$
$$x_1 + x_2 + x_3 + x_4 + x_7 \geq 16$$
$$x_1 + x_2 + x_3 + x_4 + x_5 \geq 19$$
$$x_2 + x_3 + x_4 + x_5 + x_6 \geq 18$$
$$x_3 + x_4 + x_5 + x_6 + x_7 \geq 11$$
$$x_i 1 \geq 0$$
for all i

Workforce modeling is a well developed area. Note that our model has only one type of shift, but the model is easily extended to other types of shifts, with differing shift costs.

FINANCIAL PORTFOLIO

In your finance cources, you will learn a number or techniques for creating "optimal" portfolios. The optimality of a portfolio depends heavily on the model used for defining risk and other aspects or financial instruments. Here is a particularly simple model that is amenable to linear programming techniques.

Consider a mortgage term with $100.000,000 to finance various investment. There are five categories of loans, each with an associated return and risk (1-10, 1 best)

Loan / Investment	Return(%)	Risk
Frist Mortgages	9	3
Second mortggages	12	6
Personal Loans	15	8
Commcerial Loans	8	2
Goverment Securitics	6	1

Any uninvested money goes into into a savings account with no risk and 3% return. The goal for the mortgage team is to allocate the money to the categories so as to:

(a) Maximize the average return per dollar

(b) Have an average risk of no more than 5 (all averages and fractions taken over the invested money (not over the saving account)).

(c) Invest at least 20% in commercial loans.

(d) The amount in second mortgages and personal loans combined should be no higher than the amount in first mortgages.

Let the investments be numbered 1...5, and let x_i be the amount invested in investment i. Let x_s be the amount in the savings account. The objective is to maximize

$$9x_1 + 12x_2 + 15x_3 + 8x_4 + 6x_5 + 3x_5$$

subject to

$$x_1 + x_2 + x_3 + x_4 + x_5 + x_5 = 100,000,000.$$

Now, let's look at the average risk. Since we want to take the average over only the invested amount, a direct translation of this constraint is:

$$\frac{3x_1 + 6x_2 + 8x_3 + 2x_4 + x_5}{x_1 + x_2 + x_3 + x_4 + x_5} \le 5$$

This constraint is not linear, but we can cross multiply, and simplify to get the equivalent linear constraint:

$$-2x_1 + x_2 + 3x_3 - 3x_4 - 4x_5 \leq 0$$

Similarly we need

$$x_4 \geq 0.2(x_1 + x_2 + x_3 + x_4 + x_5)$$

or

$$-0.2x_1 - 0.2x_2 - 0.2x_3 - 0.8x_4 - 0.2x_5 \geq 0$$

The final constraint is

$$x_2 + x_3 - x_1 \leq 0$$

Together with nonnegativity, this gives the entire formulation.

Optimal portfolios do not just happen: they must be calculated, and there is a constant interplay between models and solvability. Linear programming models provide great modeling power with a great limit: the handling of risk must be done in a linear fashion (like our Risk factors here). Other models you will see in finance will look at the co-variance of returns between investments, a fundamentally nonlinear effect. This can give rise to nonlinear models like those that try to minimize variance subject to return requirements. It is very difficult to embed idiosyncratic constraints (like (c) and (d) here) in such models.

PRODUCTION OVER TIME

Many problems are multiperiod, where a series of decisions have to be made over time. For instance, in our very first Sil Computer example, production decisions for computers have to be made with the future in mind. In this example, it would be easy to work with both desktop and notebook computers but let's work just with notebook computers.

Sil Computer needs to meet the demand of its largest corporate and educational customers for notebook computers over the next four quarters (before its current model becomes obsolete). SilComputer currently has 5,000 notebook computers in inventory. Expected demand over the next four quarters for its notebook is 7,000; 15,000; 10,000; and 8,000. Sil Computer has sufficient capacity and material to produce up to 10,000 computers in each quarter at a cost of $2000 per notebook. By using overtime, up to an additional 2,500 computers can be produced at a cost of $2200 each. Computers produced in a quarter can be used either to meet that quarter's demand, or be held in inventory for use later. Each computer in inverntory is charged $100 to reflect carying costs.

How should Sil Computer meet its demand for notebooks at minimum cost?

The decisions seem to be how many of each computer to produce in each period at regular time, how many to produce at overtime, and how much inventory to carry in each period. Let's denote our time periods t = 1,2,3,4. Let x_t be the number of notebooks produced in period t at regular time and y_t be the number of notebooks produced in period t at overtime. Finally, let i_t be the inventory at the end of period t.

Look at the first quater: how are these variables restructed and related?

Clearly we need $x_1 \le 10000$ and $y_1 \le 2500$ Now, anything that starts as inventory or is produced in the period must either be used to meet demand or ends up as inventory at the end of period 1. This means:

$$5000 + x_1 + y_1 = 7000 + i_t$$

For period 2, in addition to the upper bounds, we get the constraint

$$i_t + x_2 + y_2 = 15000 + i_2$$

For period 3, we get

$$i_2 + x_3 + y_3 = 10000 + i_3$$

and for period 4 (assuming no inventory at the end):

$$i_3 + x_4 + y_4 = 8000$$

Our objective charges 2000 for each x, 2200 for each y, and 100 for each i:

$2000\,x_1\ +2000\,x_2\ +2000\,x_3\ +2000\,x_4\ +2000\,y_1\ +2000\,y_2\ +2000\,y_3$ $+2000\,y_4\ +100\ i_1\ \ +100\,i_2\ \ +100\ \ i_3$

The constraints tracking where production goes are known as conservation constraints, and model the requirement that production never disappears. Whenever you have multiple types of variables in a formulation, be certain to think about whether there are necessary constraints that link them.

INVESTING OVER TIME

We are going to manage an investment portfolio over a 6 year time horizon. We begin with \$1000, and at various times we can invest in one or more of the following :

Savings account X, annual yield 5%.

Security Y, 2- year maturity, total yield 12% if bought now, 11% there for

Security Z, 3- year maturity, total yield 18%.

Security W, 4- year maturity, total yield 24%

To keep things simple we will assume that each security can be bought in any denomination. (This assumption can be relaxed if one uses integer or dynamic programming) We can make savings deposits or withdrawals anytime. We can buy Security Y any year but year 3. We can buy Secutity Z anytime after the first year. Security W, now available, is a one-time opportunity.

We let x_t be the amount of money invested in the savings account X at the beginning of year t, and similarly for y_t, z_t and w_t We will put any money not tied up in securities into the savings account. The situation is summed up in the figure.

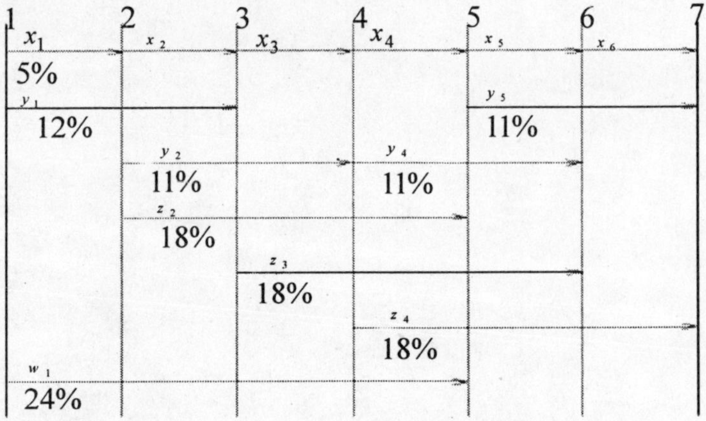

Figure 6: Possible investments over a 6-year horizon

The problem is really a kind of inventory problem. In a given year, the amount of money carried forward from the previous year (in savings), plus the yield from securities that mature that year, equals the amount invested in new securities plus the amount of money left over for next year. There is one twist: inventory grows while in storage. (In real inventory problems, stock often decreases over time due to spoilage, etc., and this can be reflected in negative "interest" rates.) Let v be the final yield when all securities are cashed in at the end of the sixth year. Then if the objective is to maximize final yield, the LP is,

$$
\begin{aligned}
&\max\ v \\
&s.t\ .x_1 + y_1 + w_1 = 1000 \\
&\quad x_2 + y_2 + z_2 = 1.05\,x_1 \\
&\quad x_3 + z_3 = 1.05\,x_2 + 1.12\,y_1 \\
&\quad x_4 + y_4 + z_4 = 1.05\,x_3 + 1.11\,y_2 \\
&\quad x_5 + y_5 = 1.05\,x_4 + 1.18\,z_2 + 1.24\,w_1 \\
&\quad x_6 = 1.05\,x_5 + 1.11\,y_4 + 1.18\,z_3 \\
&\quad v = 1.05\,x_6 + 1.11\,y_5 + 1.18\,z_4, \\
&\quad x_t, y_t, z_t, w_t \geq 0
\end{aligned}
$$

The Final assets come ot \$1387.6 an average annual yield of 5.61%

19

Sampling Methods

A population is the entire set of items or people that form the subjects of study in an investigation and a sample is a subset of a population. Companies need to know about the populations they deal with: populations of customers, employees, suppliers, products and so on. Typically these populations are very large, so large that they are to all intents and purposes infinite.

Gathering data about such large populations is likely to be very expensive, time-consuming and to a certain extent impractical. The scale of expense can be immense; even governments of large countries only commit resources to survey their entire populations, that is, to conduct a census, about every ten years.

The amount of time involved in surveying the whole population means that it may be so long before the results are available that they are completely out of date. There may be some elements within the population that simply cannot be included in a survey of it; for instance, a car manufacturer may want to conduct a survey of all customers buying a certain model three years before in order to gauge customer satisfaction. Inevitably a number of those customers will have died in the period since buying their car and thus cannot be included in the survey.

To satisfy their need for data about the populations that matter to them without having to incur great expense or wait a long time for results companies turn to sampling, the process of taking a sample from a population in order to use the sample data to gain insight into the entire population. Although not as accurate as the results of a population survey, sample results can be precise enough to serve the purposes of the investigation.

The downside of sampling is that many different samples can be taken from the same population, even if the samples are the same size. You can work out the number of samples of n items that could be selected from a population of N items:

$$\text{Number of samples size n} = \frac{N!}{n!(N-n)!}$$

We can use this to work out the number of samples of size 6 that could be selected from a very small population of just 20 items:

$$\text{Number of samples size 6} = \frac{20!}{6!14!}\ 38{,}760$$

You can imagine that the number of samples that could be selected from a much larger population will be so very large as to border on the infinite. Each of the samples you could select from a population inevitably excludes much of the population, so sample results will not be precisely the same as those from the entire population. There will be differences known as sampling errors between sample results and the results of a population survey and furthermore different samples will yield different results and hence different sampling errors.

In this chapter you will find details of a variety of sampling methods, but before we look at them we need to consider what companies might look for in sampling, and what they would prefer to avoid.

BIAS IN SAMPLING

The point of selecting a sample from a population is to study it and use the results to understand the population. To be effective a sample should therefore reflect the population as a whole. However, there is no guarantee that the elements of the population that are chosen for the sample will collectively reflect the population. Even if the population is quite small there will be an enormous number of combinations of elements that you could select in a sample. Inevitably some of these samples will represent the entire population better than others.

Although it is impossible to avoid the possibility of getting an unrepresentative sample, it is important to avoid using a sampling method that will almost invariably lead to your getting an unrepresentative sample. This means avoiding bias in selecting your sample.

Effective methods of sampling are those that minimize the chances of getting unrepresentative samples and allow you to anticipate the degree of sampling error using appropriate probability distributions. Such methods should give every element of the population the same chance of being selected in a sample as any other element of the population, and consequently every possible sample of a certain size the same chance of selection as every other sample of the same size.

If some elements of the population have a greater chance of being selected in a sample than others, then we have bias in our sampling method. Bias has to be avoided as the samples that can result will be extremely unlikely to reflect the population as a whole and such misleading results may have disastrous consequences.

Biased samples will mislead, no matter how large the samples are; in fact, the larger such samples are, the greater the danger of misrepresentation since it is always tempting to attach more credibility to a large sample.

The most effective way of avoiding bias in sample selection is to use probabilistic methods, which ensure that every element in the population has the same chance of being included in the sample. In the next section we will look at sampling methods that yield samples from which you can produce unbiased estimators of population measures, or parameters such as a mean or a proportion.

PROBABILISTIC SAMPLING METHODS

Perhaps the obvious way of giving every element in a population the same chance of being selected in sample is to use a random process such as those used to select winning numbers in lottery competitions. Lotteries are usually regarded as fair because every number in the population of lottery numbers has an equal chance of being picked as a winning number.

SIMPLE RANDOM SAMPLING

Selecting a set of winning numbers in a lottery is an example of simple random sampling, whether the process involves elaborate machines or simply picking the numbers from the proverbial hat. You can use the same approach in drawing samples from a population.

Before you can undertake simple random sampling you need to establish a clear definition of the population and compile a list of the elements in it. In the same way as all the numbers in a lottery must be included if the draw is to be fair, all the items in the population must be included for the sample we take to be random. The population list is the basis or framework of our sample selection so it is known as the sampling frame.

Simple random sampling has several advantages; it is straightforward and inexpensive. Because the probability of selection is known it is possible to assess the sampling error involved and ensure that estimates of population parameters based on the sample are unbiased. A potential disadvantage of simple random sampling is that in a case such as Example 15.3 the sample may consist of elements all over the country, which will make data collection expensive. Another is that whilst it is an appropriate method for largely homogenous populations, if a population is subdivided by, for instance, gender and gender is an important aspect of the analysis, using simple random sampling will not ensure suitable representation of both genders.

SYSTEMATIC RANDOM SAMPLING

A faster alternative to simple random sampling is systematic sampling. This involves selecting a proportion of elements from the sampling frame by choosing elements at regular intervals through the list. The first element is selected using a random number.

As well as being cheap and simple, systematic sampling does yield samples with a definable sampling error and therefore able to produce unbiased estimates. This is true as long as the population list used to select the sample is not drawn up in such a way as to give rise to bias.

Systematic sampling has the same disadvantages as simple random sampling; expensive data collection if the sample members are widely dispersed, and the possibility of sub-sections of the population being under-represented.

STRATIFIED RANDOM SAMPLING

One problem with both sampling methods we have looked at so far is that the samples they produce may not adequately reflect the balance of different constituencies within the population. In the long run this unevenness will be balanced out by other samples selected using the same methods, but this is little comfort if you only have the time or resources to take one sample.

To avoid sections of a population being under-, or for that matter over-represented you can use stratified random sampling. As the name implies, the sample selection is random, but it is structured using the sections or strata in the population. The starting point is to define the size of the sample and then decide what proportion of each section of the population needs to be selected for the sample. Once you have decided how many elements you need from each section, then use simple random sampling to choose them. This ensures that all the sections of the population are represented in the sample yet preserves the random nature of the selection and thus your ability to produce unbiased estimators of the population parameters from your sample data.

CLUSTER SAMPLING

If the investigation for which you require a sample is based on a population that is widely scattered you may prefer to use cluster sampling. This method is appropriate if the population you wish to sample is composed of geographically distinct units or clusters. You simply take a complete list of the clusters that make up your population and take a random sample of clusters from it. The elements in your sample are all the individuals in each selected cluster.

The advantages of cluster sampling are that it is cheap, especially if the investigation involves face-to-face interviews, because the number of locations to visit is small and you only need sampling frames for the selected clusters rather than the entire population. The disadvantages are that you may well end up with a larger sample than you need and there is a risk that some sections of the population may be under-represented.

MULTI-STAGE SAMPLING

Multi-stage is a generic term for any combination of probabilistic sampling methods. It can be particularly useful for selecting samples from populations that are divided or layered in more than one way.

The advantage of multi-stage sampling is that you can customize your approach to selecting your sample; it enables you to benefit from the advantages of a particular method and use others alongside it to overcome its disadvantages.

OTHER SAMPLING METHODS

Wherever possible you should use probabilistic sampling methods, not because they are more likely to produce a representative sample (which is not always true) but because they allow you to make a statistical evaluation of the sampling error and hence you can use the results to make predictions about the population the sample comes from that are statistically valid. Doing this with samples obtained by other methods does not have the same validity.

Why then is it worth looking at other methods at all? There are several reasons: some populations that you might wish to investigate simply cannot be listed, such as the potential customers of a business, so it is impossible to draw up a sampling frame; secondly, some of these methods are attractive because they are convenient; and thirdly, they are used by companies and therefore it is a good idea to be aware of them and their limitations.

QUOTA SAMPLING

In one respect quota sampling is similar to stratified random sampling: you start by working out what proportion of the population you want to include in your sample and then apply that proportion to the sections of the population to work out the quota of respondents needed from each section of the population. You then fill each quota by finding enough elements from each section of the population.

The advantages of quota sampling are that the resulting sample should be representative, and that the process is cheaper and easier than using stratified sampling. In addition there is no need to find named individuals, who may, once found, decline to participate. Quota sampling is particularly useful for sampling from large populations for which an accurate sampling frame is unavailable, a situation that polling organizations typically face.

The disadvantages are that it is susceptible to bias and the results from quota samples are not unbiased estimators of population parameters as the sample selection process is not based on probability. The bias might arise inadvertently from the researcher.

JUDGEMENTAL SAMPLING

In judgemental sampling the selection of the sample is based entirely on the expertise of the investigator, who uses their judgement to select a sample they consider representative.

The advantage of judgemental sampling is that it does allow you to customize your approach to sample selection. The disadvantage is that it is entirely subjective and non-random and as such does not yield results that can be used to predict the features of the population with any statistical rigour.

SNOWBALL SAMPLING

This method involves starting by finding a relatively few respondents who have a particular feature of interest to the investigator and using them to identify others who share the same feature. The sample 'snowballs' to include these others and perhaps yet more potential respondents whom they identify.

Snowballing is a useful means of obtaining a sample of a population that may be difficult to access by other means, such as small-scale building contractors. It is open to bias because the initial respondents or contacts decide whose names to pass on to you and there is no valid way of assessing the sampling error so any generalization from the results is not statistically valid.

CONVENIENCE SAMPLING

This method is very simple: samples are chosen purely on the basis of accessibility.

Convenience sampling, as the name suggests, is easy and cheap. It can be a useful means of conducting an initial exploratory investigation but the sample is unlikely to be representative of the whole population and results from it should certainly not be used for estimating population parameters as they lack statistical validity.

SELF-SELECTION

This is sample selection by invitation; you might send an email or display a notice asking for people to participate in an interview or complete a questionnaire. The advantages are that it is cheap and easy, and what is more you are guaranteed to get willing respondents.

Unfortunately this approach to sampling is almost invariably prone to bias; usually it is the people who have stronger feelings on the issues under investigation who put themselves forward and the sample composition is therefore biased against those with more neutral views.

20

Sampling Theory, Estimation and Hypothesis Testing

In the previous chapters we reviewed the methods that can be used to select samples from populations in order to gain some understanding of those populations. In this chapter we wil' consider how sample results can be used to provide estimates of key features, or parameters, of the populations from which they were selected. It is important to note that the techniques described in this chapter, and the theory on which they are based, should only be used with results of samples selected using probabilistic or random sampling methods. The techniques are based on knowing, or at least having a reliable estimate of, the sampling error and this is not possible with non-random sampling methods.

In previous chapters we looked at the normal distribution, an important statistical distribution that enables you to investigate the very many continuous variables that occur in business and many other fields, whose values are distributed in a normal pattern. What makes the normal distribution especially important is that it enables us to anticipate how sample results vary. This is because many sampling distributions have a normal pattern.

SAMPLING DISTRIBUTIONS

Sampling distributions are distributions that show how sample results vary. They depict the 'populations' of sample results. Such distributions play a crucial role in quantitative work because they enable us to use data from a sample to make statistically valid predictions or judgements about a population. There are considerable advantages in using sample results in this way, especially when the population is too large to be accessible, or if investigating the population is too expensive or time-consuming.

A sample is a subset of a population, that is, it consists of some observations taken from the population. A random sample is a sample that consists of values taken at random from the population.

You can take many different random samples from the same population, even samples that consist of the same number of observations. Unless the population is very small the number of samples that you could take from it is to all intents and purposes infinite. A 'parent' population can produce an effectively infinite number of 'offspring' samples.

These samples will have different means, standard deviations and so on. So if we want to use, say, a sample mean to predict the value of the population mean we will be using something that varies from sample to sample, the sample mean ($\overline{x}$), to predict something that is fixed, the population mean.

To do this successfully we need to know how the sample means vary from one sample to another. We need to think of sample means as observations, $\overline{x}$ s, of a variable, X, and consider how they are distributed. What is more we need to relate the distribution of sample means to the parameters of the population the samples come from so that we can use sample statistics to predict population measures. The distribution of $\overline{X}$, the sample means, is a sampling distribution.

We will begin by considering the simplest case, in which we assume that the parent population is normally distributed. If this is the case, what will the sampling distributions of means of samples taken from the population be like?

If you were to take all possible random samples consisting of n observations from a population that is normal, with a mean ¼. and a standard deviation Ã, and analyse them you would find that the sample means of all these samples will themselves be normally distributed.

You would find that the mean of the distribution of all these different sample means is exactly the same as the population mean, ¼. You would also find that the standard deviation of all these sample means is the population standard deviation divided by the square root of the size of the samples, Ã/ $\sqrt{n}$.

So the sample means of all the samples size n that can be taken from a normal population with a mean ¼ and a standard deviation Ã are distributed normally with a mean of ¼ and a standard deviation of Ã/ $\sqrt{n}$. In other words, the sample means are distributed around the same mean as the population itself but with a smaller spread.

We know that the sample means will be less spread out than the population because n will be more than one, so Ã/ $\sqrt{n}$ will be less than Ã. For instance, if there are four observations in each sample, Ã/ $\sqrt{n}$ will be Ã/2, that is the sampling distribution of means of samples which have four observations in them will have half the spread of the population distribution.

The larger the size of the samples, the less the spread in the values of their means, for instance if each sample consists of 100 observations the standard deviation of the sampling distribution will be Ã/10, a tenth of the population distribution.

This is an important logical point. In taking samples we are 'averaging out' the differences between the individual values in the population. The larger the samples, the more this happens. For this reason it is better to use larger samples to make predictions about a population. Next time you see an opinion poll look for the number of people that the pollsters have canvassed. It will probably be at least one thousand. The results of an opinion poll are a product that the polling organization wants to sell to media companies. In order to do this they have to persuade them that their poll results are likely to be reliable. They won't be able to do this if they only ask a very few people for their opinions!

The standard deviation of a sampling distribution, Ã/ $\sqrt{n}$, is also known as the standard error of the sampling distribution because it helps us anticipate the error we will have to deal with if we use a sample mean to predict the value of the population mean.

If we know the mean and standard deviation of the parent population distribution we can find the probabilities of ranges different sample means as we can do for any other normal distribution, by using the Standard Normal Distribution.

As long as the population the samples come from is normal we can be sure that the sampling distribution will be distributed normally with a mean of ¼ and a standard deviation of Ã/ $\sqrt{n}$.

But what if the population is not normal? There are many distributions that are not normal, such as distributions of wealth of individuals or distributions of waiting times.

Fortunately, according to a mathematical finding known as the

Central Limit Theorem, as long as n is large (which is usually interpreted to mean 30 or more) the sampling distribution of sample means will be normal in shape and have a mean of ¼ and a standard deviation of Ã/ $\sqrt{n}$. This is true whatever the shape of the population distribution.

If the samples taken from a population that is not normal consist of fewer than 30 observations then the Central Limit Theorem does not apply. The sampling distributions of means of small samples taken from such populations do not have a normal pattern.

ESTIMATING THE STANDARD ERROR

The main reason for being interested in sampling distributions is to help us use samples to assess populations because studying the whole population is not possible or practicable. Typically we will be using a sample, which we do know about, to investigate a population, which we don't know about. We will have a sample mean and we will want to use it to assess the likely value of the population mean.

So far we have measured sampling distributions using the mean and the standard deviation of the population, ¼ and Ã. But if we need to find out about the population using a sample, how can we possibly know the values of ¼ and Ã?

The answer is that in practice we don't. In the case of the population mean, ¼, this doesn't matter because typically it is something we are trying to assess. But without the population standard deviation, Ã, we do need an alternative approach to measuring the spread of a sampling distribution.

Because we will have a sample, the obvious answer is to use the standard deviation, s, in place of the population standard deviation, Ã. So instead of using the real standard error, Ã/ $\sqrt{n}$, we estimate the standard error of the sampling distribution with s/ $\sqrt{n}$.

Using the estimated standard error, s/ $\sqrt{n}$, is fine as long as the sample concerned is large (in practice, that n, the sample size, is at least 30). If we are dealing with a large sample we can use s/ $\sqrt{n}$ as an approximation of Ã/ $\sqrt{n}$. The means of samples consisting of n observations will be normally distributed with a mean of ¼ and an estimated standard error of s/ $\sqrt{n}$. The Central Limit Theorem allows us to do this even if the population the sample comes from is not itself normal in shape.

It is important to remember that $s/\sqrt{n}$ is not the real standard error, it is the estimated standard error, but because the standard deviation of a large sample will be reasonably close to the population standard deviation the estimated standard error will be close to the actual standard error.

THE T=DISTRIBUTION

In previous section we looked at how you can analyse sampling distributions using the sample standard deviation, s, when you do not know the population standard deviation, Ã. As long as the sample size, n, is 30 or more the estimated standard error will be a sufficiently consistent measure of the spread of the sampling distribution, whatever the shape of the parent population.

If, however, the sample size, n, is less than 30 the estimated standard error, $s/\sqrt{n}$, is generally not so close to the actual standard error, Ã/ $\sqrt{n}$, and the smaller the sample size, the greater will be the difference between the two. In this situation it is possible to model the sampling distribution using the estimated standard error, as long as the population the sample comes from is normal, but we have to use a modified normal distribution in order to do it.

This modified normal distribution is known as the t distribution. The development of the distribution was a real breakthrough because it made it possible to investigate populations using small sample results. Small samples are generally much cheaper and quicker to gather than a large sample so the t=distribution broadened the scope for analysis based on sample data.

The t=distribution is a more spread out version of the normal distribution.

The greater spread is to compensate for the greater variation in sample standard deviations between small samples than between large samples.

The smaller the sample size, the more compensation is needed, so there are a number of versions of the t=distribution. The one that should be used in a particular context depends on the number of degrees of freedom, represented by the symbol ½ (nu, the Greek letter n), which is the sample size minus one, $n-1$.

To work out the probability that the mean of a small sample taken from a normal population is more, or less, than a certain amount we first need to find its t-equivalent, or t=value. The procedure is very similar to the way we work out a z-equivalent.

$$t = \frac{\bar{x} - \mu}{s / \sqrt{n}}$$

You will find that the way the t distribution is used in further work depends on tail areas. For this reason, and also because the t distribution varies depending on the number of degrees of freedom, printed tables do not provide full details of the distribution in the same way that Standard Normal Distribution tables give full details of the Standard Normal Distribution.

CHOOSING THE RIGHT MODEL FOR A SAMPLING DISTRIBUTION

The normal distribution and the t distribution are both models that you can use to model sampling distributions, but how can you be sure that you use the correct one? This section is intended to provide a brief guide to making the choice.

The first question to ask is, are the samples whose results make up the sampling distribution drawn from a population that is distributed normally? In other words, is the parent population normal? If the answer is yes then it is always possible to model the sampling distribution. If the answer is no then it is only possible to model the sampling distribution if the sample size, n, is 30 or more.

The second question is whether the population standard deviation, Ã, is known. If the answer to this is yes then as long as the parent population is normal the sampling distribution can be modelled using the normal distribution whatever the sample size. If the answer is no the sampling distribution can be modelled using the normal distribution only if the sample size is 30 or more. In the absence of the population standard deviation, you have to use the sample standard deviation to approximate the standard error.

Finally, what if the parent population is normal, the population standard deviation is not known and the sample size is less than 30? In these circumstances you should use the t=distribution and approximate the standard error using the sample standard deviation. Note that if the parent population is not normal and the sample size is less than 30 neither the normal distribution nor the t=distribution can be used to model the sampling distribution, and this is true whether or not the population standard deviation is known.

STATISTICAL INFERENCE: ESTIMATION

Businesses use statistical analysis to help them study and solve problems. In many cases the data they use in their analysis will be sample data. Usually it is too expensive, or too time-consuming or simply impossible to obtain population data.

So if there is a problem of customer dissatisfaction they will study data from a sample of customers, not all customers. If there is a problem with product quality they will study a sample of the products, not all of them. If a large organization has a problem with staff training they will study the experiences of a sample of their staff rather than all their staff.

Of course, they will want to analyse the sample data in order to draw general conclusions about the population. As long as the samples they use are random samples, in other words they consist of observed values chosen at random from the population, it is quite possible to do this. The use of sample data in drawing conclusions, or making deductions, about populations is known as statistical inference from the word infer which means to deduce or conclude. Statistical inference that involves testing claims about population parameters is known as statistical decision-making because it can be used to help organizations and individuals take decisions.

In the last section we looked at sampling distributions. These distributions are the theoretical foundations on which statistical inference is built because they connect the behaviour of sample results to the distribution of the population the samples came from. Now we will consider the procedures involved in statistical inference.

There are two types of statistical inference technique that you will encounter in this chapter. The one we shall look at in this section is estimation, the using of sample data to predict population measures like means and proportions. The other is hypothesis testing, using sample data to verify or refute claims made about population measures.

Collecting sample data can be time-consuming and expensive so in practice organizations don't like to gather more data than they need, but on the other hand they don't want to end up with too little in case they haven't enough for the sort of conclusive results they want. You will find a discussion of this aspect of planning statistical research in this section.

STATISTICAL ESTIMATION

Statistical estimation is the use of sample measures such as means or proportions to estimate the values of their population counterparts. The easiest way of doing this is to simply take the sample measure and use it as it stands as a prediction of the population equivalent. So, we could take the mean of a sample and use it as our estimate of the population mean. This type of prediction is called point estimation. It is used to get a 'feel' for the population value and is a perfectly valid use of the sample result.

The main shortcoming of point estimation is given away by its name; it is a single point, a single shot at estimating one number using another. It is a crude way of estimating a population measure because not only is it uncertain whether it will be a good estimate, in other words close to the measure we want it to estimate, but we have no idea of the probability that it is a good estimate.

The best way of using sample information to predict population measures is to use what is known as interval estimation, which involves constructing a range or interval as the estimate. The aim is to be able to say how likely it is that the interval we construct is accurate, in other words, how confident we are that the interval does include within it the population measure. Because the probability that the interval includes the population measure, or the confidence we should have in the interval estimate, is an important issue, interval estimates are often called confidence intervals.

Before we look at how interval estimates are constructed and why they work, it will be helpful if we reiterate some key points about sampling distributions. For convenience we will concentrate on sample means for the time being.

- A sampling distribution of sample means shows how all the means of the different sample of a particular size, n, are distributed.
- Sampling distributions that describe the behaviour of means of samples of 30 or more are always approximately normal.
- The mean of the sampling distribution of sample means is the population mean, ¼.
- The standard deviation of the sampling distribution of sample

means, called the standard error, is the population standard deviation divided by the square root of the sample size, Ã/ $\sqrt{n}$.

The sampling distributions that are normal in shape, the ones that show how sample means of big samples vary, have the features of the normal distribution. One of these features is that if we take a point two standard deviations to the left of the mean and another point two standard deviations to the right of the mean, the area between the two points is roughly 95% of the distribution.

To be more precise, if these points were 1.96 standard deviations below and above the mean of the distribution the area would be exactly 95% of the distribution. In other words, 95% of the observations in the distribution are within 1.96 standard deviations from the mean. This is also true for normal sampling distributions; 95% of the sample means in a sampling distribution that is normal will be between 1.96 standard errors below and 1.96 standard errors above the mean.

The limits of this range or interval are: ¼ – 1.96 Ã/ $\sqrt{n}$ on the left-hand side and ¼ + 1.96 Ã/ $\sqrt{n}$ on the right-hand side.

The greatest difference between any of the middle 95% of sample means and the population mean, ¼, is 1.96 standard errors, 1.96 Ã/ $\sqrt{n}$. The probability that any one sample mean is within 1.96 standard errors of the mean is:

$$P(\mu - 1.96\sigma/\sqrt{n} < \mu + 1.96\sigma/\sqrt{n}) = 0.95$$

The sampling distribution allows us to predict values of sample means using the population mean. But in practice we wouldn't be interested in doing this because we don't know the population mean. Indeed, typically the population mean is the thing we want to find out about using a sample mean rather than the other way round. What makes sampling distributions so important is that we can use them to do this.

As we have seen, adding and subtracting 1.96 standard errors to and from the population mean creates an interval that contains 95% of the sample means in the distribution. But what if, instead of adding this amount to and subtracting it from the population mean, we add it to and subtract it from every sample mean in the distribution?

We would create an interval around every sample mean. In 95% of cases, the intervals based on the 95% of sample means closest to the population mean in the middle of the distribution, the interval would contain the population mean itself. In the other 5% of cases, those means furthest away from the population mean, the interval would not contain the population mean.

So, suppose we take the mean of a large sample and create a range around it by adding 1.96 standard errors to get an upper figure, and subtracting 1.96 standard errors to get a lower figure. There is a 95% chance that the range between the upper and lower figures will encompass the mean of the population. Such a range is called a 95% interval estimate or a 95% confidence interval because it is an interval that we are 95% confident, or certain, contains the population mean.

As long as the sample mean is among the 95% of the distribution between the lowest 21/2% and the highest 21/2%, the interval they produce will include the population mean, in other words it will be an accurate estimate of the population mean.

Of course, usually when we carry out this sort of research we don't actually know what the population mean is, so we don't know whether the sample mean we have is among the 95% that will give us accurate interval estimates or whether it is among the 5% that will give us inaccurate interval estimates. The important point is that if we have a sample mean and we create an interval in this way there is a 95% chance that the interval will be accurate. To put it another way, on average 19 out of every 20 samples will produce an accurate estimate, and 1 out of 20 will not. That is why the interval is called a 95% interval estimate or a 95% confidence interval.

We can express the procedure for finding an interval estimate for a population measure as taking a sample result and adding and subtracting an error. This error reflects the uncertainties involved in using sample information to predict population measures.

Population measure estimate = sample result $\pm$ error.

The error is made up of two parts, the standard error and the number of standard errors. The number of standard errors depends on how confident we want to be in our estimation. Suppose you want to estimate the population mean. If you know the population standard deviation, Ã, and you want to be (100 – að)% confident that your interval is accurate, then you can obtain your estimate of ¼ using:

$$\overline{x} \pm (z_{\alpha/2} * \sigma / \sqrt{n})$$

The letter 'z' appears because we are dealing with sampling distributions that are normal, so we can use the Standard Normal Distribution, the z distribution, to model them. You have to choose which z value to use on the basis of how sure you want or need to be that your estimate is accurate.

If you want to be 95% confident in your estimate, that is (100 – að)% = 95%, then að is 5% and að /2 is 21/2% or 0.025. To produce your estimate you would use z0.025, 1.96, the z value that cuts off a 21/ 2% tail in the Standard Normal Distribution. This means that a point 1.96 standard errors away from the mean of a normal sampling distribution, the population mean, will cut off a tail area of 21/2% of the distribution. So:

95% interval estimate of $\mu = \overline{x} \pm (1.96 * \sigma / \sqrt{n})$

The most commonly used level of confidence interval is probably 95%, but what if you wanted to construct an interval based on a higher level of confidence, say 99%? A 99% level of confidence means we want 99% of the sample means in the sampling distribution to provide accurate interval estimates.

To obtain a 99% confidence interval the only adjustment we make is the z value that we use. If (100 – að)% = 99%, then að is 1% and að/2 is 1/2% or 0.005. To produce your estimate use z 0.005, 2.576, the z value that cuts off a 1/2% tail in the Standard Normal Distribution:

99% interval estimate of $\mu = \overline{x} \pm (2.576 * \sigma / \sqrt{n})$.

DETERMINING THE SAMPLE SIZE FOR ESTIMATING A POPULATION MEAN

All other things being equal, if we want to be more confident that our interval is accurate we have to accept that the interval will be wider, in other words less precise. If we want to be more confident and retain the same degree of precision, the only thing we can do is to take a larger sample.

In the examples we have looked at so far the size of the sample was already decided. But what if, before starting a sample investigation, you wanted to ensure that you had a big enough sample to enable you to produce a precise enough estimate with a certain level of confidence? To see how, we need to start with the expression we have used for the error of a confidence interval:

$$z_{\alpha/2} * \sigma / \sqrt{n}$$

Until now we have assumed that we know these three elements so we can work out the error. But what if we wanted to set the error and find the necessary sample size, n? We can change the expression for the error around so that it provides a definition of the sample size:

$$\text{error} = z_{\alpha/2} * \sigma / \sqrt{n}$$

Exchange error and $\sqrt{n}$: $\sqrt{n} = z_{\alpha/2} * \sigma / \text{error}$

So

$$n = (z_{\alpha/2} * \sigma / \text{error})^2$$

This means that as long as you know the degree of precision you need (the error), the level of confidence (to find $z_{a/2}$), and the population standard deviation (Ã), you can find out what sample size you need to use.

ESTIMATING WITHOUT Ã

Practical interval estimation is based on sample results alone, but it is very similar to the procedure we saw in our previous section. The main difference is that we have to use a sample standard deviation, s, to produce an estimate for the standard error of the sampling distribution the sample belongs to. Apart from this, as long as the sample we have is quite large, which we can define as containing 30 or more observations, we can follow exactly the same procedure as before.

That is, instead of

$$\text{Estimate of } \mu = \bar{x} \pm (z_{\alpha/2} * \sigma / \sqrt{n})$$

we use

$$\text{estimate of } \mu = \bar{x} \pm (z_{\alpha/2} * s / \sqrt{n})$$

ESTIMATING WITH SMALL SAMPLES

If we want to produce an interval estimate based on a smaller sample, one with less than 30 observations in it, we have to be much more careful.

First, for the procedures we will consider in this section to be valid, the population that the sample comes from must be normal. Second, because the sample standard deviation of a small sample is not a reliable enough estimate of the population standard deviation to enable us to use the z= distribution, we must use the t=distribution to find how many standard errors are to be added and subtracted to produce an interval estimate with a given level of confidence.

Instead of

$$\text{estimate of } \mu = \overline{x} \pm (z_{\alpha/2} * \sigma / \sqrt{n})$$

we use

$$\text{estimate of } \mu = \overline{x} \pm (t_{\alpha/2} * s / \sqrt{n})$$

The form of the t=distribution you use depends on ½, the number of degrees of freedom, which is the sample size less one (n –1).

ESTIMATING POPULATION PROPORTIONS

Although so far we have concentrated on how to estimate population means, these are not the only population parameters that can be estimated. You will also come across estimates of population proportions, indeed almost certainly you already have.

If you have seen an opinion poll of voting intentions, you have seen an estimate of a population proportion. To produce the opinion poll result that you read in a newspaper pollsters have interviewed a sample of people and used the sample results to predict the voting intentions of the entire population.

In many ways estimating a population proportion is very similar to the estimation we have already considered. To start with you need a sample: you calculate a sample result around which your estimate will be constructed; you add and subtract an error based on the standard error of the relevant sampling distribution, and how confident you want to be that your estimate is accurate.

We have to adjust our approach because of the different nature of the data.. When we estimate proportions we are usually dealing with qualitative variables. The values of these variables are characteristics, for instance people voting for party A or party B. If there are only two possible characteristics, or we decide to use only two categories in our analysis, the variable will have a binomial distribution.

As you will see, this is convenient as it means we only have to deal with one sample result, the sample proportion, but it also means that we cannot produce reliable estimates from small samples, those consisting of less than 30 observations. This is because the distribution of the population that the sample comes from must be normal if we are to use the t distribution, the device we have previously used to overcome the extra uncertainty involved in small sample estimation.

The sampling distribution of sample proportions is approximately normal in shape if the samples involved are large, that is, more than 30, as long as the sample proportion is not too small or too large. In practice, because we do not know the sample proportion before taking the sample it is best to use a sample size of over 100. If the samples are small, the sampling distribution of sample proportions is not normal.

Provided that you have a large sample, you can construct an interval estimate for the population proportion, À (pi, the Greek letter p), by taking the sample proportion, p, and adding and subtracting an error. The sample proportion is the number of items in the sample that possess the characteristic of interest, x, divided by the total number of items in the sample, n.

Sample proportion, p = x/n

The error that you add to and subtract from the sample proportion is the z value appropriate for the level of confidence you want to use multiplied by the estimated standard error of the sampling distribution of the sample proportion. This estimated standard error is based on the sample proportion:

$$\text{estimated standard error} = \sqrt{\frac{p(1-p)}{n}}$$

So the interval estimate of $\pi = p \pm z_{a/2} * \sqrt{\frac{p(1-p)}{n}}$.

DETERMINING THE SAMPLE SIZE FOR ESTIMATING A POPULATION PROPORTION

If you know how confident you want to be that your interval estimate is accurate and you need your estimate to have a certain precision, in other words the error has to be a particular amount, you can work out the sample size you will need to use.

The precision of the test depends on the estimated standard error of the sample proportions, $\sqrt{p(1-p)/n}$. The value of this depends on p, the sample proportion. Clearly you won't know this until the sample data have been collected, but you can't collect the sample data until you have decided what sample size to use. You therefore need to make a prior assumption about the value of the sample proportion.

To be on the safe side we will assume the worst-case scenario, which is that the value of p will be the one that produces the highest value of p (1 – p). The higher the value of p (1– p) the wider the interval will be, for a given sample size. We need to avoid the situation where p (1 – p) turns out to be larger than we have assumed it is.

What is the largest value of p (1 – p)? If you work out p (1 – p) when p is 0.1, you will get 0.09. If p is 0.2, p (1 – p) rises to 0.16. As you increase the value of p you will find that it keeps going up until p is 0.5, when p (1 – p) is 0.25, then it goes down again.

The error in an interval estimate of a population proportion is:

$$\text{error} = z_{\alpha/2} * \sqrt{\frac{p(1-p)}{n}}$$

If p is 0.5, in other words we assume the largest value of p (1 – p):

$$\text{error} = z_{\alpha/2} * \sqrt{\frac{0.5(1-0.5)}{n}}$$

$$= z_{\alpha/2} * \sqrt{\frac{0.5*0.5}{n}}$$

$$= z_{\alpha/2} * \frac{0.5}{\sqrt{n}}$$

This last expression can be re-arranged to obtain an expression for n:

$$\text{error} = z_{\alpha/2} * \frac{0.5}{\sqrt{n}}$$

so

$$= \sqrt{n} = \frac{z_{\alpha/2} * 0.5}{\text{error}}.$$

$$n = \left[\frac{z_{\alpha/2}}{2 * \text{error}}\right]^2$$

STATISTICAL INFERENCE: HYPOTHESIS TESTING

Usually when we construct interval estimates of population parameters we have no idea of the actual value of the parameter we are trying to estimate. Indeed the purpose of estimation using sample results is to tell us what the actual value is likely to be.

Sometimes we use sample results to deal with a different situation. This is where the population parameter is claimed to take a particular value and we want to see whether the claim is correct. Such a claim is known as a hypothesis, and the use of sample results to investigate whether it is true is called hypothesis testing. To begin with we will concentrate on testing hypotheses about population means using a single sample. Later in this section you will find hypothesis testing of population proportions and a way of testing hypotheses about population medians.

Hypothesis testing begins with a formal statement of the claim being made for the population parameter. This is known as the null hypothesis because it is the starting point in the investigation, and is represented by the symbol H_0, 'aitch-nought'.

We could find that a null hypothesis appears to be wrong, in which case we should reject it in favour of an alternative hypothesis, represented by the symbol H_1, 'aitch-one'. The alternative hypothesis is the collection of explanations that contradict the claim in the null hypothesis.

A null hypothesis may specify a single value for the population measure, in which case we would expect the alternative hypothesis to consist of other values both below and above it. Because of this 'dual' nature of the alternative hypothesis, the procedure to investigate such a null hypothesis is known as a two-sided test.

In other cases the null hypothesis might specify a minimum or a maximum value, in which case the alternative hypothesis consists of values below, or values above respectively. The procedure we use in these cases is called a one-sided test.

The type of null hypothesis that should be used depends on the context of the investigation and the perspective of the investigator.

After establishing the form of the hypotheses we can test them using the sample evidence we have. We need to decide if the sample evidence is compatible with the null hypothesis, in which case we cannot reject it. If the sample evidence contradicts the null hypothesis we reject it in favour of the alternative hypothesis.

To help us make this decision we need a decision rule to apply to our sample evidence. The decision rule is based on the assumption that the null hypothesis is true. If the population mean really does take the value specified in the null hypothesis, then as long as we know the value of the population standard deviation, Ã, and the size of our sample, n, we can identify the sampling distribution that our sample belongs to.

The next stage is to compare our sample mean to the sampling distribution it is supposed to come from if H_0 is true. If it seems to belong to the sampling distribution, in other words it is not too far away from the centre of the distribution, we consider the null hypothesis plausible. If, on the other hand, the sample mean is located on one of the extremes of the sampling distribution we consider the null hypothesis suspect.

We can make this comparison by working out the z-equivalent of the sample mean and using it to find out the probability that a sample mean of the order of the one we have comes from the sampling distribution that is based on the null hypothesis being true. Because we are using a z-equivalent, this type of hypothesis test is called a z=test.

Once we know how likely it is that a sample mean of this order belongs to the sampling distribution implied by the null hypothesis, we can make a judgement about the null hypothesis. We have to distinguish between 'acceptable' sample results, those that are compatible with the null hypothesis, and 'unacceptable' sample results, those that conflict with the null hypothesis.

If the probability that a sample mean of this order belongs to the sampling distribution that H_0 implies is quite high then it would be 'acceptable'. If it were quite low it would be 'unacceptable'. But what exactly are 'quite high' and 'quite low' probabilities? When you get used to hypothesis testing you may well develop an intuitive 'feel' for what the appropriate dividing line is in a given situation, but until then you need to apply a decision rule.

In many practical applications this type of testing is a way of establishing that goods and services meet standards agreed between a supplier and a customer, or between a head office and local management. In these circumstances it is important that a decision rule that defines acceptable sample test results is agreed between the parties.

A decision rule should define how low the likelihood of a sample mean (or a more extreme sample mean in the sampling distribution) has to be before we consider it 'unacceptable'. 'Unacceptable' sample results are often described as significant, in the sense that they are significantly different to what the null hypothesis says they should be. The decision rule specifies what is called the level of significance. If we say that we will use a 5% level of significance in our testing we are saying that if there is less than a 5% chance that a sample mean (or a more extreme one) belongs to the sampling distribution based on H_0 then we will consider it 'unacceptable'. We need to turn this around because it is really the null hypothesis that we would have found to be unacceptable in the light of the sample evidence. So if our sample result is 'unacceptable' we should reject the null hypothesis.

A 5% level of significance means that if the chance that the sample mean our investigation produces (or a more extreme one) does come from the sampling distribution H_0 implies is less than one in twenty, then it is such an unlikely result we believe that the sample evidence suggests the null hypothesis is wrong. Another way of putting it is to say that if our sample mean is amongst the 5% least likely to come from the sampling distribution that it should belong to if H_0 were true, then we will reject H_0.

The implication of rejecting H_0 is that the sample mean we have belongs to a different sampling distribution, because it is very unlikely to belong to the one that H_0 implies. It is very unlikely, but not impossible. The sort of sample mean that our decision rule says is significant, or 'unacceptable', could, just possibly, belong to the sampling distribution H_0 implies. In that case the decision to reject H_0 would be wrong, a mistake known as a Type I error (accepting H_0 when it is false is a Type II error). The level of significance that we specify in a decision rule is also therefore the risk we are prepared to take that we wrongly reject H_0.

When we apply our decision rule we need to take into account the type of null hypothesis we are dealing with. If it suggests that the population mean equals a particular figure we should conduct a two-sided test in order to assess it. That is, if the sample mean we produce is either too high or too low, then we should reject H_0.

In two-sided tests there are two types of 'unacceptable', or significant sample result. Because of this, if we use a 5% level of significance, the 5% least likely sample means that would lead us to reject the null hypothesis will consist of the lowest 2.5% of sample means and the highest 2.5% of sample means. If therefore the probability that our sample mean (or a more extreme one) belongs to the sampling distribution were less than 2.5%, or 0.025, we would reject H_0. But because the test is two-sided, we would say that we reject it at the 5% level.

These lowest and highest extremes of the sampling distribution are called the rejection regions, since we reject the null hypothesis if our sample mean is located in one of those parts of the distribution. Another way of applying the decision rule is to use the z values that cut off the tails on the Standard Normal Distribution equivalent to the rejection regions as benchmarks that we compare to the z-equivalent of the sample mean. In this context the z-equivalent of the sample mean is called the test statistic and the z values that mark off the limits of the rejection regions are called the critical values of z.

In a two-sided, or two-tail, test using a 5% level of significance the rejection regions of the furthest 2.5% on the left and right sides of the sampling distribution are the areas of the Standard Normal Distribution beyond the critical z values, – 1.96 and + 1.96 respectively. If the z-equivalent of our sample mean, the test statistic, is either less than –1.96 or greater than + 1.96, we should reject H_0.

If the null hypothesis suggests that the population mean is less than or equal to a particular figure we conduct a one-sided, or one-tail, test. If we do this using a 5% level of significance we reject the null hypothesis if our sample mean is amongst the highest 5% of samples in the sampling distribution that H_0 implies.

Since the null hypothesis includes the possibility that the population mean is lower than a particular value, a very low sample mean is compatible with the null hypothesis. It is only if the sample mean is very high that we would reject H_0.

The decision rule in this case means that if the probability that the sample mean (or a more extreme one) comes from the sampling distribution implied by H_0 is less than 5% or 0.05 and the sample mean is higher than the population mean specified in Ho, then we reject H_0. Alternatively, we could say that if the test statistic, the z-equivalent of our sample mean, is higher than 1.645, the z=value that cuts off a tail of 5% on the right-hand side of the Standard Normal Distribution, we will reject H_0.

If the null hypothesis states that the population mean is greater than or equal to a particular value, we would also conduct a one-tail test. But this time we would reject the null hypothesis if our sample mean were among the lowest 5% of samples in the sampling distribution that H_0 implies.

If the null hypothesis includes the possibility that the population mean is higher than a particular value, a very high sample mean is compatible with the null hypothesis. It is only if the sample mean is very low that we would reject H_0.

The decision rule is that if the probability that the sample mean (or a more extreme one) comes from the sampling distribution implied by H_0 is less than 5% or 0.05 and the sample mean is lower than the population mean specified in H_0, then we reject H_0. Alternatively we could say that if the test statistic were less than – 1.645, the z=value that cuts off a tail of 5% on the left-hand side of the Standard Normal Distribution, we would reject H_0.

In the same way that you can use different levels of confidence in estimation, you can use different levels of significance in hypothesis testing. The most commonly used levels of significance are 10%, 5%, 1% and 0.1%. The lower the level of significance you use, the more rigorous the test. In circumstances where it is important that the result of a hypothesis test is robust, such as testing pharmaceutical products, it would be appropriate to use the 0.1% level of significance.

The level of significance you use determines the size of the rejection region and the critical value of z. Once you have decided which level of significance to use you can obtain the critical value by looking for the appropriate values of að ð(for a one-tail test) or að/2 (for a two-tail test) in the body and finding the z values associated with them. Alternatively, you can find the probability that the sample result (or a more extreme one) occurs if the null hypothesis is true by working out its z-equivalent and then referring critical value.

You may find that at first the most difficult thing about hypothesis testing is the decision rule, and in particular making sure you use the appropriate critical value. It may help if you remember the connection between the type of null hypothesis and the critical value.

If you are testing $H_0: \mu = \mu_0$, reject it if the test statistic is below $-z_{a\eth/2}$ or above $z_{a\eth/2}$.

If you are testing $H_0: \mu \leq \mu_0$, reject it if the test statistic is above $z_{a\eth}$.

If you are testing $H_0: \mu \geq \mu_0$, reject it if the test statistic is below $-z_{a\eth}$.

HYPOTHESIS TESTING WITHOUT Ã

In the hypothesis testing we have looked at so far we have assumed that we know the population standard deviation, Ã. This could be the case, particularly if you are trying to find out whether a change had an effect by comparing sample data collected after the change with a previous situation that was well established and known. Perhaps a brewery wants to know if the refurbishment of a pub has had a significant effect on trade. In such a case the brewery records are likely to be comprehensive and they could be used to calculate the population standard deviation of the turnover per week. You could then use this figure to calculate the standard error of the sampling distribution that would provide the context for the test.

However, in many cases we won't know the population standard deviation. In these situations the sample size is the first key factor. If our sample evidence comes from a sample that consists of 30 or more observations, the sample standard deviation will be sufficiently close to the population standard deviation to allow us to use a z test; that is, to base our decision rule on the Standard Normal Distribution. We simply use the sample standard deviation in place of the population distribution when we calculate the estimated standard error; instead of $\sigma \sqrt{n}$, we use $s \sqrt{n}$.

HYPOTHESIS TESTING WITH SMALL SAMPLES

Suppose we want to test a hypothesis using the mean of a sample that consists of less than 30 observations and we don't know the population standard deviation. We can do this but we have to be reasonably sure that the population that the sample comes from is normal.

We cannot rely on the sample standard deviation from a small sample being close enough to the population standard deviation to allow us to simply substitute s for Ã as we could do with larger samples. This means we have to use the t=distribution for benchmarks to use in comparing sample results to sampling distributions that null hypotheses imply. Because the t=distribution is used hypothesis tests based on small samples are called t=tests.

TESTING HYPOTHESES ABOUT POPULATION PROPORTIONS

The procedure for testing hypotheses about population proportions is similar to the way we test hypotheses about population means. We begin with a null hypothesis that specifies a population proportion to be tested, which we represent by the symbol π_0 (the Greek letter pi, π, is the symbol for the population proportion). If the null hypothesis is one of the 'equal to' type we conduct a two-tail test. If it is 'less than' or 'greater than', we conduct a one-tail test.

We calculate the test statistic from the sample proportion, represented by the symbol p, which comes from the sample data that we want to use to test the hypothesis. We assume that the sample proportion belongs to a sampling distribution that has a mean of π_0 and a standard error of:

$$\sqrt{\frac{\pi_0(1-\pi_0)}{n}}$$

Note that we use the proportion from the null hypothesis to calculate the standard error, not the sample proportion.

The test statistic is:

$$z = \frac{p - \pi_0}{\sqrt{\pi_0(1-\pi_0)/n}}$$

Sample proportions are distributed normally if they come from large samples. As long as the sample size is large, preferably over 100, we can use the Standard Normal Distribution as the benchmark for the test; in other words, it will be a z test.

As we have done before, we use a decision rule that specifies a level of significance in order to assess the validity of the null hypothesis.

A HYPOTHESIS TEST FOR THE POPULATION MEDIAN

For most of this section we have concentrated on testing population means. When sample sizes are large this is a generally applicable way of assessing the central tendency of populations. But as we have seen, it is not so straightforward when using small samples, samples that contain less than 30 items.

If you want to test a hypothesis about a mean using a small sample you have to be able to assume that the population that the sample comes from is normal. In many situations this is not a reasonable assumption; patterns of wealth and income, for instance, do not typically form a normal distribution.

When a distribution is skewed the sampling distributions for small samples based on it will also be skewed. Here we will look at a test for the population median known as the sign test, which can be used with small samples drawn from non-normal populations.

The idea at the heart of the sign test is quite a simple one. The median is the midway point in the population. Exactly one-half of the values in the population are above the median and the other half are below it. This means that the probability a randomly selected value is less than the median is 0.5 and the probability it is more than the median is 0.5. If we have a random sample the values in it will be either above or below the median. The total number of values in the sample that are above and below the median can therefore be modelled using the binomial distribution, with say 'success' being defined as a value above the median, and p, the probability of success being 0.5.

You start with null and alternative hypotheses like those we have already looked at, except that they involve the population median. As before, the null hypothesis must identify the specific value of the population median to be tested. You then have to allocate a plus to each value in the sample that is above the median and a minus to each value that is below the median. In the unlikely event that your sample contains a value exactly the same as the null hypothesis population median, you can allocate a sign on the basis of the toss of a coin or simply ignore it.

Once every value has been assigned a plus or minus, you then count up the number of plus signs and the number of minus signs. Finally, use the appropriate binomial distribution to define the rejection region in keeping with the desired level of significance.

The sign test is one of a range of tests that can be applied in a broader range of contexts than the more traditional or classical methods we looked at earlier in the section. These tests are known as nonparametric tests because they are not generally based on the parameters used in the classical methods, the mean and the standard deviation. They are also referred to as distribution-free methods because they do not depend on assumptions about the population distribution.

Nonparametric methods are simpler to use and more widely applicable than classical methods, but they are not as efficient. Typically a nonparametric test requires more data than a classical test for the same degree of rigour. We have only considered one of the many nonparametric tests that are available. You can find out more about them in Sprent (1989).

21

Comparing Population Means and Bivariate Data

In the previous chapter we looked at statistical inference in relation to univariate data, estimating and testing single population parameters like the mean using single sample results. In this chapter we will consider statistical inference methods that enable us to compare means of two or more populations, to test population correlation coefficients, to make predictions from simple linear regression models and to test for association in qualitative data.

TESTING HYPOTHESES ABOUT TWO POPULATION MEANS

In the previous chapter we looked at tests of the population mean based on a single sample mean. In this section we will consider tests designed to assess the difference between two population means. In businesses these tests are used to investigate whether, for instance, the introduction of a new logo improves sales.

To use these tests you need to have a sample from each of the two populations. For the tests to be valid the samples must be random, but they can be independent or dependent. Independent samples are selected from each population separately. Suppose a domestic gas supplier wanted to assess the impact of a new charging system on customers' bills. The company could take a random sample of customers and record the size of their bills under the existing charging system then, after the new system is introduced, take another random sample of customers and record the size of their bills. These samples would be independent.

Dependent samples consist of matched or paired values. If the gas supplier took a random sample of customers and recorded the size of their bills both before and after the introduction of the new charging system they would be using a paired or dependent sample. The choice of independent or dependent samples depends on the context of the test. Unless there is a good reason for using paired data it is better to use independent samples. We will begin by looking at tests for use with independent samples and deal with paired samples later in this section.

As with single sample tests, the size of the samples is important because it determines the nature of the sampling distribution. In this section we will assume that the population standard deviations are not known.

LARGE INDEPENDENT SAMPLES

The null hypothesis we use in comparing population means is based on the difference between the means of the two populations, ¼$_1$ – ¼$_2$.

The hypotheses assume that the focus of the test is that there is no difference between the population means. This is very common but the same formats can be used to test whether the difference between two population means is a non-zero constant, e.g. H_0: ¼$_1$ – ¼$_2$ = 6.

If both samples contain 30 or more items the difference between their means, $\bar{x}_1 - \bar{x}_2$, belongs to the sampling distribution of $\bar{X}_1 - \bar{X}_2$.

This sampling distribution is normally distributed with a mean of ¼$_1$ – ¼$_2$, and a standard error of:

$$\sqrt{\frac{\sigma_1^2}{n_1}+\frac{\sigma_2^2}{n_2}}$$

where Ã$_1$ and Ã $_2$ are the standard deviations of the first and second populations, and n1 and n_2 are the sizes of the samples from the first and second populations.

We will assume that the population standard deviations are not known, in which case the estimated standard error of the sampling distribution is:

$$\sqrt{\frac{s_1^2}{n_1}+\frac{s_2^2}{n_2}}$$

The test statistic is:

$$z=\frac{(\overline{x}_1-\overline{x}_2)-(\mu_1-\mu_2)}{\sqrt{\frac{s_1^2}{n_1}+\frac{s_2^2}{n_2}}}$$

If the null hypothesis suggests that the difference between the population means is zero, we can simplify this to:

$$z=\frac{(\overline{x}_1-\overline{x}_2)}{\sqrt{\frac{s_1^2}{n_1}+\frac{s_2^2}{n_1}}}$$

Once we have calculated the test statistic we need to compare it to the appropriate critical value from the Standard Normal Distribution.

SMALL INDEPENDENT SAMPLES

If the size of the samples you want to use to compare population means is small, less than 30, you can only follow the procedure outlined in the previous section if both populations are normal and both population standard deviations known. In the absence of the latter it is possible to test the difference between two population means using small independent samples but only under certain circumstances.

If both populations are normal and their standard deviations can be assumed to be the same, that is $\tilde{A}_1 = \tilde{A}_2$, we can conduct a two-sample t=test. We use the sample standard deviations to produce a pooled estimate of the standard error of the sampling distribution of $\overline{X}_1-\overline{X}_2$, s_p.

$$s_p=\sqrt{\frac{(n_1-1)s_1^2+(n_2-1)s_2^2}{n_1+n_2-2}}$$

The test statistic is

$$t=\frac{(\overline{x}_1-\overline{x}_2)}{s_p * \sqrt{\frac{1}{n_1}+\frac{1}{n_2}}}$$

We then compare the test statistic to the appropriate critical value from the t distribution. The number of degrees of freedom for this test is $n_1 + n_2 - 2$, one degree of freedom is lost for each of the sample means.

PAIRED SAMPLES

If you want to test the difference between population means using dependent or paired samples the nature of the data enables you to test the mean of the differences between all the paired values in the population, ¼$_d$. This approach contrasts with the methods described in the earlier parts of this section where we have tested the difference between population means, ¼$_1$ – ¼$_2$.

The procedure involved in testing hypotheses using paired samples is very similar to the one-sample hypothesis testing we discussed in previous chapter. We have to assume that the differences between the paired values are normally distributed with a mean of ¼$_d$, and a standard deviation of Ã$_d$. The sampling distribution of sample mean differences will also be normally distributed with a mean of ¼$_d$ and a standard error of $\sigma_d / \sqrt{n}$, where n is the number of differences in the sample. Since we assume that Ã$_d$ is unknown we have to use the estimated standard error $s_d / \sqrt{n}$, where sd is the standard deviation of the sample differences.

Typically samples of paired data tend to be small so the benchmark distribution for the test is the t distribution.

The test statistic is:

$$t = \frac{\overline{x}_d - \mu_{d0}}{s_d / \sqrt{n}}$$

where $\overline{x}_d$ is the mean of the sample differences.

We then compare the test statistic to the appropriate critical value from the t=distribution with n – 1 degrees of freedom.

TESTING HYPOTHESIS ABOUT MORE THAN TWO POPULATION MEANS – ONE-WAY ANOVA

In some investigations it is important to establish whether two random samples come from a single population or from two populations with different means. The techniques we looked at in the previous section enable us to do just that. But what if we have three or more random samples and we need to establish whether they come from populations with different means?

You might think that the obvious answer is to run t tests using each pair of random samples to establish whether the first sample came from the same population as the second, the first sample came from the same population as the third and the second sample came from the same population as the third and so on. In doing this you would be testing the hypothesis:

$$H_0\text{: ¼}_1 = \text{¼}_2$$

$$H_0\text{: ¼}_1 = \text{¼}_3$$

$$H_0\text{: ¼}_2 = \text{¼}_3 \text{ etc.}$$

Although feasible, this is not the best way to approach the investigation. For one thing the more random samples that are involved the greater the chance that you miss out one or more possible pairings. For another, each test you conduct carries a risk of making a type 1 error, wrongly rejecting a null hypothesis because you happen to have a sample result from an extreme end of its sampling distribution. The chance of this occurring is the level of significance you use in conducting the test. The problem when you conduct a series of related tests is that the probability of making a type 1 error increases; if you use a 5% level of significance then the probability of not making a type 1 error in a sequence of three tests is, using the multiplication rule of probability, 0.95 * 0.95 * 0.95 or 0.857. This means the effective level of significance is 14.3%, considerably greater than you might have assumed.

To establish whether more than two samples come from populations with different means we use an alternative approach, analysis of variance, usually abbreviated to ANOVA (analysis of variance). At first sight it seems rather odd to be using a technique based on variance, a measure of spread, to assess hypotheses about means, which are measures of location. The reason for doing this is that it enables us to focus on the spread of the sample means, after all the greater the differences between the sample means the greater the chance that they come from populations with different means. However, we have to be careful to put these differences into context because, after all, we can get different samples from the same population. Using ANOVA involves looking at the balance between the variance of the sample means and the variance in the sample data overall.

So how we can test whether the samples come from the same population, in other words that there is no difference between the population mean amounts of cash dispensed per period in the three towns? For convenience we will use ¼$_G$, ¼$_H$ and ¼$_I$ to represent the population means for Gloucester, Huddersfield and Ipswich respectively.

The hypothesis we need to test is:

$$H_0: \tfrac{1}{4}_G = \tfrac{1}{4}_H = \tfrac{1}{4}_I$$

The alternative hypothesis is that there is a difference between at least two of the population means for the three towns.

If the null hypothesis is true and the three samples all come from a single population the best estimate of the mean of that population is the mean of the values in all three samples, the overall mean. Since we already know the three sample means we can work this out by taking the mean of the sample means, being careful to weight each mean by the number of observations in the sample.

The test statistic we will use is based on comparing the variation between the sample means with the variation within the samples.

The basis of the variance is the sum of the squared deviations between each observation and the sample mean. This amount, which is usually abbreviated to the sum of squares, is used to measure variation in analysis of variance.

When you calculate a sample variance you have to divide the sum of squared deviations by the sample size less one, n – 1. This is the number of degrees of freedom left in the data; we lose one degree of freedom because we use the mean in working out the deviations from it. Before we can use the sums of squares we have determined above to test the hypothesis of no difference between the population means we need to incorporate the degrees of freedom associated with each sum of squares by working out the mean sum of squares. This makes the variation within the samples directly comparable to the variation between samples.

The mean sum of squares within the samples, MSW, is the sum of squares within the samples divided by the number of observations in all three samples, in this case 14, less the number of samples we have, 3. You may like to think of subtracting three as reflecting our using the three sample means in working out the sum of squares within the samples.

There are several assumptions that apply when we use analysis of variance to test differences between population means. To begin with the populations from which the samples are drawn should be normal and the populations should have the same variance. Furthermore, the samples must be random and independent. In this section we have used one-way analysis of variance; one-way because we have only considered one factor, geographical location, in our investigation. There may be other factors that may be pertinent to our analysis, such as the type of location of the cash dispensers. ANOVA is a flexible technique that can be used to take more than one factor into account.

TESTING HYPOTHESES AND PRODUCING INTERVAL ESTIMATES FOR QUANTITATIVE BIVARIATE DATA

In this section we will look at statistical inference techniques that enable you to estimate and test relationships between variables in populations based on sample data. The sample data we use to do this is called bivariate data because it consists of observed values of two variables. This sort of data is usually collected in order to establish whether there is a relationship between the two variables, and if so, what sort of relationship it is.

Many organizations use this type of analysis to study consumer behaviour, patterns of costs and revenues, and other aspects of their operations. Sometimes the results of such analysis have far-reaching consequences. For example, if you look at a tobacco product you will see a health warning prominently displayed. It is there because some years ago researchers used these types of statistical methods to establish that there was a relationship between tobacco consumption and certain medical conditions.

The quantitative bivariate analysis that we considered in previous chapter consisted of two related techniques: correlation and regression. Correlation analysis, which is about calculating and evaluating the correlation coefficient, enables you to tell whether there is a relationship between the observed values of two variables and how strong it is. Regression analysis, which is about finding lines of best fit, enables you to find the equation of the line that is most appropriate for the data, the regression model.

Here we will address how the results from applying correlation and regression to sample data can be used to test hypotheses and make estimates for the populations the sets of sample data belong to.

TESTING THE POPULATION CORRELATION COEFFICIENT

The sample correlation coefficient, represented by the letter r, measures the extent of the linear association between a sample of observations of two variables, X and Y. You can find the sample correlation coefficient of a set of bivariate data using the formula:

$$r = \frac{\text{Cov}_{XY}}{(s_x * s_y)}$$

where

$$\text{Cov}_{XY} = \frac{\sum (x - \overline{x})(y - \overline{y})}{(n-1)}$$

and s_x and s_y are the standard deviations of the x and y values respectively.

If we select a random sample from populations of X and Y that are both normal in shape, the sample correlation coefficient will be an unbiased estimate of the population coefficient, represented by the Greek r, the letter rho, Á. In fact the main reason for calculating the sample correlation coefficient is to assess the linear association, if any, between the X and Y populations.

The value of the sample correlation coefficient alone is some help in assessing correlation between the populations, but a more thorough approach is to test the null hypothesis that the population correlation coefficient is zero:

$$H_0: Á = 0$$

The alternative hypothesis you use depends on what you would like to show. If you are interested in demonstrating that there is significant correlation in the population, then use:

$$H_1: Á \neq 0$$

If you want to test for significant positive correlation in the population then:

$$H_1: Á > 0$$

If you want to test for significant negative correlation in the population then:

$$H_1: < 0$$

If we adopt the first of these, H_1: ≠ 0, we will need to use a two-tail test, if we use one of the other forms we will conduct a one-tail test. In practice it is more usual to test for either positive or negative correlation rather than for both.

Once we have established the nature of our alternative hypothesis we need to calculate the test statistic from our sample data. The test statistic is:

$$t = \frac{r\sqrt{n-2}}{\sqrt{1-r^2}}$$

Here r is the sample correlation coefficient and n is the number of pairs of observations in the sample.

As long as the populations of X and Y are normal the test statistic will belong to a t distribution with n – 2 degrees of freedom and a mean of zero, if the null hypothesis is true and there is no linear association between the populations of X and Y.

TESTING REGRESSION MODELS

The second bivariate quantitative technique we looked at in a previous chapter was simple linear regression analysis. This allows you to find the equation of the line of best fit between two variables, X and Y. Such a line has two distinguishing features, its intercept and its slope. In the standard formula we used the intercept is represented by the letter a and the slope by the letter b:

$$Y = a + bX$$

The line that this equation describes is the best way of representing the relationship between the dependent variable, Y, and the independent variable, X. In practice it is almost always the result of a sample investigation that is intended to shed light on the relationship between the populations of X and Y. That is why we have used ordinary rather than Greek letters in the equation.

The results of a sample investigation can provide you with an understanding of the relationship between the populations. The intercept and slope of the line of best fit for the sample are point estimates for the intercept and slope of the line of best fit for the populations, which are represented by the Greek equivalents of a and b, að and bð:

$$Y = \alpha + \beta X$$

The intercept and slope from the sample regression line can be used to test hypotheses about the equivalent figures for the populations. Typically we use null hypotheses that suggest that the population values are zero:

H_0: að ð= 0 for the intercept

and

H_0: bð ð= 0 for the slope.

If the population intercept is zero, the population line of best fit will be represented by the equation Y = 0 + bðX, and the line will begin at the origin of the graph.

If we wanted to see whether the population intercept is likely to be zero, we would test the null hypothesis H_0: að = 0 against the alternative hypothesis: H_1: að ≠ 0.

When you use regression analysis you will find that investigating the value of the intercept is rarely important. Occasionally it is of interest, for instance if we are looking at the relationship between an organization's levels of operational activity and its total costs at different periods of time then the intercept of the line of best fit represents the organization's fixed costs.

Typically we are much more interested in evaluating the slope of the regression line. The slope is pivotal; it tells us how the dependent variable responds to changes in the independent variable. For this reason the slope is also known as the coefficient of the independent variable. If the population slope turns out to be zero, it tells you that the dependent variable does not respond to the independent variable. The implication of this is that your independent variable is of no use in explaining how your dependent variable behaves and there would be no point in using it to make predictions of the dependent variable.

If the slope of the line of best fit is zero, the equation of the line would be Y = að + 0X, and the line would be perfectly horizontal.

We usually want to use regression analysis to find useful rather than useless models – regression models that help us understand and anticipate the behaviour of dependent variables. In order to demonstrate that a model is valid, it is important that you test the null hypothesis that the slope is zero. Hopefully the sample evidence will enable you to reject the null hypothesis in favour of the alternative, that the slope is not zero.

The test statistic used to test the hypothesis is:

$$t = \frac{b - 0}{s_b}$$

Where b is the sample slope, 0 is the zero population slope that the null hypothesis suggests, and s_b is the estimated standard error of the sampling distribution of the sample slopes. To calculate the estimated standard error, s_b, divide s, the standard deviation of the sample residuals, the parts of the y values that the line of best fit does not explain, by the square root of the sum of the squared deviations between the x values and their mean,

$$\bar{x}\ .\ s_b = \frac{s}{\sqrt{\sum (x - \bar{x})^2}}$$

Once we have the test statistic we can assess it by comparing it to the t=distribution with n – 2 degrees of freedom, two fewer than the number of pairs of x and y values in our sample data.

CONSTRUCTING INTERVAL PREDICTIONS

The problem with single-figure predictions is that we do not know how likely they are to be accurate. It is far better to have an interval that we know, with a given level of confidence, will be accurate. Before looking at how to produce such intervals, we need to clarify exactly what we want to find. We can construct an interval estimate, or confidence interval, of the mean level of sales on days when the temperature is at a particular level by taking the point estimate and adding and subtracting an error. The error is the product of the standard error of the sampling distribution of the point estimates and a figure from the t=distribution. The t=distribution should have n – 2 degrees of freedom, n being the number of pairs of data in our sample, and the t value we select from it is based on the level of confidence we want to have that our estimate will be accurate.

We can express this procedure using the formula:

Confidence interval

$$\hat{y} \pm t_{\alpha/2, n-2} * s \sqrt{\frac{1}{n} + \frac{(x_0 - \bar{x})^2}{\sum (x - \bar{x})^2}}$$

Here $\hat{y}$ is the point estimate of the mean of the y=values associated with the x=value of interest, x_0, and s is the standard deviation of the sample residuals.

If we produce a confidence interval for the mean of the y=values associated with an x=value outside the range of x=values in the sample it will be both wide and unreliable.

If you want to produce a prediction of an individual y=value associated with a particular x=value rather than an estimate of the mean y=value associated with the x=value, with a given level of confidence, you can produce what is called a prediction interval. This is to distinguish this type of forecast from a confidence interval, which is a term reserved for estimates of population measures like means.

The procedure used to produce prediction intervals is very similar to the one we used to produce confidence intervals for means of values of dependent variables. It is represented by the formula:

$$\text{Prediction interval} = \hat{y} \pm t_{\alpha/2,n-2} * s\sqrt{\frac{1}{n} + \frac{(x_0 - \bar{x})^2}{\sum (x - \bar{x})^2}}$$

If you look carefully you can see that the difference between this and the formula for a confidence interval is that we have added one to the expression beneath the square root sign. The effect of this will be to widen the interval considerably. This is to reflect the fact that individual values vary more than statistical measures like means, which are based on sets of values.

Just like confidence intervals produced using regression models, prediction intervals are more dependable if they are based on x=values nearer the mean of the x=values. Prediction intervals based on x=values that are well outside the range of the sample data are of very little value. The usefulness of the estimates that you produce from a regression model depends to a large extent on the size of the sample that you have. The larger the sample on which your regression model is based, the more precise and confident your predictions and estimates will be.

As we have seen, the width of the intervals increases the further the x=value is away from the mean of the x=values, and estimates and predictions based on x=values outside the range of x=values in our sample are useless. So, if you know that you want to construct intervals based on specific values of x, try to ensure that these values are within the range of x=values in your sample.

WHEN SIMPLE LINEAR MODELS WON'T DO THE JOB

So far we have concentrated on the simple linear regression model. Although it is used extensively and is the appropriate model in many cases, some sets of quantitative bivariate data show patterns that cannot be represented adequately by a simple linear model. If you use such data to test hypotheses about the slopes of linear models you will probably find that the slopes are not significant. This may be because the relationship between the variables is non-linear and therefore the bestfit model will be some form of curve.

In this case to find an appropriate model you would have to look to the methods of non-linear regression. The variety of non-linear models is wide and it is not possible to discuss them here, but they are covered in Bates and Watts (1988) and Seber and Wild (1989). Non-linear models themselves can look daunting but in essence using them may involve merely transforming the data so that the simple linear regression technique can be applied; in effect you 'straighten' the data to use the straight-line model.

The simple linear regression model you produce for a set of data may not be effective because the true relationship is non-linear. But it might be that the two variables that you are trying to relate are not the whole story; perhaps there are other factors that should be taken into account. One way of looking into this is to use residual plots.

One type of residual plot is a plot of the residuals against the fits (the values of the Y variable that should, according to the line, have occurred). It can be particularly useful because it can show you whether there is some systematic variation in your data that is not explained by the model.

CONTINGENCY ANALYSIS

To investigate association involving qualitative variables, which consists of different categories of attributes or characteristics, you can apply contingency analysis. This tests whether one characteristic is associated with, or contingent upon, another. It can also be used with quantitative data as long as the data are discrete and have only a very few values or are sorted into relatively few categories.

If you have to analyse the results of questionnaire research, you may want to find out how different characteristics are related to each other. For instance, you may want to assess the possible connection between the socio-economic class of respondents and the newspapers they buy. You would need to conduct a contingency test in order to ascertain whether a connection you might find in your sample results is strong enough to enable you to conclude that there is a connection in the population at large, in other words to see if the sample results are significant.

Contingency tests are conducted in the same way as the hypothesis tests we looked at previously. You begin with a null hypothesis, H_0, which in contingency analysis is always that there is no association between the characteristics, and an alternative hypothesis, H_1, which is that there is an association between them. The next stage is to analyse the sample results that we want to use to decide which hypothesis is the more plausible. The first step is to put the data into a contingency table.

To test the hypotheses the sample results must be consolidated into a test statistic in the form of a measure of contingency. This test statistic is known as chi-square after the Greek letter chi, Ç, and the benchmark distribution used to assess its value is the chi-square ($Ç^2$) distribution.

You find the value of chi-square by comparing the sample results, referred to as the observed frequencies and represented by the letter O, to the results that you would expect if the null hypothesis were true. These values, which you have to work out, are known as the expected frequencies and are represented by the letter E.

$$\text{exp ected frequency} = \frac{\text{row total} * \text{column total}}{\text{overall total}} = \frac{50 * 40}{100} = 20$$

We compare the expected frequencies to the observed frequencies, the actual sample results, by putting them together in a single table.

The procedure can be represented using the following formula.

$$Ç^2 = £\ (O - E)^2/E$$

The distribution we use to assess the test statistic is the chi-square distribution, and the procedure is referred to as a chi-square test. This distribution describes the behaviour of the measure of contingency that we have used.

There are different versions of the chi-square distributions. The one to use depends on the number degrees of freedom you have in your sample results. You can work this out by taking the number of rows in the contingency table, subtracting one, and then multiplying by the number of columns in the contingency table minus one. If we use r to represent the number of rows and c to represent the number of columns:

degrees of freedom = (r – 1) * (c – 1)

Once you specify a level of significance for the contingency test you need to find the appropriate critical value from the chi-square distribution. The test is a one-tail test; if your test statistic is greater than the critical value then it is less likely to arise from a population with no association than your level of significance.

The first is that more rows and columns mean more degrees of freedom, so you must use the correct version of the 2 distribution. The second point concerns the amount of data. Like other types of statistical testing the more data you have the firmer your conclusions will be. We should have enough data to ensure that none of the expected frequencies is less than 5; otherwise our results may be unreliable. If any expected frequencies are less than 1, the results of the test will be useless.

If one or more expected frequencies are too low there are two possible solutions; obtain more data or merge categories so that there are fewer rows and columns. If you are managing the project yourself you can avoid the problem by planning the research carefully.

Bibliography

Abelson, R. P. 1995. *Statistics as Principled Argument.*

Adkins, A. C. 1984. EOQ in the real world. *Production and Inventory Management* (4th quarter): 50-54.

Bamber, E. M. and J. H. Bylinski. 1984. Attribute sampling: A review in light of SAS no. 39. *Journal of Accounting Education* 2(1): 83-97.

Baran, J. J. 1965. Exponential smoothing. *N.A.A. Bulletin* (May): 51-52.

Barenbaum, L. and T. Monahan. 1983. Utilizing terminal values in teaching time value analysis. *Journal of Accounting Education* 1(2): 79-88.

Bene, K. J. 1966. Clerical work measurement. *Management Accounting* (October): 29-34.

Benjamin, W. 2004. *Introduction to Online Competitive Intelligence Research*. South-Western Educational Publishing.

Berger, J. O. 1985. *Statistical Decision Theory and Bayesian Analysis (Springer Series in Statistics)*. Springer-Verlag.

Berhold, M. 1970. It's permutations or combinations. *Decision Sciences* 1(3-4): 513-515.

Boot, J. C. G. 1961. Notes on quadratic programming: The Kuhn-Tucker and Theil-Van de Panne conditions, degeneracy, and equality constraints. *Management Science* (October): 85-98.

Bradbury, M. E. and P. Rouse. 2002. An application of data envelopment analysis to the evaluation of audit risk. *Abacus* 38(2): 263-279.

Bradley, H. E. 1969. Setting and controlling budgets with regression analysis. *Management Accounting* (November): 31-34, 40.

Brown, T. W., E. D. White and M. A. Gallagher. 2002. Weibull-based forecasting of R&D program budgets. *The Journal of Cost Analysis & Management* (Winter): 41-54.

Brownlee, E. R. II. 1985. Actuarial cost methods: A primer. *Journal of Accounting Education* 3(2): 163-169.

Candler, W. and R. J. Townsley. 1964. The maximization of a quadratic function of variables subject to linear inequalities. *Management Science* (April): 515-523.

Capettini, R. and G. L. Salamon. 1977. Internal versus external acquisition of services when reciprocal services exist. *The Accounting Review* (July): 690-696.

Chenhall, R. H. and K. Langfield-Smith. 1998. The relationship between strategic priorities, management techniques and management accounting: An empirical investigation using a systems approach. *Accounting, Organizations and Society* 23(3): 243-264. (Summary).

Churchman, C. W., R. L. Ackoff and E. L. Arnoff. 1957. *Introduction to Operations Research*. New York: John Wiley.

Clarke, P. J. 1984. Optimal solution? Try the linear programming way. *Accountancy* (December): 119-120, 122.

Dantzig, G. B. 1960. A machine-job scheduling model. *Management Science* (January): 191-196.

Dantzig, G. B. 1960. On the shortest route through a network. *Management Science* (January): 187-190.

Dantzig, G. B. and J. H. Ramser. 1959. The truck dispatching problem. *Management Science* (October): 80-91.

Dash, J. W. 2004. *Quantitative Finance and Risk Management: A Physicist's Approach*. World Scientific Publishing Company Inc.

Davall, B. M. and J. W. Wilkinson. 1971. Simulating an accounting information system model. *Management Accounting* (January): 26-30, 35.

Deakin, E. B. and M. H. Granof. 1974. Regression analysis as a means of determining audit sample size. *The Accounting Review* (October): 764-771.

Deakin, E. B. and M. H. Granof. 1976. Regression analysis as a means of determining audit sample size: A reply. *The Accounting Review* (April): 402-407.

Dean, B. V. 1958. Application of operations research to managerial decision making. *Administrative Science Quarterly* 3(3): 412-428.

Deming, W. E. 1944. A view of the statistical method. *The Accounting Review* (July): 254-260.

Deming, W. E. 1953. Statistical techniques in industry. *Advanced Management* 18(11): 8-12.

Dietzenbacher, E. (ed) and M. L. Lahr (ed). 2005. *Wassily Leontief and Input-Output Economics.*. Cambridge University Press.

Dillon, G. J. 1984. Getting the most from your forecasting system. *Management Accounting* (April): 28-32.

Dillon, J. D. 1956. Geographical distribution of production in multiple plant operations. *Management Science* (July): 353-365.

Dinkelbach, W. 1967. On nonlinear fractional programming. *Management Science* (March): 492-498.

Dino, R. N. and L. W. Dino. 1980. A sure-fire method to improve budget cycling. *Management Accounting* (January): 34-41.

Dittman, D. and P. Prakash. 1979. Cost variance investigation: Markovian control versus optimal control. *The Accounting Review* (April): 358-373.

Freimer, M. and L. S. Simon. 1967. The evaluation of potential new product alternatives. *Management Science* (February): B279-B292.

Gutjahr, A. L. and G. L. Nemhauser. 1964. An algorithm for the line balancing problem. *Management Science* (November): 308-315.

Gynther, R. S. 1963. Improving separation of fixed and variable expenses. *N.A.A. Bulletin* (June): 29-38. (Using the least squares method and correlation analysis).

Hadley, S. W. 2004. Safety inventory analysis: Why and how? *Strategic Finance* (September): 26-33.

Hale, J. A. and L. J. Ryan. 1979. Decision science and the management accountant. *Management Accounting* (January): 42-45.

Hall, E. J. and R. J. Kolkmann. 1976. A vote for the probabilistic pro forma income statement. *Management Accounting* (January): 45-48.

Hamlen, S. S. 1980. A chance-constrained mixed integer programming model for internal control design. *The Accounting Review* (October): 578-593.

Hamlen, S. S., W. A. Hamlen, Jr. and J. Tschirhart. 1980. The use of the generalized Shapley allocation in joint cost allocation. *The Accounting Review* (April): 269-287.

Hanna, R. A. 1953. Applying statistics to checking of venders' invoices. *N.A.C.A. Bulletin* (December): 503-511.

Hansen, D. R. and T. L. Shaftel. 1977. Sampling for integrated auditing objectives. *The Accounting Review* (January): 109-123.

Hayes, R. H., and K. B. Clark. 1985. Explaining Observed productivity differentials between plants: Implication for operations research. *Interfaces* (November-December): 3-14.

Hicks, H. G. 1960. An approach to quantitative analysis for organization. *The Journal of the Academy of Management* 3(3): 155-160.

House, W. C. Jr. 1966. The usefulness of sensitivity analysis in capital investment decisions. *Management Accounting* (February): 22-29.

Ijiri, Y. and R. S. Kaplan. 1971. A model for integrating sampling objectives in auditing. *Journal of Accounting Research* (Spring): 73-87.

Ijiri, Y. and R. S. Kaplan. 1978. Sampling for integrated audit objectives - A reply. *The Accounting Review* (July): 773-774.

Irish, R. R. 1965. Managerial use of operations research. *N.A.A. Bulletin* (April): 19-24.

Isbell, J. R. and W. H. Marlow. 1961. On an industrial programming problem of Kantorovich. *Management Science* (October): 13-17.

Jensen, R. E. 1967. A multiple regression model for cost control - Assumptions and limitations. *The Accounting Review* (April): 265-273.

Jensen, R. E. 1968. Sensitivity analysis and integer linear programming. *The Accounting Review* (July): 425-446.

Jensen, R. E. 1971. A cluster analysis study of financial performance of selected business firms. *The Accounting Review* (January): 36-56.

Jensen, R. E. and C. T Thomsen. 1968. Statistical analysis in cost measurement and control. *The Accounting Review* (January): 83-93.

Jensen, W. S. 1973. Problem identification in accounting research. *Management Accounting* (December): 49-52. (Uses Venn diagrams).

Johnson, G. L. and S. S. Simik, II. 1971. Multiproduct C-V-P analysis under uncertainty. *Journal of Accounting Research* (Autumn): 278-286.

Kinney, W. R. Jr. 1978. ARIMA and regression in analytical review: An empirical test. *The Accounting Review* (January): 48-60.

Kinney, W. R. Jr. 1979. Integrating audit tests: Regression analysis and partitioned dollar-unit sampling. *Journal of Accounting Research* (Autumn): 456-475.

Kinney, W. R. Jr. and A. D. Bailey, Jr. 1976. Regression analysis as a means of determining audit sample size: A comment. *The Accounting Review* (April): 396-401.

Kircher, P. 1961. Translator's note on "Mathematical methods in economics". *Management Science* (July): 335-336.

Klein, M. 1961. On production smoothing. *Management Science* (April): 286-293.

Reiter, S. and D. B. Rice. 1966. Discrete optimizing solution procedures for linear and nonlinear integer programming problems. *Management Science* (July): 829-850.

Reneau, J. H. 1978. CAV bounds in dollar unit sampling: Some simulation results. *The Accounting Review* (July): 669-680.

Shapiro, J. F. 1968. Turnpike planning horizons for a Markovian decision model. *Management Science* (January): 292-300.

Sharpe, I. G. 1974. Econometric model building in financial management. *Abacus* 10(1): 55-73.

Shehata, M. 1991. Self-selection bias and the economic consequences of accounting regulation: An application of two-stage switching regression to SFAS No. 2. *The Accounting Review* (October): 768-787. (Part of a forum on the use of limited-dependent variables in accounting research).

Vance, L. L. 1952. An experience with small random samples in auditing. *The Accounting Review* (October): 472-474.

Vance, L. L. 1955. Capsule cases in statistical cost control. *N.A.C.A. Bulletin* (January): 682-688. (Statistical sampling).

Vance, L. L. 1960. A review of developments in statistical sampling for accountants. *The Accounting Review* (January): 19-28.

Vanecek, M. T. 1978. An overview of decision theory for management accountants. *Management Accounting* (January): 41-48.

Vatter, W. J. 1961. Accounting and statistics. *The Accounting Review* (October): 589-597.

Vatter, W. J. 1967. The use of operations research in American companies. *The Accounting Review* (October): 721-730.

Vazsonyi, A. 1954. The use of mathematics in production and inventory control. I. *Management Science* (October): 70-85.

Vazsonyi, A. 1955. The use of mathematics in production and inventory control. II. *Management Science* (April-July): 207-223.

Ventura, E. 1960. Sur L'Utilisation des Integrales de Contour dans les Problemes de Stocks et de Delais d'Attente. *Management Science* (July): 423-443.

Walgenbach, P. H. and W. G. Frank. 1971. A simulation model for applying

Welch, P. R. 1984. A generalized distributed lag model for predicting quarterly earnings. *Journal of Accounting Research* (Autumn): 744-757.

Welker, R. B. 1974. Discriminant analysis as an aid to employee selection. *The Accounting Review* (July): 514-523.

Werolin, A. E. 1942. The cost accountant and time and motion studies. *N.A.C.A. Bulletin* (May 15): 1217-1224.

Zannetos, Z. S. 1964. Standard costs as a first step to probabilistic control: A theoretical justification, an extension and implications. *The Accounting Review* (April): 296-304.

Zionts, S. 1968. On an algorithm for the solution of mixed integer programming problems. *Management Science* (September): 113-116.

Index

D

E

H

I

L

M

N

O

P

Q

R

S

T

U

V